I Want to Make a Difference – but I Don't Like Politics

To my parents

I Want to Make a Difference – but I Don't Like Politics

The Crisis in Party Politics

John Redwood

POLITICO'S

First published in Great Britain 2006 by
Politico's Publishing Ltd, an imprint of
Methuen Publishing Ltd
11–12 Buckingham Gate
London
SW1E 6LB

10 9 8 7 6 5 4 3 2 1

A CIP catalogue record for this book is available from the British Library.

ISBN-10: 1-84275-182-4
ISBN-13: 978-1-84275-182-4

Printed and bound in Great Britain by Cromwell Press, Trowbridge,
Wiltshire

Contents

Introduction

People are fed up with political parties. The polls tell us that, the public tells politicians that. Even the government admits it, and asked Baroness Kennedy to study the problem. It is a worrying trend in a representative democracy, where party organisation has been fundamental to how we are governed throughout the period of mass franchise.

The electors express their frustration and anger in different ways. Some explode on the doorstep to visiting party representatives. Many choose not to vote. Many more now vote for candidates who do not represent the three main parties.

People say 'It won't make any difference' or 'Nothing will change' if they vote. Some fear the main parties are becoming too similar to offer them a real choice. Some think all parties lie – they will say anything to get elected, then do something else. Some think politicians and even parties may want to do what they say, but once in office will discover they are unable to do so.

The mass abstentions that characterise local elections are now matched by the fact that as many people fail to vote in a general election as vote for the two main parties, who win the vast majority of the seats. Just one in five voters wanted the present government enough to go and vote for it in 2005. A local council ruling group may be elected to power by as few as one in seven of the voters.

This does not mean, however, that people have ceased to care about political issues. Many people are very aware of what is going on in the world about them. Locally, they worry about planning, traffic, the journey to work and school, and local public services. Internationally they see on television the poverty in Africa or flooding in Asia. They want to do something about it, or they want their government to help solve the problem. They are more likely to take the issue up themselves with the media and friends, or to work with a campaigning organisation, than they are to join a political party.

All the main parties have lost thousands of members in the last couple of decades. For a long time parties put it down to changing lifestyles. Women who used to do voluntary work for the Conservatives or Labour now have paid employment. Men who gave their occasional evening to the local committee now work longer hours, or feel the need to be at home with their families. Parties need to consider the possibility that the drop in their membership is also a commentary on how people feel about this way of organising and doing politics.

For sixteen years now we have been governed by 'Blajorism'. The idea that politics was about what appeared in the media started to dominate with the advent of John Major. He announced he wanted a grammar school in every town but built none of them, and promised the abolition of inheritance tax but did not get around to it. Under Tony Blair spin not action became a total preoccupation with New Labour. Blair took what Major did on a bad day at the office and made it routine. In the last nine years people have seen a growing gap between what ministers say is happening and what is happening in practice. They see that ministers only seem to attend to a problem if the media are highly critical of them. The ministers tell us the problem of asylum seekers has gone away, only to reveal they haven't a clue how many illegals there are in the country. They promised no increase in taxes, whilst putting through a large number of stealth taxes. They said they would be the party of manufacturing, only to ignore the million manufacturing jobs that have disappeared on their watch.

The message is simple. If you want to influence them, hit them in the headlines. Why join the local Labour Party, where it appears your views will be ignored and your loyalty taken for granted, if you can back a national professional campaign, organised by a pressure group you agree with, that could drag ministers through the fire of bad press coverage?

Voters and politicians are now engaged in a dangerous game of misleading each other. Political parties all spend too much money on endless polling and focus group research to find out what the audience believes and wants. They use this to send back the messages that their party has understood and is doing something about the concerns or will do something about them given power. Unfortunately people often mislead the focus groups, just as the government seeks to mislead the people about what it is up to.

Focus groups and polls usually say people would be happy to pay more tax for better services. They don't really mean that. The Conservatives gave people the chance to make a bigger contribution to local services through the community charge, to be driven back by public opinion. Labour faced a serious revolt over higher petrol taxes, and have never felt it would be a winning ticket to promise higher income tax. The Liberal Democrats show you stay in third place if you offer higher income tax.

The focus group culture creates a vacuum in political leadership. Politicians who want to take the argument to the people, who want to change public opinion, are thought to be dangerous or maverick. They should calm down, and just play back the tried and tested 'safe' words that the experts have derived from the research. What's the point of doing that? If all three parties do it, using similar techniques and consultants, they will all be saying something similar. If the research tells you your party is not popular enough to win, surely that means you need to be bold in trying to change public opinion, rather than meekly accepting the unpopularity your party has inherited?

The public will not trust political parties unless they start to tell them things they do not want to hear as well as things the research says they do want to hear. No party will break out of the current debilitating cycle of cynicism unless it starts to tell people things they do not believe, with a view to making them think and move the debate on, as well as things they do already believe.

So much modern political 'debate' is puerile, stereotyped, boring and low grade. The party game is dictated by Labour's professional spin machine. To them you either spend as much or more in the public sector as Labour currently do, or you wish to sack teachers and nurses. It's pathetic. The idea is to close down any debate of how you might get more for less, and any debate of whether we need some of the parts of the public sector that are not teaching our children to read or performing operations in the emergency ward. Their treatment of Europe is even worse. You either agree with every concession and deal Labour have made in the EU, or you wish to withdraw unilaterally. If you did withdraw, apparently Germany would no longer sell us her BMWs.

Of course caricaturing opponents' positions, and presenting your own as virtuous, is a necessary part of democratic debate, and has been done effectively by all governments over the years. It is just that this time round the monotonous repetition of the same myths and lies corrupts the whole debate, and makes an increasingly well-educated electorate say 'That's not for me, I don't believe a word of it'. Labour are finding that their lies about others are undermining their own credibility more than they are damaging their opponents.

One of the ironies of the present predicament is that some electors turn to campaigning organisations, who also distort and exaggerate in the same way as political parties. People supporting them usually don't notice, because they share the prejudices of the campaigning organisation, or don't seem to care, because, they reason to themselves, it takes one to stop one. Why not play the politicians at their own game?

The campaigning bodies have understood the need for instant gratification. They usually ask for small sums of money from the many who contact them, paying their big media and opinion research bills from a multitude of small donations. In return they offer an easy answer. 'Send this card to your MP' and then you have done your bit to achieve whatever outcome they are seeking. It's a new form of takeaway politics – you can fill it in whilst eating the takeaway pizza, and pop it into the office post tray. That's the job done, conscience cleared, responsibility transferred.

Elected politicians need to remind people that things are not that easy. If you want to delegate your compassion or subcontract your political involvement, then the best way should be to vote in someone who can represent your view. Just voting once in a while may be enough for you. If you want to live in a vital democracy that really works, it does need many people to express their view, to write to their MP, to talk to their councillors, to attend the public meeting or send in the interesting e-mail. It does require a big army of people to join political parties and make their voices heard within the party coalitions. Successful parties do debate policy, have arguments over the way ahead, and hold strongly contested elections for who should lead and represent them.

Those who advise political parties often seem to want acquiescence. They see party members as unpaid sales personnel who will take any old product onto the doorsteps if it has tested well with the focus groups. This attitude is putting talented people off joining political parties. Members want to know that the product will reflect the brand values of the party they joined. If you join Labour you don't bargain on the leadership recommending privatisation of the health service or introducing selection in state schools. If you join the Conservatives you don't volunteer for higher taxes or more European government. There are limits to how far the leadership can stretch the brand without losing members. Members expect to be involved, consulted, nurtured. Taking them for granted can lose them altogether, impoverishing the party. Members properly used are a source of ideas, a means of market-testing new policies, and a means of communicating with the electorate. They are a pool of talent to find candidates for councils, Parliament, and quango boards. They are a source of funds.

The Conservative Party upset its membership in the early 1990s by joining the European Exchange Rate Mechanism, which did so much damage. The fact that this was a policy recommended by the Liberal Democrats and Labour made it worse for activists. It compounded the error by forcing through an unpopular European treaty. The Labour Party is now upsetting its membership by requiring them to support city academies, private treatment centres, privatised dentistry and selection by aptitude in state schools, as well as upsetting all of us by its willingness to destroy civil liberties in many fields.

In this book I show the extent of the disillusion with modern political parties. I demonstrate how people have discovered that the Emperor has no clothes. Many people have realised that the EU and the quangos have so much power that there are real limits on what any well-intentioned government could achieve. Many realise that the treadmill of seeking re-election and believing that so much money needs to be raised for national campaigns limit what political parties can say and do about anything.

Is there a way out? There is, but it will require many changes by many people. It will require constitutional reform. More things need to be settled by elected ministers and elected councillors. That means fewer things should be settled in Brussels, in quangos and without proper parliamentary debate. It means legislating and regulating less, and debating more. It means political parties offering some leadership and being prepared to venture the unpopular truth as well as the pleasing popular policy.

It also means improving what a political party offers to its members. If members see they can make a difference within their party, that will encourage more better people to join. This does not mean a leader having to take dictation from the rank and file. It does mean a leader taking the rank and file seriously, and using them as a sounding board before instructing them to be the sales force for a given view.

I don't think the end of the political party would represent a better way forward. Parties do allow for more orderly conduct of business in elected assemblies and for clearer choices in elections, if done well. What we must prevent is the introduction of proportional representation. Most of the systems of PR strengthen the power of parties at the expense of their elected members. List systems destroy necessary independence of mind by MPs. This would increase disillusion with parties and Parliament still further. Coalition governments undermine politicians' reputation for truthfulness from day one, because you can only create a coalition by reneging on the more interesting features of your manifesto which the other parties dislike.

People want a more honest politics. They want to feel their elected representative understands them and stands up for them. Parties need to allow this to happen, so their members have a worthwhile job. If parties seek too much false loyalty, they will continue to undermine the party system itself. If parties start to put things right, more people will enjoy their politics by joining and influencing from within. If parties remain wholly owned subsidiaries of pollsters and experts, many people will opt out altogether or will take pleasure in taking pot shots at the whole party-political show.

1

Where have all the voters gone?

I WANT TO MAKE A DIFFERENCE
I will give voting another try
I will read the leaflets they send round
I will have questions ready to ask the candidates/canvassers
I will contact the candidates through the website or address if there is something I want to clarify or press them on
If I don't like the views of any of them, I will tell the leading candidates why I am unhappy
I will consider writing to the paper saying what I want if none of them are offering it

Maybe it does make a difference which person gets elected
I will see who looks as if they intend to work hard for us, the voters
I will see who I can rely on, who seems to be telling the truth

I do see that I will never find the perfect candidate (unless I stand myself!)
Each party will have something in it I don't like
Each candidate will say something or have something in their background I don't like
Voting is about making a choice from among what is on offer

It's a bit like going shopping without as much money as you would like
You know which car you would really like
But you only have half the money you need
You still buy a car – you compromise on what you want
You discover there are important choices between the cars you can afford
So you exercise what choice you can

Some people feel strongly that one particular party should be elected – probably more feel strongly about a party they do not want to see elected
Some people feel strongly about individuals who put their names forward

If you want to live in a democracy maybe you should take a little time to give voting another chance

In the general election of June 2001 only twenty-six million voters chose to cast their vote, out of a total electorate of forty-four million. The turnout was under 60 per cent for the first time in a UK general election. Some people argued that the low turnout was no surprise as everyone knew who was going to win. It is true that in 2001 very few people expected an upset. Most confidently expected the one-term Labour government to sweep to victory again. Some supporters remained enthusiastic, others merely gave it the benefit of the doubt.

In May 2005 the feeling was different. There was a mood of growing disillusion with the ruling party. The Prime Minister, once a great asset to his party's cause, had become a very contentious figure. The second term of Labour government was dominated by supporting the United States in the Iraq war. Many people felt let down that we had gone to war at all. Many electors felt lied to when it was revealed that the intelligence on which the case for war was based was faulty. At the very least commentators expected there to be a shift against Labour in the House of Commons after the general election. Despite this, turnout again remained obstinately low. Just over 27 million people voted in May 2005 out of the 44.25 million who were eligible, edging up from the 59.4 per cent of June 2001 to 61.3 per cent. Scottish voters remained the most reluctant. In 2001 the turnout in Scotland was only 58.2 per cent. It rose to 60.6 per cent in May 2005. In Northern Ireland turnout actually fell in 2005, down from the respectable 68 per cent of June 2001 to 62.5 per cent. Elsewhere glacial progress was made towards greater voter participation in the later election.

In June 2001 Labour polled 10.74 million votes. By May 2005 this had fallen to 9.5 million. The Conservative vote, down at only 8.4 million in 2001, rose slightly to 8.8 million in 2005. In 2005 Labour polled less than they had achieved in 1992, when they lost for the fourth time in a row to the Conservatives. In that year the Tories polled fourteen million votes, half as much again as Labour in 2005. In 1992 the two main parties together polled 25.6 million votes. In 2005 this was down to 18.3 million, seven million fewer despite a rise of over a million in the number of electors. Voters choosing candidates from parties other than Labour, Conservative or Liberal Democrat rose from two million to 2.8 million between 1992 and 2005 despite the lower turnout.

Table 1.1: General elections 1992–2005

	1992	1997	2001	2005
Turnout, England	78.1%	71.3%	59.1%	61.2%
Turnout, Scotland	77.9%	71.3%	58.2%	60.6%
Turnout, Wales	80.9%	73.5%	61.6%	62.4%
Turnout, Northern Ireland	69.8%	67.3%	68.0%	62.5%
Labour votes, UK	11.56m	13.55m	10.74m	9.55m
Conservative votes, UK	14.09m	9.59m	8.36m	8.77m
Lab & Con votes as % of total votes cast	76.3%	73.9%	72.4%	67.5%
Lab & Con votes as % of electorate	59.3%	52.8%	43.0%	41.4%

Conventional analysis of British elections assumes a two-party model. Commentators presume that national election campaigns have a fairly uniform impact around the country, and assume they are the dominant factor affecting whether an individual candidate is elected or not in a particular constituency. Defined in this way, June 2001 saw a swing of a mere 1.8 per cent from Labour to the Conservatives, whilst May 2005 saw a further swing of 3.1 per cent from Labour to the principal opposition party. Such an analysis encourages parties to concentrate their attention upon the seats requiring the smallest swing, whilst pursuing a national strategy designed to maximise support for their own cause and highlight the weaknesses of their principal opponent. Labour and Conservative are the dominant firms in the marketplace. They specialise in attacking each other, usually ignoring the Liberal Democrats altogether.

In elections prior to the current century this has broadly worked. The strategists advise the political parties to head for the middle ground, and believe that the party that wins is the one that makes the most successful pitch for the middle, doing most to distance itself from its left in the case of the Labour Party or from its right in the case of the Conservatives. This thinking still predominates in the two major parties' central campaign units. It is reflected very strongly in the interesting book published by Michael Ashcroft shortly after the third Conservative general election defeat, entitled *Smell the Coffee*.

Reading his book and others like it you can see the point of trying to apply the old-fashioned logic and analysis to current conditions. It is comfortable and it appears to fit the reality on the ground. Yet on more careful inspection you see how three-, four- and five-party politics is complicating matters, how low turnout is now very crucial, and how individual, local contests seem to matter more and more. What was remarkable about the May 2005 election was not the modest national swing and the relatively few seats that changed hands in the circumstances but the enormous variation of swings recorded around the country. If you look at the target board of seats that the Conservatives were hoping to win in the conventional, two-party swing model, you see that they won some seats that looked fairly unlikely, given the average low level of swing, whilst failing to gain some seats that should have fallen quite easily. The Conservatives failed to win the Labour seat with the smallest majority, South Dorset. They also failed to take Selby, where the Labour majority was only 4.3 per cent in 2001; South Thanet, where it was only 4.5 per cent; Gillingham, where it was only 5.4 per cent; and Enfield North, where it was only 6 per cent. Yet the Conservatives succeeded in taking next-door Enfield Southgate, which had a Labour majority of 13.2 per cent in 2001; Reading East, which had a majority of 12.8 per cent; Gravesham, with a majority of 11.1 per cent; and St Albans, with a majority of 10.2 per cent.

There was a more limited but similar trend in Conservative against Liberal Democrat contests. The Conservatives failed to take Cheadle, North Norfolk and Mid Dorset & North Poole, all with majorities of under 1 per cent, and Somerton & Frome and Brecon & Radnorshire, with majorities of 2 per cent or less. Yet they succeeded in taking Newbury, with a 4.75 per cent majority, and Ludlow, with a 3.78 per cent majority.

How do we account for these divergences in the seats which the Conservatives managed to win and did not manage to win, in a world usually described by national campaigns and uniform national swings? In each case the major parties would, I suspect, agree with my account which gives a prominent position to local campaigns and local people. In the case of South Dorset, the very active and energetic Conservative candidate, Ed Matts, was caught during the campaign using photographs in his literature which had been doctored. Labour succeeded in exposing this and it clearly put off local voters, even though Matts appeared to have the easiest task of all the Conservative candidates seeking to prise a seat from an incumbent Labour MP.

In the case of Cheadle, the former Conservative MP, Stephen Day, well known and reasonably respected in the local area, failed to dislodge the incumbent Liberal Democrat MP, Patsy Calton, defending a majority of only thirty-three. Calton was terminally ill with cancer at the time but had a good reputation as a very active local campaigner. The combination of sympathy and respect for her work as an MP swept her to victory with an increased majority against the odds. She recorded a swing of 4.2 per cent to herself and boosted the majority to 4,020. In the subsequent by-election following the sad death of the Liberal Democrat MP, the Conservatives again fielded Day. The nationally influenced campaign literature was thought to be insensitive by the electorate, and so once again the Conservatives failed to take what should have been an easy target seat, even though the very popular local MP was no longer available.

In North Norfolk the incumbent Liberal Democrat had a majority of only 483 based on the 2001 result. The Conservatives put up the very model of a modern Conservative candidate: the media-friendly and very energetic Iain Dale. Dale ran an extremely active campaign, gained a lot of local publicity but ended up with one of the worst results achieved by the Conservatives; the Liberal Democrat majority shot up from 483 to 10,606, a swing of 8.5 per cent. There was something about the local campaign that upset local voters. The best explanation I have heard from those who observed it more closely than me is that they felt that Dale's campaign was too negative concerning the Liberal Democrat incumbent, who turned out to be a more popular MP than the challenger realised.

There were similar troubles for the Conservatives in the once safe seat of Solihull. The seat had been held for many years by John Taylor in the Conservative interest. In June 2001 he achieved a majority of 9,407, 19.5 per cent of those voting. Lorely Burt succeeded in overturning his majority at her first attempt, winning the seat by the wafer-thin margin of 279 votes, and in the process recording a swing of 10 per cent to the Liberal Democrats. In this case an aggressive Liberal Democrat campaign, targeting what they perceived to be the weaknesses of the incumbent Conservative MP, paid off with the local electorate. The electors decided they wanted somebody younger and felt it was time for a change, which showed that there are occasions when negative campaigning against an incumbent can work in favour of the challenger rather than backfiring.

The Conservatives often benefited from diverging swings. The strong swing of 6.9 per cent from Labour to the Conservatives in Reading East overturned a Labour majority of 5,595, and gave the seat to the Conservative challenger, Robert Wilson, with a majority of 475. The swing here was better than in the other Labour–Conservative contests in Berkshire, including the marginal Reading West and the safe Conservative seat of Bracknell. Again, local people passed judgement upon the incumbent. Jane Griffiths had not had a happy time as the Labour MP for Reading East since her first election in 1997. She had fallen out with her Labour neighbour in Reading West, Martin Salter, and had also fallen out with other Labour Party figures. She was deselected. The replacement Labour candidate was well known locally and had a controversial background. Electors came to their own conclusion, feeling that the endless Labour rows, coupled with Labour's decision that their own MP was no longer suitable to represent the town, meant they might as well move on to a different party altogether.

In Hammersmith & Fulham Greg Hands recorded one of the best swings for the Conservatives, 7.4 per cent from Labour, to convert a Labour majority of 2,015 into a Conservative one of 5,029. Grant Shapps in Welwyn Hatfield went one better and achieved a 8.1 per cent swing, to convert a 1,196 Labour majority into a 5,946 Conservative majority. It was active local campaigning on a consistent basis for many months that seemed to make the big difference to these results. In Feltham a Conservative challenger achieved an 8.4 per cent swing against the incumbent Labour MP, Alan Keen; Keen held on to his seat but with his majority almost halved from 12,657 to 6,820. David Burrows, the Conservative candidate in Enfield Southgate, achieved the heroic swing of 8.7 per cent to the Conservatives to unseat the incumbent Labour MP, Stephen Twigg.

The result in Enfield Southgate was a particularly interesting one. Twigg had been the well-publicised victor of 1997, overturning Michael Portillo's large majority in a single night to take the seat. This event became a favourite television clip for the ensuing eight years. Burrows's energetic campaign exposed just how personal the vote against Michael Portillo had been, restoring more of the Conservative vote from the pre-1997 period than many other Conservative candidates were able to do in adjacent or more distant parts of the country. Twigg had been an education minister and was not a particularly unpopular local MP, but the seat he held had a lot of latent Conservative support. The Conservative vote was boosted from 38.6 per cent of those voting in 2001 to 44.6 per cent in 2005, whilst the Labour vote fell from 51.8 per cent of those voting to only 40.5 per cent four years later. It was not just the rise in the Liberal Democrat vote that accounted for the Conservative victory, as in some other places, but it was a positive affirmation of the virtues of the Conservative cause. Meanwhile, in the neighbouring Enfield North Labour achieved one of their best results of the night, limiting the swing to the Conservatives to a mere 0.7 per cent.

Andrew Rosindell in Romford showed what a popular, hard-working, campaigning incumbent could achieve against Labour that night. Rosindell had a good result in 2001, when he took the seat for the first time in the Conservative interest with 53 per cent of the votes. In 2005 he added another six percentage points to his tally, taking his vote up to a remarkably good 59.1 per cent of those voting, whilst the Labour vote fell a further nine points, down to only 27.3 per cent. His majority, at 11,589 or 31.8 per cent, was one of the strongest Conservative majorities recorded in 2005. Rosindell has a unique campaigning style based on his belief in Romford and the United Kingdom, and continuous communication with his electors. In nearby Rochford and Southend East, a good candidate for the Conservatives, James Duddridge, contesting the seat for the first time, showed that it was not a general or regional swing that accounted for Rosindell's result. Duddridge held the seat for the Conservatives but he saw his share of the vote fall from his predecessor's 53.6 per cent to 45.3 per cent, and the majority drop a little from 7,034 to 5,494, a Conservative-to-Labour swing of 2.5 per cent. Doubtless he will record a better result next time when he has the advantage of telling people of the good service he provides as a member of Parliament. He had the misfortune this time to fight against the background of a very popular predecessor, Teddy Taylor, who was retiring.

Elsewhere incumbent Conservatives were sometimes able to achieve remarkably good results. John Greenway in Ryedale managed a 6.4 per cent swing from the Liberal Democrats, boosting his majority from an adequate 4,875 to a good 10,469. Mark Simmons achieved a similar swing from Labour as the Conservative MP retained the Conservative stronghold of Boston & Skegness. This took his majority from 515 to 5,907.

In a reasonable evening for the Conservatives there was more than a 10 per cent difference between the best and the worst Conservative–Labour swings. There was no regional pattern to it, with both good and bad results being recorded in the north, the west, the south and the east. For Conservatives against the Liberal Democrats there was a 17 per cent divergence between the best and the worst swings.

These swings were comparatively modest compared with the huge swings seen elsewhere between Labour, the Liberal Democrats, new parties and independents. The biggest of the night was a dramatic 49 per cent swing from Labour to independent in Blaenau Gwent. Before 2005 Blaenau Gwent was the safest Labour seat in Wales with a long Labour pedigree. It had returned Michael Foot and Aneurin Bevan to Parliament, Labour idols in their day. Including the towns of Ebbw Vale and Tredegar, it was the kind of seat Labour aspirants dreamed of contesting. People would joke that they weighed the votes for Labour in Blaenau Gwent, there were so many of them. Others joked, wrongly as it turned out, that Labour could put up a donkey in Blaenau Gwent with a red rosette and it would be elected. On this occasion Labour put up a better candidate than a donkey but he was very contentious with the local Labour establishment. The result was shocking for the Labour Party. Labour's vote of 22,855 or 72 per cent of those voting in 2001 plunged to 11,384 or 32.3 per cent of those voting in 2005. The independent Peter Law, of Labour provenance himself, managed a massive 20,505 votes or 58.2 per cent of those voting to take the seat with a handsome majority of 9,121, 25.9 per cent of those voting. The Labour-to-independent swing is off the scale of any swingometer and showed the government could no longer rely on the loyalty of the electorate.

In some inner city areas large swings occurred from Labour to Respect. In Bethnal Green & Bow George Galloway, the former Labour member of Parliament, stood as the leader of his embryo party against the media-friendly incumbent Labour MP, Oona King. King was defending a majority of 10,057 or 26.2 per cent of those voting in 2001. She saw a swing of 26.2 per cent against her to deliver the seat to Galloway with a small majority of 823. An election which had been bedevilled by the issue of the Iraq war had made King the local scapegoat for the unpopularity of the Prime Minister's policy. Although Galloway did not get any of his other Respect candidates home to accompany him to the House of Commons, they were able to achieve big swings elsewhere. In Birmingham Sparkbrook the incumbent Labour member of Parliament, Roger Godsiff, saw his 2001 majority of 16,246, or 44.3 per cent of those voting, collapse to a mere 3,289 on a swing of 24.5 per cent to the Respect candidate, who came from nowhere to take 27.5 per cent of the votes cast. It was only the Liberal Democrats who saved Godsiff as their vote also leapt by seven percentage points to 20.2 per cent, just preventing the Respect candidate unseating the Labour member.

With a few exceptions, Liberal Democrats were losing to the Conservatives. Indeed they were on the defensive. Weston-super-Mare, Guildford, Devon West & Torridge, Ludlow and Newbury passed to the Conservatives following hard-fought campaigns. The Liberal Democrats did not take any of the high-profile scalps they wanted through their clumsily named decapitation strategy, directed against Michael Howard, the Conservative leader, David Davies, the Shadow Home Secretary, and Oliver Letwin, the Shadow Chancellor of the Exchequer. All three held their seats with increased majorities, probably aided by the unpleasant nature of the Liberal Democrat campaign. It is true the Liberal Democrats did unseat Tim Collins in Westmorland on a swing of 3.6 per cent, again showing how unpredictable and erratic this particular election was.

The Liberal Democrats achieved their very large swings in contests against Labour in inner city areas. Brent East was their best result, where a swing of a massive 30.7 per cent from Labour to the Liberal Democrats made Sarah Teather the member of Parliament, following her by-election success in 2003 when Ken Livingstone gave up the seat for Labour. The final figures gave Teather a majority of 2,712, compared with the Labour majority of 13,047 four years earlier for Livingstone. In Birmingham Ladywood the Liberal Democrats achieved a swing of 22.2 per cent against Clare Short, slashing her majority from 18,143 to 6,801. This was an interesting result because Short had resigned from the Cabinet in protest over the Iraq war, seeking to build bridges with her constituents who felt similarly. Maybe it was her delay in resigning which undermined some of the beneficial effect the resignation might have had.

Outside the inner cities the Liberal Democrats did best in the old university towns of Oxford and Cambridge. A 15 per cent Labour-to-Liberal Democrat swing threw Anne Campbell, the Labour MP, out of her job in Cambridge and gave the new Liberal Democrat MP, David Howarth, a useful 4,339 majority. In Oxford East an 11.9 per cent swing to the Liberal Democrats was not enough to unseat Andrew Smith but it did take his comfortable majority of 10,344 down to a perilously slim 963. The Liberals picked up Bristol West on a Labour-to-Liberal Democrat swing of 8.4 per cent.

In Northern Ireland a completely different election was underway. A seismic shift occurred in Ulster politics. The Ulster Unionist Party (UUP), the traditional dominant party of the north, lost all of its seats save North Down, usually through very large swings to the Democratic Unionist Party (DUP). The DUP picked up Antrim East, Antrim South, Upper Bann and, most spectacularly, Lagan Valley on a massive swing of 38.2 per cent. There Jeffrey Donaldson had changed party from UUP to DUP and took many of his voters with him. Just as the Protestant forces realigned around the less moderate option, so in Newry & Armagh, a largely Catholic area, Sinn Fein took the seat on an 11.4 per cent swing from the more moderate Social Democratic and Labour Party. Opinion on both sides of the sectarian divide was hardening.

In Wyre Forest Richard Taylor was defending his seat as the only independent member of the 2001 parliament. He had won it in a surprise result in the 2001 general election, campaigning on local health issues against the Labour incumbent. On that occasion he had won it with a majority of 17,630. He saw his majority drastically cut to 5,250 with a sharp fall in his own vote, as a result of an extremely good Conservative performance compared with the poor one in 2001. The Labour vote stayed virtually constant at just over a fifth of those voting.

★

It is difficult looking at this very divergent set of results to believe strongly in the theory of national swings. Of course, it is still possible to show that the Conservatives were more likely to take a seat off Labour where the Labour majority was smaller than where it was bigger, and to show that the main things that happened that night were a loss of seats by Labour and a gain of seats by the Conservatives. If there was any predominant swing it was a transfer of votes from

Labour to the Liberal Democrats, which in some cases was helpful to the Conservatives, where they were in second place to Labour. Even this, however, is a very partial account of a very complicated general election. I would suggest that a better way of looking at the general election of May 2005 is as a series of by-elections, only loosely connected by national campaigns and by the national general election itself.

The electors of Brent East, Blaenau Gwent and Bethnal Green & Bow were not swayed by the big argument between Conservative and Labour over who should govern the country. In Brent East the voters wished to reaffirm their by-election choice, which had been designed to deliver a strong message to the incumbent Labour government at the time in 2003. In Blaenau Gwent Labour voters wanted to show the Labour Party they were not going to be taken for granted, and they would far rather have an independent member of Parliament than someone not of their choosing, even if he did come from their own clan. In Bethnal Green & Bow electors were so angry about the issue of the war that they decided to vote for a colourful outsider who had broken with Labour, rather than participating in the general choice of whether the Conservatives or Labour should run the country.

These were just the outriders of a mood which was present in a large number of constituencies around the country. People decided to make up their own minds on local issues and local candidates in many cases. In other cases they made up their mind on national issues but not around the competing claims of the Labour and Conservative parties, who disagreed with the electorate over what the main national issue should be. Both major parties decided that the Iraq war should not be the principal issue of the election or even an important one. Indeed, with the exception of the occasion when Michael Howard accused the Prime Minister of lying over the war, to try and raise the issue of trust and accountability, neither major party willingly talked about the subject at all. Respect kept the issue of the war alive and showed it mattered to a substantial number of voters.

In the UK as a whole 2,234,256 votes, or 8.2 per cent of the total number of votes cast, were given to parties and individuals other than Labour, Conservative, Liberal Democrat or nationalist. This was well up on the 1,794,246 votes, or 6.8 per cent, cast for such people and parties in 2001, and represents a rising trend compared with the elections of the previous century. Within this a large number of voters decided that the issue of Europe was so important that they wished to vote for a pull-out-of-Europe party, when all three major national parties decided the issue of.Europe was not an important consideration in the general election. Meanwhile 587,105 votes, or 2.2 per cent of the total, were cast for nationalist candidates. This showed that in Scotland and Wales there remained a minority of voters who regarded more independence within the UK, or complete independence for their own country, as the most important issue. This gave the Scottish Nationalists six seats, including the capture of the old Western Isles seat on a 9.3 per cent swing from Labour. In Wales Plaid Cymru kept three seats but lost Ceredigion to the Liberal Democrats on a 6 per cent swing.

At the very least, analysts of the UK political scene now need a three-party model to understand the complexity. They need to adjust the three-party model for the possibility in any given constituency, or group of constituencies, of a fourth, fifth or sixth party or independent entering the race who could have a decisive influence. In a world where even in a general election an independent can achieve a 50 per cent swing and a new party can achieve a 25 per cent swing, there are no safe seats.

After the general election a group of new Conservative MPs came to the shadow Cabinet to explain to us why they thought they had won. They began their presentation by saying they did not think the national campaign had helped them at all. Their own results showed that they had been able to gain much bigger swings than the party average. Their experience on the ground told them that the Conservative campaign, based upon rigorous discipline and clear, simple messages, was not working for them. Honest Labour MPs and candidates would tell a similar story. Indeed they might tell it in an even more heartfelt way, given the number of seats they had lost and the huge divergences of result achieved by Labour candidates and MPs against all comers.

The Conservative Party under Michael Howard produced its most disciplined and focused campaign for many years. The leader had complete control with his immediate advisers, and kept the party to consistent messages around the ten words of 'cleaner hospitals, school discipline, more police, lower taxes and controlled immigration'. There was practically no dissension. The one person, Howard Flight, who was thought to have said something out of line was instantly dismissed not only from the front bench but also as a candidate. The Conservative campaign proved beyond doubt that message discipline, based around propositions that tested well with the focus groups and opinion pollsters, is not a guaranteed way to win a general election.

Labour had considerable message discipline as well. They too had checked the tea leaves, consulted the focus groups, and spent a fortune on opinion polling. Their basic message was that they offered a way forward rather than going backwards with the Tories. They kept repeating that they could be trusted with the economy, combining economic dynamism with social justice. They too did surprisingly badly for a disciplined party with a well-researched message. Labour polled only 9,547,944 votes throughout the UK, compared with 10,740,648 in June 2001. They were outpolled in England by the Conservatives: the Conservatives polled 8.1 million votes while Labour secured a little over eight million. Labour staggered to victory with only 35 per cent of the votes cast, compared with the 43 per cent or 44 per cent it normally took for a party to win in the previous century.

If the Liberal Democrats were ever going to break through in post-war British politics, 2005 was the time for them to do it. They had been the only one of the three main parties against the very unpopular war that Tony Blair had waged. They sought every opportunity to highlight this in their campaign. They did see their vote rise by a little over a million from 4.8 million in 2001 to just under six million in 2005 but at 22.1 per cent it was still more than ten percentage points below the Conservative vote, miles away from their far-fetched claims that they were about to replace the Conservatives as the principal opposition party and the main challenger to Labour. Indeed, their vote fell below the level it reached under a Conservative government in the 1980s.

Why should this be? It seems to be because the Liberals went out with a very unpopular policy of imposing a local income tax in every area, and then destroyed their own policy through a particularly inept press conference, where the Liberal Democrat leader was unable to give the basic figures of the consequences of the tax change. Because the Liberal Democrats were taken more seriously they were subject to rather tougher cross-questioning by the media than had been the case before, and they too became afflicted by the general political problem, that people do not trust political parties and think they lie to them. In many parts of the country people had experience of majority or minority Liberal Democratic local government. They had discovered that, far from it being squeaky clean, well run and good value, it often let them down in the same old way. Reality had caught up with the Liberal Democrats and they blew their best opportunity in fifty years to make a breakthrough.

Since the election the electorate has learnt much more about the Liberal Democrats. Those of us who were close to them in the House of Commons knew that there were great tensions between the so-called modernising Liberal Democrats, who wished to move their party much closer to the Conservative position of lower taxes, less regulation and less government, and the more traditional Liberal Democrat majority of MPs, who believe in the beneficial effects of government and would like more of it than Labour are currently offering. They had managed to paper over the cracks by keeping Charles Kennedy as their leader. Kennedy assumed a studied ambiguity about many of the important issues, enabling Liberal Democrat candidates in Conservative areas to move to the more Conservative end of the Liberal Democrat spectrum, and encouraging Liberal Democrat candidates in the Labour areas to move to a much more left-wing position. Post-election, both factions became frustrated with Kennedy's procrastination and indecisiveness whilst supporters of Sir Menzies Campbell became even more impatient, wishing to see their champion replace Kennedy as leader. The resulting campaign to oust Kennedy, followed by the divisive leadership election, has deflated Liberal Democratic ambitions to replace the Conservatives.

The mood throughout the 2005 election was one of dis-enchantment by the electorate. Whilst it is quite normal for a fifth or more of the electorate not to bother to vote because they are not very interested in politics, it is unusual for two-fifths not to vote. A sizeable proportion of the electorate were aggressive abstainers. When you spoke to them on the doorsteps they were well informed about political issues. They had read articles about the political situation, they had seen representatives of the principal parties on television or heard them on the radio, and were aware of the main issues and campaign themes. They made a positive decision not to vote because they did not like anything on offer. They commonly told canvassers that they did not think it would make any difference how they voted. This did not necessarily mean that the outcome of the race in their constituency was a foregone conclusion because one party had a large inherited majority. Many of them were quite canny enough to understand that in the current fickle world of politics there is no safe seat, and it is quite possible for tides of opinion within an individual constituency to unseat even the Labour candidate for Blaenau Gwent. What they meant by their phrase was that they did not think their individual MP, whoever he or she might be, would have influence if he or she wished to move things in the direction they wanted. They were sceptical about whether any of the candidates locally would be true to their word and stand up for their voters' interests.

Where the electorate was persuaded to make a change, where they found a candidate they liked who they thought might make a difference, turnout rose. In Hammersmith & Fulham, where the Conservatives took the seat, turnout was up by six percentage points. In Brent East, where the Liberal Democrats held their by-election gain, turnout rose by 5.3 points, and in Newbury, where the Conservatives unseated the incumbent Liberal Democrat David Rendell, turnout was boosted by 4.7 points. It was possible for a good candidate or campaign to add another five percentage points to the turnout, which could make all the difference to the result. Nowhere did the boost to turnout get it back to the levels that were traditional in twentieth-century elections.

These successes in local campaigning do not seem to be matched by enthusiasm for the national campaigns, which must take the main blame for the very low turnout overall. The Conservative and

Labour campaigns were models of discipline. For some eight months leading Conservatives just kept repeating their ten words, with the addition of 'accountability' into the script from time to time. These words appeared on every e-mail sent out by party representatives, on quite a few letter headings and on most leaflets, and were used in every broadcast where the shadow spokesperson remembered his or her lines. They informed the day-by-day press conferences, launches and events during the election campaign itself, and had also dominated the Conservatives' offerings from the party conference in the autumn of 2004 right through to the May election the following year.

Despite the tight discipline and the consistency of the message, it had very little impact. During the period between the beginning of March and the announcement of a general election, less than 1 per cent of electors remembered the Conservative phrase or point on schools, hospitals, police or tax, and even immigration was mentioned by fewer than those who voted Conservative. Recall of the Conservative message was little better during the election campaign itself and tailed off towards the end of the campaign, probably reflecting the fact that people had made up their minds. Polling also shows that the Labour national campaign, in a poll taken just a few days before the general election, fared no better. Voters in the 130 Labour marginals said by a margin of 27 per cent to 13 per cent that the Labour national campaign had made them less inclined to vote Labour, with 57 per cent saying it made no difference. The Conservative national campaign had inclined a fifth of the target seat voters towards the Conservatives but more than a third, 36 per cent, had become less favourable. Local campaigns had had a more even impact upon both types of voter.

The polls showed that people did not trust the political parties. Around 30 per cent thought that Conservatives or Labour would deliver and less than 35 per cent the Liberal Democrats. By a big margin, people did not trust the Prime Minister, nor did they think he had been a particularly good Prime Minister. Unfortunately for the Conservatives they had no more faith in them.

By general agreement of the public, the election campaign was lacklustre. As one who fought it day by day on the doorsteps, I remember endless conversations with people complaining about the media election they were seeing on television. They felt it was all dumbed down and not discussing in an open and frank way the things that mattered most to them. Their frustration could have been directed at the media as well as the politicians. In an effort to make the election exciting, the media treated most party politicians as likely liars and subjected them to bruising and consistent cross-examination on the same point or points, allowing little scope for any of the parties to develop a more mature argument. They made it difficult to discuss issues that the electorate were interested in but which did not happen to dominate the media and party agendas of the day.

On the doorstep people were talking about world poverty, fair trade, the environment, local planning issues, quality of life in their community, the Iraq war, the follow-up to the tsunami, and the other big issues that had dominated in the press over previous months. Meanwhile Labour were insistent on talking about the economy, health and education and the Conservatives continued with their five themes, laying especial emphasis upon immigration and crime.

Neither main party wanted to spend a lot of time on taxation, even though lower taxation was one of the Conservatives' chosen five themes. The electorate wanted to talk about the council tax. The election took place against the backdrop of large council tax bills, often reflecting substantial increases in individual areas, dropping on to the doormat. The Liberal Party thought they were on to a winner with their proposal to scrap the council tax and replace it with local income tax. People's experiences of new taxes was unpleasant and there was a natural scepticism about how the numbers might work out. When the Liberal Democrat leader, Charles Kennedy, failed to answer basic questions about the financial impact of his changes in one of the news conferences, the public got the idea that in many places a local income tax would put their bill up rather than reducing it.

Labour spent the election claiming that the economy was in such a good shape that they would not need to increase taxes, despite the many forecasts from independent forecasters that there was a big gap between revenue and expenditure that would need plugging after the election. The Conservatives offered some relief from council tax bills for pensioners, which was popular on the doorsteps but had to be marketed door by door, street by street, through local campaign literature as it received little national prominence. For the rest of the electorate the Conservatives seemed to be offering nothing on taxation.

Many electors decided this was an election to miss. They did not particularly like Labour or Tony Blair. They did not believe many of the things Blair told them. They did not like his war in Iraq, and they thought Labour would probably put taxes up if re-elected. However, they also did not trust the Conservatives, did not think they would provide a better answer, remembered that they had supported the war, and thought that, whatever they might say about taxes, they too would end up increasing them. On this basis the largest block of voters stayed at home and the two major parties slumped to a uniquely low level for their combined efforts in a general election.

People did expect an energetic, local campaign. Whilst many were not at home or were not keen to have an extensive doorstep conversation with a canvasser, the prevailing mood was against voting for parties that did not bother. Contact with the electorate was extremely important. Parties discovered that direct letters and e-mails supplementing the general leaflets were important means of communicating and encouraging those who did support to come out to vote. The election degenerated into frantic efforts by each of the major parties to mobilise their core supporters against a general background of disillusion and dislike of the political offering.

British democratic politics has been brought low by a combination of forces. The fact that both the Conservative and Labour parties have misled people with regard to taxation over the last fifteen years is one of the most important influences. The Conservative decision to increase taxes after the debacle of the Exchange Rate Mechanism favoured by all parties in the early 1990s wiped out their reputation for good economic management and honest dealing. The slump in Conservative fortunes at the polls can be dated to that event. Labour similarly misled the public by telling them at each of the general elections they fought they would not increase taxes. They then went on to do so, through big increases in national insurance, council tax, pensions taxation, utility taxation and a host of other ways. Labour have been caught misleading the public in a number of other areas. Blair won the 2001 election on the promise of no student fees but was busily legislating to introduce them by the end of the parliament. Although he kept the letter of his promise by not imposing them within that parliament, people felt he had broken the spirit of what he said. Labour said they would scale down the quango state but instead built it up. They promised to end sleaze but then fell prey to a whole series of difficulties in ministers' public and private lives, which led to a spate of resignations – just like the government before them. The Liberal Democrats have also fallen foul of scepticism about their honesty in places where they have won control of a council and failed to deliver. They too will struggle following the revelation that they had all been misleading the public over Kennedy's drinking problem.

The only thing a politician has which is worth having is his or her word. If you use it casually and get a reputation for misleading people, you lose the most precious thing you have in politics. Why should people believe you if in the past you have misled them? How can you expect people to trust you as a political leader if your actions reveal an untrustworthiness in your heart?

This breakdown in trust has been reinforced by the growth of the European institutions and the quango state. People now recognise that there are quite a lot of politicians who seek to do the right thing, seek to represent them, and seek to tell the truth. Unfortunately, all too often the elected politician in the Westminster Parliament discovers that they are not able to get the result they want on behalf of their electors because an independent quango in Britain, or the member states of the European Union, make the decision instead. Allied to perceptions of the unreliability of political parties has come a strong perception that in many cases, even if well intentioned, the political parties lack the power that is needed.

People also stay at home when they do not think their vote will count in the particular place where they are voting. The Liberal Democrats make a great point about this as part of their incessant campaign for proportional representation (PR). People in so-called safe seats are now often encouraged to believe that there's no point in voting because the outcome is a foregone conclusion. The outcome is only inevitable if those people do go and vote. Parties with so-called safe seats now have to work very hard in them, to make sure that their electorate does not become so complacent that they lose the seat by default on a low turnout. The problem with PR is that, far from solving the problem of the perceived issue of dishonesty in politicians, it makes politicians far more dishonest. As the German election of 2005 showed, under a PR system the apparent winners, the Christian Democrats, had to ditch most of their campaign promises in order to form a coalition with their principal rivals. In a PR world, policy gets decided after the election when the electorate has no influence on it, in a process of bargaining which entails the loss of principle and breaking promises by the leading players. This would not seem to be a good model for tackling the underlying British malaise, the lack of trust in politics and politicians.

Disillusion with the party political system in general elections is not the same as a complete lack of political interest in the country at large. Many of the abstainers were very interested in the issues. They were frustrated rather than uncommitted. It is our task now to look at the ways in which people are in fact participating in active politics in our community and our country, despite the growing disillusion with the party political system at its top.

2

Anyone for a protest?

I WANT TO MAKE A DIFFERENCE

Campaigning
I still think joining a campaigning organisation or joining in one
of their campaigns is right for me

It may well be – it's as much a part of politics as joining a party,
and very similar
You should always ask before you commit:

- How much do I have to give to join?
- What do they do with my money?
- How does the action required by this campaign really make a
  difference?
- Is it directed to the people who have the power to change
  things for the better?
- Does it understand the people in power well enough to make
  it likely they will change their minds?
- Do I have to get very involved in the campaign?
- Will I appear in the local media if I join in?
- How do I know it will be more than a one-day media wonder?
- What action is being taken to see the campaign through?
- What is the likelihood of success?

Many people are growing to like their politics more from campaigning organisations than from political parties. At the same time as
the number of voters turning out at the polling stations is in decline,
we are seeing strong growth in the number of people prepared to

write to their MP, send in a campaign postcard or join up for a campaign run by one of the large campaigning organisations.

Issues that affect people's local environment are the ones likely to bring out the strongest interest in politics. Threaten a green field next to a settlement with major development and a couple of hundred people are likely to turn up to the protest meeting. Threaten overdevelopment of a whole settlement and a sizeable proportion of the residents will write their own individual letters to the local council and to the local MP, asking them to resist the incursions. Hold a meeting about cleaning up the local river or improving the look of the town, and again a hundred people may well turn out and express enthusiasm for the project. People can understand the issue, and they hope that their individual action when lumped together with their neighbours' will make some difference.

People are also prepared to take an interest in the bigger issues and global concerns. Two of the most successful campaigning organisations operating in Britain are Friends of the Earth and Greenpeace. They've captured the mood. People understand that we only have a leasehold interest in the earth. We wish to pass it on in good order to our children. We're becoming increasingly aware of the impact that man's settlement and living habits can have upon the natural environment around us. Friends of the Earth and Greenpeace in their different ways campaign to keep the seas clean, the rivers pure, the fields free of dangerous chemicals, and the air above us in good order. It is difficult to disagree with their aims.

An increasingly common feature of an MP's postbag is the standardised campaign card. Well-funded, successful campaign organisations issue tens of thousands of these cards to their members and their friends. It is a simple act to put your name at the bottom of a card and send it to your MP. A card of early 2006 from Friends of the Earth is typical. It states:

Parliament will debate the Company Law Reform Bill this spring. This is a unique opportunity to help deliver trade justice and make UK companies accountable for the impact of their activities in the UK and overseas.

At present the proposed Bill only obliges company directors to deliver profits to shareholders. It denies justice to people overseas whose health, livelihoods and environment are being harmed by irresponsible UK companies.

Whether it's rainforests being cleared to produce palm oil for British supermarkets, or communities in Nigeria suffering because of Shell's harmful activities, there are countless examples of why we need legislation urgently to make companies work for people and planet. Please back amendments to the Bill so that: companies are legally obliged to minimise any damage their company does to local communities and the environment. People overseas who were harmed by the activities of a UK company are able to take action against them in a UK court.

Please sign an Early Day Motion 697 modernising company law and write to Alan Michael, MP, Minister for Industry. Please urge him to amend the Company Reform Bill and to hold companies accountable for their impact on workers, communities and the environment.

People across the country are invited to put a stamp on one of these cards and write their name and address on the bottom, so that the MP knows they are a constituent and may like to reply to them.

This card is typical of the genre developed by these campaigning organisations. It is hard-hitting and presents complex matters in an oversimplified way. We are left unclear as to why a company law reform Bill in one medium-sized country in the world is 'a unique opportunity to help deliver trade justice'. Surely the unique opportunity to deliver trade justice occurred when the United Kingdom simultaneously chaired the G8 and held the European Union presidency, and was conducting high-level talks with the leaders of all the world's countries over trade rules and trade management. It is also difficult to understand the comment 'the proposed Bill only obliges company directors to deliver profits to shareholders'. I see no such reference in the Bill. It would be quite absurd for a Bill or Act of Parliament to oblige company directors to deliver profits. Many companies trade at breakeven or at a loss. Some of them do not wish to make losses and it would compound their difficulties if they were then breaking the law by failing to deliver a profit. Who would be a director in these circumstances if companies had to make profits?

It is also beyond comprehension how the UK Companies Bill denies justice to people overseas. British companies operating outside UK jurisdiction in foreign countries are clearly subject to the law of the land in which they are operating. If Friends of the Earth are not happy with the standards required of British companies operating in a third country, surely the correct thing to do is to lobby that third country to change its law to bring its standards up to acceptable international practice. Like Friends of the Earth, I'm very unhappy to see large chunks of rainforest being cleared. The sad truth of life is that if Britain did manage to find some legal means of stopping, limiting or fining British companies who were in some way complicit in it, it would do nothing to stop all the companies from other parts of the world assisting the countries in their clearance programmes. Again, surely the campaign should be targeted on the governments of the countries responsible for destroying the rainforest?

Even if you accept the terms of Friends of the Earth's complaint and argument, it is difficult to see how their supposed remedy would solve their problem. If directors were under a legal obligation to minimise any damage their company does, it would be a matter of judgement as to whether they had carried this out in any particular case. If a British multinational invests in a developing-world economy, it is usually because there are people and government officials in the host economy that wish to see the British multinational operating there. They presumably do so because they believe the balance of advantage lies in accepting the investment. The British multinational would create jobs, it would supply more product to the local market, it may offer additional facilities to the local economy, and it would usually be seen as an improvement on what had gone before. Directors would be able to pray this all in aid. It would be unlikely that a successful case could be brought, given the complex judgements involved. Any given company would claim it was buying produce from areas where rainforest had been destroyed long ago. How could you trace something to the most recent plantation without the help of the host country?

These cards usually ask MPs to sign an early day motion (EDM).

EDMs are a kind of parliamentary graffiti. There are hundreds of them on the list at any given time. What the campaigning group rarely explains is that EDMs are rarely or never debated and have little impact on the political process. If you wish to get an EDM debated you have to persuade either the government or one of the leading opposition parties to table a new motion for debate, in time which is theirs to allocate.

The only conceivable use of an EDM would be to demonstrate the strength of disquiet amongst the government's own MPs about something which the government was doing. No government minister is going to be very surprised or interested if a couple of hundred opposition MPs all sign the same EDM censuring the government or urging it to do something different. They might be a bit more interested if more than 100 government MPs also signed an EDM critical of the government or urging it to do something else, although it is more likely that this pressure of opinion would have been come clear through whips' soundings and conversations before the EDM attracted such support.

Friends of the Earth had a similar campaign which set out to save the orang-utan. The argument ran that British companies were buying palm oil from new plantations. These new plantations resulted from wholesale clearance of rainforest in the Equatorial belt. This reduced the habitat for the orang-utans and, therefore, cut their population. Like Friends of the Earth I would love to see a way to keep more rainforest and with it the flora and fauna. I'm sure the orang-utans are very fine creatures and it is a pity if they are being routed out of house and home by wholesale logging. However, it is difficult to see how signing an EDM in the UK Parliament, with a view to changing British company law, would be sufficient to ride to the rescue of the orang-utan. British companies buying palm oil could always claim that they were doing so from sustainable plantations that had been put in some years earlier. It is difficult to identify which company is buying the marginal palm oil from the newest plantation which has resulted from the most recent cut in the forest. Even if it were possible to find a legal means of nailing down British-registered companies, any Act of Parliament would have absolutely no jurisdiction or impact on the thousands of companies from around the world not registered in the UK who are also buying palm oil.

Sometimes an MP gets a campaign card which makes rather more sense. The Democracy Movement in early 2006 issued one concerning fraud and waste in the EU. It took the form of a mock cheque from the Treasury to the EU of £115 million every week, the British net contribution to the EU from 2007. On the other side it states:

> The European Union's accounts have not been approved by EU auditors for 11 years running.
>
> Marta Andreasen, the EU's former Chief Accountant, was sacked by former EU Commissioner Neil Kinnock for revealing that accounting systems were open to fraud. She said, 'Opportunities for fraud are open and they are taken advantage of. The most elementary precautions are neither taken or even contemplated.'
>
> Yet the government still pays £4.3 billion to the EU every year, even taking into account the EU grants received back. Now, Tony Blair has agreed to increase payments to £6 billion a year from 2007 – that's £115 million every week. ... As my MP please explain why you feel it's acceptable to hand astonishing amounts of public money to an organisation beset by fraud and whose accounts have not been approved by auditors for 11 years running.
>
> Or, alternatively, what urgent action are you taking to stop payments to the EU, at least until we can be certain that public money is protected from fraud.

This card is short and to the point. It gives references for its quotations and cites Treasury sources for its figure work. It does not suggest there is an easy answer or invite an MP merely to sign an EDM to condemn it. Instead it puts legitimate pressure on the MP to ask what he or she is doing to tackle the problem of fraud and waste in the EU, and to protect taxpayers' interests here in Britain.

The Friends of the Earth website is a good example of the new, large, global campaigning organisations. It is slick and well presented. The front page on the day I checked told you to join Campaign Express for free. It told you that they are running campaigns on global trade, climate and other matters. It asked you to get involved, to act local, to volunteer, to donate.

Money is at the heart of much of what they do. The page on donations told you that if you give £15 it will help pay for campaign postcards and other forms of individual action 'to show business and industry the strength of our voice'. If you give £25 it will help to pay for a campaigner's time, lobbying MPs and meeting with key business people. If you give £50 it will help pay for research 'so we can give government and industry the real facts'. The page asked for your financial details and offered you the chance of paying by a range of international credit cards.

One of the recent Friends of the Earth campaigns is about palm oil. The site told us that palm oil is found in one in ten of the goods we buy from supermarkets, including soap, chocolate, toothpaste, biscuits, cosmetics and muesli. Friends of the Earth believe that palm oil plantations are now often grown on land that was once rainforest, and this in turn is endangering species such as tigers, elephants and orang-utans. Friends of the Earth think that British business should be more careful about where it buys its palm oil from, and it should be helping to source and develop sustainable palm oil production. Their answer to this huge international problem is to demand new rules for big business from the British Parliament.

Their site prominently attacked Shell. Shell have recently announced that they are going to sponsor the British Wildlife Photographer of the Year competition, retitled the Shell Wildlife Photographer of the Year. Friends of the Earth, in hard-hitting prose, stated:

> The new sponsorship deal will undermine everything the competition stood for. Shell has frequently been criticised for the damaging impacts of its operations around the world ... If Shell put half the effort into cleaning up its act as it puts into promoting a green image then it might be entitled to trumpet its support for global biodiversity. The sad reality is that after years of making green claims this company is still causing unacceptable damage to wildlife, it's polluting local communities and is helping to accelerate climate change.

The site then listed a whole series of reports and studies of Shell's conduct around the world, and invited you to leaf through the archive that shows a pattern of alleged behaviour from Shell that Friends of the Earth condemn, dating back to 1994.

Friends of the Earth ran a campaign called 'The Big Ask'. They told us it is about tackling the biggest question the world faces: 'How do we stop dangerous climate change?' They said, 'The most important part of the question is – is the government doing enough about climate change? . . . Are you ready to get the government to tackle the big question? It's a huge obstacle to climb – but together we can do it.' The main aim of the campaign was to get MPs to pass a Bill mandating government to make annual 3 per cent CO_2 emission cuts year on year.

What strikes one most about Friends of the Earth in the UK is that practically everything is seen in terms of a top-down campaign, centring around the British Parliament. There is not the same fascination with EU legislation, even though success in this area would affect so many more people and countries at a single go. The site shows less enthusiasm to get people to do things for themselves. It is true that under Local Campaigns and Groups on the website we're told, 'There are around 200 local groups in the Friends of the Earth network in England, Wales and Northern Ireland, including the Channel Islands and Isle of Man.' However, if you wish to find out about that you have to log on to a community website with no address supplied on the national site.

After exploring Links you can discover the contact of your local group. When I logged on to mine for Wokingham in January 2006, it was displaying Wokingham Friends of the Earth meeting dates for 2005 and was advertising the Wokingham Friends of the Earth newsletter for January 2005. It contained a plea for help with the Trade Justice campaign of 16 April 2005, and it supplied my name and address as MP. The site was trying to persuade the members to write to me to get me to sign Early Day Motion 406, concerning biotech products.

On the part of the site which tells you what you can do as an individual to make a difference, considerable emphasis is again placed on writing to MPs. They tell you, 'If an MP gets five letters on a subject it's a big deal (though obviously more is better). So a handful of your neighbours could kick your MP's ass by writing letters with a personal touch.' The Friends of the Earth top tip for a green Christmas, still on their website in the middle of January 2006, was: 'Buy your loved ones a year's support to Friends of the Earth – they receive gifts including *Earth Matters*, seeds and the *Little Green Book of Big Green Ideas*, and you know you've helped us with our vital work to protect the environment.' Their top tip for 'saving cash and saving the planet' was to spend £12.99 on the Friends of the Earth-recommended book of the same name. And the Friends of the Earth tip of the day was to 'subscribe to receive a free tip of the day Monday to Friday by e-mail', which requires filling in a form and supplying your address.

In summary, the Friends of the Earth website is a good, state-of-the-art, global company website encouraging people by all sorts of means to divulge their e-mail address and interest, and in some cases their postal address, to Friends of the Earth and to part with their money to boost the funds and power of the campaigning corporation. It is a delicious irony of the environmental movement that it uses so many of the techniques developed by the marketing and sales programmes of large corporations which the environmental movement so strenuously attacks.

Friends of the Earth UK see themselves in very nationalistic terms, concentrating on campaigning in Britain. This is probably because they recognise that members of the Westminster Parliament are responsive to and interested in their constituents' views, an interest encouraged by the first-past-the-post electoral system and the relatively small size of constituencies. The website mentions little of Brussels and campaigns to change the views of the EU. This is particularly surprising given the growing power of the EU in the environmental sphere, and the fact that environmental issues, which most concern Friends of the Earth, clearly transcend national boundaries and are usually global in their reach.

Greenpeace are even stronger than Friends of the Earth on what they are doing. They exhort us on the front page of their website to 'stop climate change, save our seas, protect ancient forests, say no to genetic engineering, eliminate toxic chemicals, end the nuclear age

[and] encourage sustainable trade'. The front page invites us to support them, to sign up and to get involved. The front page of the UK website for Greenpeace invited us to supply our e-mail address to receive the latest news, when I logged on. It told us to join them to campaign against nuclear power stations on the grounds that they would increase the risk of a catastrophic terrorist attack, 'which could claim millions of lives'. The front page also contained an apology 'for the serious error affecting some supporters' direct debit claims over the Christmas period'. We were invited to write to our MP 'to demand a nationwide debate on the replacement of Trident'.

Like Friends of the Earth, they have views on how to get the most out of an MP, although Greenpeace do couch it in rather pleasanter terms. They stated:

Please bear in mind that an MP is a busy person who has to deal with literally thousands of letters on a daily basis. Remember to be brief, objective and relevant. This sample letter is a guide. We very much recommend that you don't just copy it. A letter in your own words expressing your own concerns will usually get a better response from your Member of Parliament than simply copying this one.

Greenpeace also invited us to send a letter or an e-mail to Asda to complain about the seafood they offer for sale. Just like Friends of the Earth, they're also keen that we support them and they thoughtfully have an ability to donate online. They tell us:

Our vision of a better future is only as strong as the people who support us. As a matter of principle we don't solicit money from business or government. Your gift will be put to work straight away to defend the environment and will help to defend ancient life, defend ancient forests and promote renewable energy.

Greenpeace is a global environmental organisation with an international council in Amsterdam and twenty-seven national and regional offices around the world. It claims a presence in forty-one countries. It claims to be 'committed to the principle of non-violence, political and economic independence in internationalism, and to run campaigns that will make a difference'. Greenpeace turns out to be a franchise with national and regional offices licensed to use the name. Each office is governed by a board usually elected by a voting membership of volunteers and activists. Greenpeace does place its EU materials prominently on its website as well as those of the national organisations, and it has some content about the legislative efforts of the EU in its chosen field. It also makes available through a link its annual reports, which give a breakdown of its income and spending.

Friends of the Earth in the UK carries out its activities through two different companies. Friends of the Earth Limited (FEL) is a campaigning company free to undertake political activity. Friends of the Earth Trust Limited (FETL) is a charitable company which has to be more circumspect in what it says and does. It is allowed to supply public information and educational materials but is not allowed to campaign politically.

Between them the two FoE companies managed to raise £8.89 million in 2005. Most of the revenue for both companies comes in the form of donations from individual supporters. FEL spent £306,227 on recruiting new supporters or donors and £228,864 on general fund raising. FETL spent an additional £197,650 on supporter recruitment and another £168,610 on fund raising. This means that Friends of the Earth, through its two organisations, spent over 10 per cent of its donations on new fund raising and the attraction of new supporters. The bulk of FEL's expenditure, around £5 million, went on campaigning whilst most of FETL's money, just over £2.5 million, was spent on information and education.

Greenpeace also takes raising cash and support very seriously and spends substantial sums on it. The Greenpeace accounts for 2004 show an income of €158.5 million from grants and donations – the over-whelming bulk of the total income of the Greenpeace movement. €43 million was spent in that year on fund-raising costs, a sizeable 27 per cent of the total income raised. Greenpeace also spent an additional €24.6 million, or over 15 per cent of the total, on administration. Worldwide Greenpeace enjoyed 2.7 million supporters, who were seen as a source of income as well as a campaigning strength, as Greenpeace spoke to governments and multinational companies.

The interaction of money and popular pressure was very clear in Greenpeace's vaunted campaign in the United States. According to its website:

> Greenpeace won a significant victory for freedom of speech after the Bush administration mounted a unique prosecution of the organisation in the US. Greenpeace was acquitted of conspiracy charges after the judge agreed the prosecution had failed to prove the case. A record number of 100,000 cyber activists sent messages to President Bush and US Attorney General John Ashcroft demanding the end of the prosecution.

It helps to have supporters and money when your activities lead you into legal disputes with powerful governments.

Greenpeace also needed its money for good legal advice in another battle in France in 2004. As its website stated: 'In a victory for freedom of expression, the French court overturned all oil giant Esso's attempts to censor Greenpeace. Esso took Greenpeace to court when we used a parody of the company's logo, as part of our "Don't buy Esso, don't buy Exxon Mobil" campaign.' These campaigning organisations live dangerously, taking on the powerful and rich, which is why they need access to substantial sums from their supporters.

This, then, is the face of the new politics. People will take their own individual action, expressing their views and worries in their own words if it applies to something local which they think their councillors and their MP may be able to influence. They will lend their voice to large campaigning organisations on issues such as toxic waste, nuclear power, animal cruelty, the rape of the rainforest, or dirty air and water. They trust campaigning organisations such as Greenpeace and Friends of the Earth more than they trust some political parties. They recognise that these organisations have an expertise, they understand that they use aggressive campaigning techniques, and they are happy for them to do so as they feel it provides some antidote to the powerful forces of government and big business.

Many MPs simply send the campaign postcards to the government, or send the standard government or opposition reply to their constituents. I find that if I write back as MP with a query or a disagreement there is often no response. People are easily persuaded to send in the cards but are often unwilling to back up the view on the card if you challenge it. Sometimes they are embarrassed that they have put their name to a card without considering other points of view. Sometimes they are angered to discover the campaigning organisation had been partial or biased in its presentation of the case. Sometimes they only put in the card to avoid saying 'no' to a friend or street campaigner, and do not want to waste time on responding.

Occasionally campaign cards judge the mood and the understanding of electors better. People who sent in anti-fox hunting cards prepared by the campaign did mean it. They understood the arguments and could back them up. Sometimes people become muddled when different campaign organisations link up without explaining the connections. The Christina Churches Fair Trade Movement has become linked with Friends of the Earth's English company law campaign in a way which has not been fully explained to all its supporters.

There is a danger in this for the political process. Whilst I often have admiration for the aims of some of the campaigns run by the campaigning organisations, they too should be careful about their techniques. If they think of themselves too much and spend too much of their money on themselves, the same disillusion will set in with them that has set in with political parties generally. A lot of the disillusion relates to the money-raising treadmill that political parties find themselves on. It has got to its most dramatic overextension in the USA, where millions of dollars have to be raised for a modest congressional race, and hundreds of millions of dollars now have to be raised to be a serious presidential runner. Everything is done by professionals. Polling, campaign themes, focus groups, communications, advertisements are all done by media-savvy professionals at considerable cost to the campaign. As a result, the campaigning politicians and parties need to raise ever-bigger sums from the public and from business to stay in the race.

The campaigning organisations have to be aware. If they're not careful they too will have to cut too many corners to raise their money and will be seen by the public not as white knights on chargers but as similar organisations to political parties, scrambling for cash and support in a very overpopulated marketplace.

3

Where does the power lie?

I WANT TO MAKE A DIFFERENCE

Influence
If you want to influence something for the better, first find out how it is run and who runs it

Say you want to influence the range of drugs available on the NHS, by adding a new one
You need to find out if the drug is not available because
- your local hospital won't buy and prescribe it
- your local health authority won't use it
- it is not recommended by NICE, the national body that approves medicines
- the NHS has a problem with it

If it is a local decision, you need first to try to influence the chief executive and the board of the local NHS trust
If they refuse to change their minds, then you can try getting the local health authority to bring influence to bear

If it is a national decision, you need to contact NICE
If they are dug in against the remedy, then try your local MP and ask him or her to engage government ministers

Does going public with the campaign help?
Yes it does – all of these NHS bodies, both local and national, are concerned about bad publicity
If you hit them in the headlines they are more likely to take notice
The central NHS and ministers are kept informed about local press and media criticisms, as well as the more prominent national ones

Does getting more people to join the campaign help?
Yes it does
Try to organise a patients'/users' group whose members want the new medicine and are prepared to talk to the press about its benefits
Get independent professional endorsements for the treatment
Show how it works in countries that have adopted it

Pressure group politics works
It works because it targets the issue, concentrates the media mind and makes the government or quango respond

The government's worry about the growing disillusion with politics and politicians led to the establishment of a committee under Baroness Kennedy to investigate the problem. Amongst her conclusions was the sensible point that people were disillusioned because they did not believe that MPs had much impact any more on what the government did. She saw the problem largely in terms of the accountability of United Kingdom ministers to the British Parliament. She was right but this is part of a much wider problem.

It's not just that people, correctly, perceive that ministers are not as answerable as they used to be to Parliament and to their local MP. They have also worked out that many things are now decided by quangos outside the reach of not just their local MP but of many of the ministers. Many more things are settled in Brussels by the European Union, which seems to have a will of its own as far as the British electorate is concerned. There is a growing worry about the lack of power and influence of local councillors and local government in general. Frustrations build up in each local community. They know what they would like. Their local councillor or their local MP may agree with them. A local MP may be active and vocal in pursuing the case but all too often the local community is thwarted. The eventual result is the opposite of what they wished or intended.

Baroness Kennedy is right that ministers in recent years have become very adept at shifting power away from Parliament and themselves, and dodging questions in Parliament. Under the traditional British constitution of the twentieth century ministers made all the important decisions and they were answerable to Parliament for them. If they wished to change the law they had to enact a new piece of legislation, which requires considerable parliamentary time and scrutiny. If they made a decision about how to spend our money or how to interpret the law, that could be challenged in Parliament and in the courts. An opposition in the twentieth-century British Parliament had considerable powers to delay, harry or get the government to change its mind. Most legislation went through without any limitation on the time for debate, allowing the opposition full scope to analyse the measure clause by clause, line by line, word by word if necessary. If an opposition was suspicious about a government action or a minister's decision, there were various ways to tease out from those in power what had happened and to bring them to account.

The new Labour government elected in 1997 decided that ministers were too exposed and too accountable. It deliberately set about reducing the ways in which Parliament could call it to account, force it to change its mind or get it to discuss what it was doing. It was only too well aware from its success in opposition of how powerful a written question could be. MPs were allowed to ask any minister any day of the week through a written question anything they liked about what that minister was doing in his or her department, what the government's policy was, what decisions had been taken, what money was being spent. It was always the duty of the minister on advice of his or her officials to answer the question. An incoming question immediately generated a file. Civil servants would go off and research the answer. They would present their findings to the minister, who would agree on the answer.

Of course, Conservative ministers in the 1979–1997 government were aware of the hazards of honest answering of parliamentary questions. We permitted ourselves the right to add to the answer additional information which could take some of the edge off the embarrassment which the strict answer might have caused. For example, if during the period of high unemployment written questions were tabled to elicit details of unemployment in the worst-affected areas, the minister approving the answer might well add some of the better news about employment in the less badly affected parts of the country. The minister did not feel he had the right to refuse the information the questioner was asking, assuming it was asked about something for which the government had responsibility and the information was in the hands of the government department concerned.

The present government seems to take a different view of written questions. As this is a government of the spinners, by the spinners, for the spinners, ministers object strongly to having to put out in the public domain answers to questions that give a different view to the line they are trying to put forward. They therefore use a number of techniques to avoid answering the most embarrassing questions. Sometimes they merely refuse to give an answer on the grounds of complexity or cost. Sometimes they answer a different question to the one that was actually being asked. Sometimes they state that the information is already in the public domain, not wishing to repeat embarrassing information in their own words. Sometimes the House authorities do not let MPs table the question they would like to ask, on the grounds that the Table Office already knows that ministers won't be answering that sort of question.

Many people think that an MP can ask anything he likes when he likes. Life in a Parliament controlled by the modern Labour government gives the lie to this. Constituents are surprised when I tell them some things they wish to ask would not be permitted at all, and that others when asked will not be answered. One of the ways round this used to be to ask an oral question. The rules of order can be less onerous in the heat of exchanges in the House of Commons than trying to deal with the cerebral Table Office in the cold light of morning, when it comes to what a minister should be prepared to answer. Parliament as a whole may have a different view to officials operating under tight rules and trying to come to a judgement about written questions. However, those of us who wish to pursue an interest or a problem through oral questions are often defeated by the same spin techniques that have changed the nature of the written answer. Ministers are usually pre-programmed to give the same answer whatever the question so that they are setting out their stall. If a questioner is persistent from an opposition party then the minister will decide to give the questioner a history lesson about things that happened fifteen or twenty years ago under a different government, rather than admit to what is going on under the one of which he is a member.

Closing down answers to questions closes down a lot of debate and greatly damages accountability. Under the pure system a minister should reveal what he knows. The information can often be embarrassing to the minister. It may reveal that the policy is not working out as planned. It could reveal that the minister made a bad judgement or failed to do something he promised to do. It is rare these days to catch ministers out by asking the right question, as it is rare to get an accurate, honest and full answer to parliamentary questions.

The problem with accountability has been compounded when it comes to probing and examining their legislation. Under the regime before 1997 very few Bills were timetabled or guillotined. Most Bills were given as long as the opposition wished in committee to discuss matters of importance. Governments only resorted to a guillotine or a timetabled motion if the opposition was being unnecessarily dilatory because it did not like the measure. If, for example, a committee had spent 50 or 60 hours discussing only the first clause of a Bill then the government might return to the floor of the House of Commons with a special timetable motion, saying there had to be some limit to the amount of time it was prepared to spend in committee, given the attitude of the opposition. Each one of these guillotine motions was usually bitterly contested and only a small fraction of the legislation went through under the unpopular guillotine. It was always in the opposition's power to avoid the guillotine by making reasonable progress in committee.

The new government elected in 1997 decided to have none of it. Having itself often in opposition used time as a weapon against legislation it did not like, it was determined to push its legislative programme through with the minimum of effort. It decided that each Bill coming before the House would have at the time of its second reading a timetable motion. This would limit the amount of time the Bill was to be considered on the floor of the House as well as in committee. It is very difficult to judge at the outset how long an opposition will need to examine a Bill properly. In some cases current timetable motions allow more time than is needed. If it turns out on examination that the Bill is not particularly contentious or that the detail of the Bill does conform with the general principles set out on second reading, there is little point in the opposition going on at great length in committee even if it dislikes the principles of the Bill.

In other cases contentious Bills may also have very contentious drafting. The opposition may genuinely think that there could be substantial improvements in the detail of the Bill, even though they are not in favour of the principle. There are often glaring errors or problems with the Bill as drafted that need to be properly explored. All too often these days large chunks of a Bill go through with no Commons scrutiny whatsoever, as the time simply runs out in the committee and the committee chairman has to conclude under the terms of the timetable motion that the committee has completed its consideration of the Bill, although many clauses have never been examined.

All primary legislation goes through several stages in each of the Commons and the Lords. The first reading means simply tabling the Bill without discussion. On second reading there is longish debate about the principles of the Bill. At this point MPs of all parties and of none can ask: is this Bill really necessary, is it a good idea, will it achieve what it sets out to achieve? In the committee stages MPs are meant to give line-by-line, word-by-word scrutiny to the detail of the legislation in the light of the government's intentions. The Bill then returns to the Commons or to the Lords at the report stage, where further important amendments can be considered prior to a shortish third reading, which goes back to the principles of the Bill in the light of the amendments achieved.

The government has intensified the difficulties with the guillotine by introducing the concept of 'knives under the guillotine'. Instead of just setting an overall time limit for consideration of the Bill in committee and on report, the government may also set specified points by which certain parts of the Bill have to be decided. This means that if the opposition genuinely has lots of problems with the first three clauses but not with the rest of the Bill, it will have a very tight timetable on those first clauses if a knife is imposed, and then rather more time than it needs to consider the remaining parts of the Bill. This compounds the essential problem of the guillotine. It takes away from the opposition the ability to decide how much time to use and how to use that time to best effect in order to highlight the weaknesses of the Bill and to suggest improvements.

The guillotine and its knives may also conspire more forcefully against backbench members of the governing party. It is true that all governing parties have discouraged their backbench members from speaking out in committee or on the floor. The government wishes to get its measure through. It does not wish to give the opposition encouragement by demonstrating that even members of the governing party think there is a need to reconsider or to adjust. However, all sensible backbenchers in a governing party recognise that it is their duty to speak up for their constituents and to exercise their judgement. Strong-minded and independent individuals on the government side are not going to be easily put off from moving their amendments or speaking about amendments proposed by others. They have a job of work to do and sensible government whips understand this.

However, where a guillotine or a knife has been imposed in order to limit debate, the government whips' position is greatly strengthened. They can use the timing available under the guillotine to make it very unlikely that a government backbench member will get a chance to speak. If they know there is a lot of backbench unrest concerning a particular measure, limiting the time will limit the numbers who are able to speak and may limit the impact of the unrest. It also means that the process can be opened to the reverse kind of abuse. Where the government is worried that the opposition has a good point, it can encourage its own backbenchers to speak, knowing that their speaking will not delay proceedings overall. It can get loyal backbenchers then to speak on the issues, to take up the time available that would otherwise be used by the opposition to make its strong points.

The government has also developed another technique to avoid unfortunate parliamentary scrutiny of their legislative activities. It decided that more and more elements of any given proposal or law should take the form of regulations under an Act of Parliament, rather than being placed in the actual Act. Parliament has always adopted less rigorous ways of scrutinising regulations as opposed to primary legislation. This was based upon the original theory that statutory instruments were less important than Acts of Parliament, covering more minor or detailed measures. Governments knew that if they had an important new law to propose it should be done by means of primary legislation. That primary legislation should contain on the face of the Bill the important matters the government wished to cover.

In recent years there has been a growing wish to legislate in more and more detail. In part this reflects the government's response to the courts making more and more decisions about primary legislation that do not meet with the approval of ministers. Ministers have retaliated by saying, 'Well, in that case, we must specify everything so precisely and in so much detail that the courts will not have the same amount of discretion.'

An Act of Parliament today is more a Christmas tree awaiting adornment. The bare branches are there in the Act of Parliament but all the important matters are added later in statutory instruments under the Act. All too often, when trying to debate a new government Bill with ministers, the answer is the same. The crucial matter that we wish to debate is not a matter for now, as it will be settled after the Bill has been enacted and included in a statutory instrument.

Statutory instruments can be handled in two different ways. The government can propose a statutory instrument to the House of Commons for approval. It would normally get one and a half hours' debate in committee, unless Parliament thought it was sufficiently important to warrant a debate, of similar duration, on the floor of the House itself. The statutory instrument cannot be amended. After a short debate the House is invited to say yes or no. It usually says yes because the government whips normally have enough power on their own side to ensure that it goes through. It is, therefore, much easier from the government's point of view to legislate by means of a statutory instrument than by a primary Act of Parliament. There is no need to discuss the principles, then to discuss the detail, then to discuss the principles again. The government doesn't have to accept any new ideas, new clauses, amendments or suggested changes to the form of the legislation, and rules out any redrafting or reconsideration. It is a take-it-or-leave-it matter.

In many cases, where a statutory instrument is proposed by way of negative resolution, the government hopes there will be no parliamentary debate on it at all. Many of our statutory instruments are proposed in this way. Unless the opposition tables a prayer seeking consideration of it in committee, the statutory instrument automatically becomes a law on the say-so of the minister of the sponsoring department.

The attractions of legislating in this way to departments of government are obvious. Ministers and officials save themselves a lot of time and trouble. They do not have to think the thing through nearly as carefully and know that it will escape proper attention from MPs and the press. Using this method, government ministers can legislate throughout the summer holidays, when there is no Parliament present. They can legislate without the sharp light of public scrutiny. Those affected by these statutory instruments often find it difficult to get press or public attention, and are often dismayed to learn that either there will be no parliamentary process at all or if there is one, it will be so short and so lacking in detail.

The present government almost caricatured itself when it announced the Legislative and Regulatory Reform Bill early in 2006. The government claimed that it was introducing a piece of legislation that would enable it to deregulate. The government wished to deregulate in a hurry, so it said it would do so without full reference to Parliament. It implied that the Bill, if passed, would enable the government to strike regulations off the statute book by a very easy process. However, on scrutinising the text, it became clear that what the Bill actually did was to increase the number of areas in which government ministers could legislate, without going through the process of proper parliamentary scrutiny for primary legislation. It represented a further large shift in power from Parliament to the executive, and reflected the general trend under this government of wanting to legislate more with less and less scrutiny.

The public are astute about what MPs can and cannot do. There is an appreciation amongst the electorate that an MP is far more powerful if his or her party allows a free vote on an issue. Some issues are a matter of conscience in all parties. For example, if Parliament wishes to consider the reintroduction of the death penalty, the age of consent for sexual acts, or whether fox hunting should be allowed, it is common across the floor of the House to allow each MP the right to make up his or her own mind. In these cases the democracy works much better than where the whips are applied. The public recognise that it is worthwhile lobbying their own MP because there is a real chance that he or she will change his or her mind in response to pressure from within the constituency. People know that on whipped votes the chances of getting a MP to alter his or her view are much less than in the case of the free vote.

One of the ways of strengthening parliamentary accountability and the importance of the local MP would be to increase the number of issues over which there are free votes. I've always favoured this, both in government and out. I thought Conservative MPs should have been given a free vote over the Maastricht Treaty, when all three major parties were whipped to support it. I urged a free vote on identity cards along with others and was delighted when the Conservatives were given that opportunity, at a time when the leadership was inclined to support this rather authoritarian measure.

The exception to the rule that people write to MPs on parliamentary matters mainly about issues subject to a free vote was the Iraq war. The two main parties were whipped. As it happens, they were both whipped to vote the same way, in favour of military action alongside the United States against Iraq. The public decided it was such an important issue, where so many of them were in disagreement with the government's line, that they treated the vote as if it were a free one anyway. The pressure they applied did help confirm some rebels to vote against, and it certainly made for a much more passionate and lively national debate. It did not achieve the desired result that the public wanted. If you look back to the correspondence and the polling at the time, you can see that the public mood shifted quite noticeably. In the run-up to the vote there was a great deal of hostility to the idea of the war. At the point of the vote opinion started to shift to a more balanced position, and once the war had started the public moved to support our troops and the action being taken. It was only when things went wrong subsequently, and there were difficulties with the post-war settlement, that the public returned to its original dislike. Something similar happened to the mood in Parliament, which on this occasion tended to follow rather than lead public opinion.

The Iraq vote did not help relations between public and Parliament, eroding more people's view of whether writing to an MP is a good idea. There has not been anything similar under this government on whipped votes. Whilst there has been a very lively debate going on within the Labour Party about the Prime Minister's education proposals, it does not seem to reflect a more general debate amongst the wider public. The question of how the Conservative opposition votes on the Education Bill mattered. If the Conservatives had shifted their position from support to opposition, then the Bill would have been voted down. In the run-up to the crucial vote I was surprised that I received no letter or e-mail about it from people, despite the fact that the Conservative Party position made a crucial difference to whether the measure went through.

The reticence on the part of many concerning the Education Bill may reflect the fact that the public realise that the Bill does not amount to very much one way or the other. The parliamentary process has been working on the Education Bill, to the extent that it has enabled left-wing Labour opinion within the House of Commons, reflecting left-wing Labour opinion in the parliamentary constituencies, to move the government away from its model based on more choice and more independence for schools. In its final shape the Bill is going to make very little difference to the way public education is run and conducted in this country, and so maybe the electorate are right to give it the cold shoulder.

The biggest volume of e-mail and postal correspondence that an

MP receives is about local matters. Despairing at the national political process, as many electors seem to do, they wish instead the MP to become a kind of super-councillor. More than half of the communications I receive are about matters under the control of the local authority. Councillors receive very few of these communications. There is a temptation in British life these days to escalate everything. If a constituent wishes to make a point about national government or national legislation, they're more likely to write direct to the Prime Minister than to write to their local MP. In a similar vein, if they are annoyed about a decision of the local education authority or the local highways board, they are very likely to rush off a letter to the MP rather than to the councillors or the senior executives on the council making the decision.

MPs face a constant daily dilemma about how to handle such correspondence. The purist would write back a courteous letter, saying these matters are decided by the local council and he or she is therefore referring them to the relevant local councillor or council committee chairman. This may leave the constituent feeling that the MP has not done his or her job, or feeling that the MP does not sympathise with them in their important case. Alternatively, the MP can take up the issue directly, either with the councillor or with council executives, showing that he or she is committed to the local community and shares many of their concerns. The danger in doing this is that the MP has no official power to alter the decision or call for a review. All too often the MP can fail to persuade the local council, leading to frustration both for him or her and for the constituent involved.

The escalation of local authority cases to MP level is further proof of growing disillusion with the whole electoral system in Britain. We elect thousands of councillors around the country to represent us and look after our interests. Many of them have senior roles, making important executive decisions about what planning policies to follow, about how to spend large public budgets locally, about local schools and the local police. Many people have the same perception of councillors as of backbench MPs – they feel they are not important and they feel they do not have the influence they should have to right wrongs and make correct decisions. The public understands that local government has become much more professional and much more complex. The unelected officials, led by the chief executive officer, are often far more powerful than the elected officials above their heads, trying to keep some control and provide a strategy for the executive team.

Things have definitely got worse for local democracy in recent years. All post-war governments have been accused of centralising too much and there is some truth in the allegation. The Conservative government from 1979 onwards set out with the intention of strengthening local government, by allowing it to raise more of its own money for itself, which naturally increases the amount of control local councillors have. This policy was brought to a grinding halt with the introduction of the community charge. The unpopularity which surrounded the charge did not succeed in broadening the taxable base in the way intended. After several years of successfully increasing the proportion of locally financed expenditure prior to the introduction of the community charge, the strong reaction against the charge meant that the government had to increase the proportion of money coming from central government taxation to pay for local spending.

The theory behind the community charge was that all adults should make a contribution to the local services they enjoyed. Polling showed that everybody thought that more should be collected in taxes to spend on local services such as schools. Given the opportunity to put their hands in their pockets, all those who had not being paying rates said very strongly that they had no wish to do so and that they had not really been honest when they had told the pollsters that they thought people ought to pay more tax to support good local services. The net result of cancelling the community charge and introducing the council tax was to reduce the proportion of locally financed expenditure yet again, increasing both the amount of central money supporting local councils and, therefore, the amount of central control.

He who has the money usually has the management. Because the local business rate has been nationalised, it is now sent back in the form of a grant to each locality rather than being collected directly by the local council. The redirected business rate along with central government grants account for a massive 75 per cent or more of local service costs. The present government has been particularly keen to direct councils in return for sending them so much central taxation. Whereas previous governments used to give most of the money to local government by means of a block grant, leaving councils free to decide whether to spend the money on education or social services or highways or the environment, this government has increasingly decided to send the money in the form of specific grants tied to particular policies that it favours.

This government has also strengthened its grip by means other than strings attached to the money. It is hyperactive in sending out guidance, advice and recommendations on everything that local government does. It runs a very centralised system, assessing councils and the work of officers through its comprehensive performance review. Councils are given marks each year for how well they run different services, with the assessment often geared to the degree to which they have followed the government model. It takes a brave group of councillors to disagree with the government's approach, especially if it means that their council then may be marked down in the comprehensive assessment and appear to be a poor performer in the league tables simply because the council thoroughly disagrees with what the government is trying to do and how it says councils should be doing it.

More insidious still is the impact this regime has upon the officers of the councils. Council officers usually wish to make their way up local authority organisations as part of their career plan. They soon come to understand that some of the biggest and highest-spending councils are under Labour control. In order to gain access to the best jobs in those high-spending councils, they would need to demonstrate that they have followed the guidelines and recommendations coming from the government. They want to show they have been successful in moving their councils up the league tables, based upon these proposals. Council officers are also worried that there could be legal action against them or their councils if they do not follow the government guidance.

In some cases the government has gone further than simply issuing guidance or strong recommendations. If we take the case of planning, in theory a local authority has an important power to decide the shape of the local community and to determine whether people can build on their fields or not. In practice, under this government most of the important decisions are taken centrally by the secretary of state and the quangos underneath the government. The government sets out housing targets. It breaks these up by region and gives them to regional planning bodies. The regional planning bodies then divide them up amongst the districts and unitary authorities in their region. It is top-down planning, deciding the most important thing that a planning committee has to determine. The government buttresses its target-driven position on housing with strong planning guidance which has to be followed in each case. If a council fails to observe the planning guidance, it is much more likely to lose a case on appeal to the secretary of state and his or her inspectors.

The same process of nationalisation is happening to a lesser extent in the field of education itself, the biggest service run by local councils. The previous Conservative government started the centralising process by introducing a national curriculum, limiting the ability of schools and local education authorities to decide what they would teach and when. The incoming Labour government loved this beginning of centralisation and decided to make it far more precise. For it the weakness in the national curriculum was that it did not specify how much time should be devoted to each of the national curriculum core subjects, or when they should be taught. The new government decided that it would make a priority out of teaching literacy, and for this purpose dictated a special literacy hour for every primary school in the country. Individual schools and local education authorities who might protest that they can teach literacy in other ways without a special dedicated hour to do it no longer have the freedom to do as they wish.

The present government also decided that new city academies would be set up, involving private sector sponsors, outside the framework of local schools as run by local education authorities. This has become a particular point of contention with Labour education authorities that wish to preserve neighbourhood comprehensives with no choice for parents, which discover they are no longer able to do so.

The limitations on the role of the MP and the eclipse of the power of local government have been hastened by the rise and rise of the quango. All post-war governments have used quangos to some extent. Most oppositions have expressed their hostility to them. When Margaret Thatcher swept to power in 1979 she laid about the quangos with a vengeance, cutting their numbers drastically. In later years under the Conservative government, especially under John Major, there was some increase in the number of power and quangos. The Labour opposition rightly railed against this, demanding that fewer things should be given to unelected, unaccountable bodies and more things should be done directly by elected councillors or elected ministers. But when Labour came to power there was no sweeping away of the quango state in the way that some of us hoped. On the contrary, the Labour government decided to set up larger, more aggressive quangos and to greatly strengthen the powers and influence of those, such as the Environment Agency, that had already been established.

Throughout this government's life its response to many a crisis in the headlines has been to offer and then to set up a new quango to handle it. On issue after issue the government has said it wishes to take things out of politics altogether. It started strongly with the question of interest rates, arguing the popular case in the business community that interest rates should be decided by an independent central bank, without ministerial involvement. I would believe this rather more if the Treasury did not have power to appoint so many members or influence members on the Monetary Committee, and if the Chancellor had not changed the guidance as to what they were trying to achieve at a crucial moment in the run-up to the 2005 general election.

Buoyed up by the apparent success of the independent central bank, which just happened to be launched at a very benign time for central banks generally and for the international interest rate environment, the government has recommended similar moves in many other fields. More and more environmental issues are determined by the Environment Agency. A quango decides which medicines the National Health Service shall buy. Another quango tries to tackle the problem of school leadership whilst the NHS is littered with dozens of quangos trying to interpret national guidance or make independent judgements.

Part of the explosion of the quango state under Labour is connected with their agenda of wishing to regionalise government. The EU has always regretted the fact that England is not split into governing regions in the way that Germany or Italy is. The EU thinks that it would be much neater if there were government regions in every part of Europe. Part of the EU strategy for reducing the power of nation states is to appeal over the heads of the nations to the regions of Europe. The EU has developed a pincer movement on national, democratic governments by taking to itself important powers and at the same time demanding that other powers be given to regional organisations to give it cover, enabling it to claim that it believes in devolution.

In the UK the government was able to achieve regional government in both Scotland and Wales. The decision to give a Scottish Parliament to people north of the border was unfinished business from the 1974-79 Labour government, which had failed to carry the referendum question in favour of a Scottish Parliament by the necessary majority. This time round there were no mistakes. The case was made more forcibly and there was considerable resentment in Scotland towards London government, which had built up over many years. The Welsh were far from enthusiastic about the idea of an assembly with more limited powers but there were just enough on the day turning out to defeat those who were against. A Welsh Assembly was established with only one-quarter of the Welsh people sufficiently in favour to go and vote for it, most thinking it wasn't worth the effort either way.

The government decided to tackle England in a more crab-like way. Its experience in Wales had winded it. It had expected the Welsh people to be clamouring for their own regional assembly, and had expected there to be a massive vote against London in the ensuing referendum. The difficulty in securing the vote the government wanted warned it off holding votes immediately in England to establish regional government elsewhere. Instead, the government decided to create unelected regional government first and then turn round some years later to explain to the English people that they really should make honest men and women of these new regional governments by having elected officials, to cross-examine them and to hold them to account.

As a result, England was encumbered with an expensive regional bureaucracy. The embryo was there from the Major government. England already had government offices of the regions, outposts of the old Department of the Environment, channelling funds to the regions and viewpoints back to Westminster. Regional government offices were strengthened. England was decked out with regional development agencies in every part. Regional planning was beefed up. Regional assemblies were established.

Armed with this strengthened regional bureaucracy, the government then decided to test the electoral position yet again. It decided to offer the people of the north-east an elected regional assembly. The government pointed out that the north-east now had regional planning, a regional development agency and a regional government office. It pointed out that just across the border Scotland had its own regional Parliament. The government hinted that the EU looked more favourably upon regions that had proper regional government when it came to the distribution of regional funds. None of these arguments proved enough. The government went down to a massive defeat, with four times as many people voting against a regional assembly in the north-east as for it. The public were too clever for the government's campaign. They realised that it meant higher council tax to pay for all the politicians and officials that the regional government would require, without necessarily delivering anything of benefit to themselves.

The government returned to the drawing board. Undeterred by the temporary setback of an angry public against their scheme, it decided to strengthen regional government still further. When challenged about this, it said that the public had rejected elected regional government but it did not mean the public was against regional government! Had the government put down on the ballot paper the proposition 'Would you like unelected regional government?', I suspect it would have had an even bigger no vote than the one it did achieve.

The government has recently been engaged on the task of trying to create regional policing structures. It came up with the idea that no police force should have fewer than 4,000 officers. It said that in order to combat terrorism successfully this was the minimum size of force that could afford to employ the specialists necessary. On probing it emerged that most of the counter-terrorist specialists are in the Metropolitan Police and will remain there, whatever happens by way of organisation around the country. It also emerged that, of course, when there is a major terrorist alert or a major terrorist incident, police forces from all round the country come together to pool their specialist resources and to tackle the problem as best they can.

The shires were up in arms in England, not wishing to lose their county police forces. Some police forces said that there might be sense in two smaller forces amalgamating, only to be told that if the new force straddled an artificial regional boundary they were not allowed to merge. The mergers had to be within the regions as defined by the government. In the case of my local police force, Thames Valley Police, the government wished it to merge with Hampshire. As Thames Valley already had more than 4,000 officers it was easy to make the case against. When we suggested that the Thames Valley force might like to amalgamate with country forces lying to the west of it, which were smaller and where there could be some advantages from a merger, the government made it clear that was not their wish. With a change of Home Secretary in May 2006 these planned mergers were suspended, but not necessarily scrapped.

In the NHS the doctrine of 'bigger is better' is also alive and well. Primary care trusts, which organise general practitioner services in each locality, tend to be around the size of a district council. The government has decided that two or three should merge together to create larger units. The health service is already run through a regional structure of strategic health authorities, which the government is reluctant to abolish.

The combination of regional offices, regional development agencies, regional planning, and police and health services with growing regional involvement points in one direction. The government wishes to come back to the electorate of England at some point in the future and say, 'Now there is so much unaccountable regional power, surely the sensible thing to do is to include a regional elected government to supervise it.' Genuflecting to those of us who are worried about the remorseless rise of the political classes and the endless expansion of bureaucracy, the government will also argue that in return for introducing elected regional government, the government will propose that instead of the counties and districts which still exist in most of England, we should have unitary councils.

If the government had its way and introduced elected regional government with no other changes, many parts of the country would then have an elected parish or town council, an elected district council, an elected country council, an elected region, an elected national government and an unelected European government, the European Commission. Six layers of government between the public and something happening in their locality does seem excessive. It's no wonder people have a sense of frustration. It is difficult even for a well-informed professional to know who exactly took a particular decision or where a result came from. For the general public who only come across these bodies when something happens in their locality that they do not like, it is a very difficult minefield to get through.

The greatest quango of them all is the EU itself. In 1975 the British people voted yes in a referendum to remaining in a common market. The assembled political parties and groups in favour of the yes vote represented the whole of the British establishment. The Confederation of British Industry and the Trades Union Congress, the Conservative Party and the Labour Party, the Liberal Party and most of the respected commentators of the day were in favour of continued membership of the European Economic Community. They stressed it was a trading club. They said that Britain needed access to Continental markets and that without EEC membership that access would be restricted. They thought that growing contact with the Continent commercially would act as an important shock to force British business into a more modern and more competitive mode. We were told we would lose jobs, that our incomes would fall and Britain would be a far less prosperous place if we voted to leave the EEC. Not surprisingly the electorate of 1975 said yes to more jobs, more prosperity and to little interference in our lives. They were assured by all the spokesmen concerned that Britain would remain a sovereign country, that all the important decisions would still be taken by government ministers answerable to the British Parliament, and that a set of trading arrangements was all that was coming from Brussels.

Thirty years on the world looks very different. Whilst we still do not have a single market in services, the most important part of the British economy, we do have a single farm policy, a single currency for the many of the countries on the Continent, the beginnings of a European defence force, a European armaments agency, common environment, agricultural, fishing and transport policies; a president, an anthem, a parliament, a flag and many of the trappings of a nation state. The EU has greatly increased its power over the intervening years. In treaty after treaty, through Rome and Maastricht, Nice and Amsterdam, the EU has taken power after power to itself. It has legislated on a colossal scale, producing some 2,500 directives every year, which have to be translated into national law quickly and accurately by the member states. In 1975 Britain had a veto over most things. In 2006 the UK has limited opportunities to veto European intentions as so many things are now decided by majority votes.

The EU is ever alert to opportunities to enhance and increase its power. When there was a series of terrorist outbreaks in the USA and the EU, the Union decided that countering terrorism required cross-border activity at EU level. It gave the rationale to break into the field of criminal justice which the EU had been hankering after for many years. The EU has taken over the whole of our trade policy, conducting trade talks on our behalf and on behalf of all the other member states with the other leading trading countries of the world. Europe runs our competition policy, regulates our business and commerce, and is now taking over regulation of the most precious of all commercial assets in the UK, the City of London. Many of the laws now passed by the British Parliament have to be passed to comply with European directives. All too often when we're debating a measure in the House, if I ask the minister if we have any freedom to make a different decision, I'm told we don't. It has already been decided in Brussels behind closed doors.

★

The sheer scale, reach and expense of government terrifies many of us. The citizen feels disenfranchised and wonders whether it's worthwhile taking it on at all. In any given situation there are great complexities in sorting out who is to blame, who makes the decisions and who might be able to put it right. Let us take a few examples that matter a lot to people in communities in Britain.

Many people like the area in which they live. They like the balance of rural and urban, of green field and developed land. They do not wish to see their local community changed too rapidly. They do not wish to lose their rural views or find too much more pressure on the road system and other public facilities. People have often spent a very large sum of money on buying their own property. They lavish a great deal of time and attention on maintaining and improving it. It is most families' largest asset and one that they naturally wish to protect and enhance.

If someone wishes to build a large number of houses nearby it is not surprising that people will want to object. They fear that the extra housing will reduce the value of their own home. They worry that it will put too much pressure on the local community, that it will ruin their local views and it will overload the local roads. If they express this view, for their pains they are called 'Nimbys' by the government and by the developers. They soon become locked in a very long battle which it is difficult for them to win.

When they take advice they will be told that the main decision about whether houses will be built near them or not will be taken by their local elected planning authority, either their district or their unitary council. This seems straightforward enough. If then they can persuade their local councillors that the development is inappropriate, surely they will be able to win their case? Further probing will reveal to them that local councillors are not able to interpret local opinion and make a decision based on it. Local councillors supervise the work of the planning experts or officers. The people are told that they cannot reverse the officers' recommendation, often in favour of new development, unless they have good planning reasons so to do. The unhappy freeholder sees then that he or she has a more important task in trying to persuade the planning officers before they frame their recommendation to go to the planning committee.

If the individual can get access to the planning officers, he or she will often be told by them that they are acting under orders from the region. The planning officer might say in conversation that he has a lot of sympathy with the individuals who do not want the housing estate built near them. He personally might well choose to turn it down and would feel as they do if he lived where they live. However, he will point out that the regional planning authority has set his council a target for a certain number of homes that have to be constructed. Unless he can find a very good planning reason why these homes should not be built on this particular site, he is under a duty to allow the development to go through. If he does not let this particular development go through the council might then not be meeting its target from the region to produce a certain number of homes.

If the individual takes his or her case to the region, the region is very likely to lay the blame both upwards and downwards. It will say that it wasn't very happy having to impose so many houses on the districts and unitary authorities beneath it but it was acting under government orders. The secretary of state has set out national guidelines. The secretary of state is very keen to see more housing development in the country as the whole, and that particular region has to play its part and take its fair share. If the complainant has a problem then maybe they should write to the secretary of state, complaining about the national planning policy under which the region is operating. Alternatively, the region might say that whilst it has set out how many homes are to be built, it has not actually decided where they should be built in any particular unitary or district council area. If challenged, the region would agree with the planning officers that they mustn't turn it down unreasonably, and if they are going to turn down one particular site they have to make sure there are enough alternative sites available so that the targets can be met.

Finally, if the frustrated constituent takes the matter up with the government minister, the minister is likely to blame both the region and the local council. The minister might in an honest moment admit that he had set overall targets but these were very general, and did not mean that the field next to the person's home had to be built on. If the constituent goes to their MP, the MP is very likely to side with the constituent and say he has every sympathy and wishes to help them make their case. The MP would doubtless write a letter both to the district council urging rejection of the scheme and to the government minister querying yet again the national targets and the national interference.

The constituent would have received five different views from five people apparently in power. They would be more confused at the end of this process about where the true power lay than at the beginning. Would they be right to blame their local councillor who apparently makes a decision in the planning committee? Would they be better off blaming the officer who had advised the councillor to do something the constituent didn't wish? Do they accept the officer's defence that he was only acting under the orders of the region? Do they accept the region's defence that it was only acting under the orders of the secretary of state? Or do they agree with the region that it really is the local councillor who has considerable flexibility within the overall totals? Why can't the local MP, who seems to agree with them, have any influence on the process as a whole? Why is it that the most senior elected official in a given district has absolutely no responsibility for making important decisions, like where new development goes, when he is probably best placed to interpret both the constituency's needs and the constituent's views? All those who have been dragged through this process often find it extremely frustrating and unsatisfactory.

Worse lies in store for the constituent. If, for example, they succeed in the first instance and gets the local council to side with them and turn down the development, there will doubtless be an appeal. The constituent then discovers that a developer on appeal may find it easier to make the case to the secretary of state's inspector and see the development approved after all, overriding the wishes not only of the local constituents but also the local elected planning authority. Time after time this happens, leading to more frustration with the elected process.

Let us take another case. Many people in Britain value the opportunity to buy vitamins and food supplements from local shops. Whilst some doctors argue that these vitamins and food supplements do not have the desired medical effects that some people ascribe to them, there has been no evidence forthcoming to suggest that vitamins and food supplements are damaging if taken in sensible quantities. The people who think they do good may be right, or it may be good for their health that they believe they do good whether they are right or wrong. A number of successful businesses were set up to make these products and a number of other successful businesses were established to sell them retail and wholesale to customers. All seemed fine until the EU decided, as a result of lobbying by the chemical pharmaceutical companies, that vitamins and food supplements needed regulating as well.

The British government decided either that it could not prevent this or that it was a good thing. It attended the Council of Ministers meeting, put various points and came out saying that it was in agreement with its partners, that regulation was needed and this particular regulation would be just fine. Very few purchasers of these products, and even fewer manufacturers and distributors, thought the regulation a good idea. Nonetheless, the British government decided to rush through Parliament a statutory instrument implementing these directives. I and others put up a strong critique of them but in the end the government used its block vote in the House of Commons to push them through.

Many constituents are unhappy about what has happened. Again, they have a question of who they should blame. They all got in touch with their local MPs in good time. Many of us lobbied the government before it signed up to the original directive. We all lobbied again before the parliamentary processes. Many MPs spoke up for their constituents, both prior to the European deal and before and during the course of the statutory instrument proceedings in Parliament.

If you challenge the government on the subject, it both blames the EU and claims that no damage is being done. It explains that it was the wish of the majority of the member states to go ahead with these proposals, and implies it had no choice. Should the public blame the pharmaceutical companies for lobbying EU officials so successfully? Should they blame the EU officials who framed the law and got it through without any apparent strong ministerial engagement to challenge them? Should one blame British government ministers for failing to see the impact the regulation would have, or failing to understand the public mood sufficiently to put the case strongly against it? Why didn't British ministers lobby the other states hard and try and get the thing struck off the agenda? Should one blame British government ministers for slamming it through the House of Commons when there was considerable unease around the country about it? Couldn't they have done more to seek derogations for Britain from the more harmful parts, or couldn't they have framed their own regulations in a less obtrusive way?

Every time there are disagreements with the results of Brussels legislation we have the same futile arguments. Very often people claim that the government has gold-plated the regulation, adding unnecessary complications and additions to the Brussels text when turning it into British law. Sometimes it has. The reason lies deep in the way the British government culture interacts with the Brussels one. Britain has a very law-abiding government culture, averse to legal challenge. Officials will give ministers very cautious advice. Only if they gold-plate the directive and go further than its minimum recommendations can they be sure that they will be safe from legal challenge in the European court. The last thing an official wants is to have down to his or her watch the experience of Britain being taken to the European Court for improperly implementing a European directive. The cards are stacked in favour of gold-plating. But one cannot get away from the fact that if there were no directive in the first place there would be no problem with gold-plating.

The thing that most frustrates us is the overactivity of the Brussels legislative machine. British ministers claim they wish to have a more deregulated Europe. The more they claim it the more they go along with Brussels legislating to a greater extent. Since Tony Blair launched his deregulatory crusade more than 2,000 new Brussels laws have gone through. I'm sure he meant it when he said he wished to deregulate Brussels but it is quite obvious he has absolutely no ability to do so.

The British public do not feel they have a say when it comes to Brussels legislation. It would be much better if British ministers highlighted the issues coming up before a Council of Ministers meeting, and encouraged public debate then. Instead of making a statement when they get back from the summit to tell Parliament what they have agreed, they should make a statement before they go to the council meeting, to see what Parliament's view is on the measures that are coming up for agreement. Instead of reluctantly permitting public debate at the time when the regulations go through as statutory instruments in the UK Parliament, they should be encouraging a much more active debate prior to anything being agreed in the first place. No wonder people are frustrated. Their parliament debates the issues that matter to them only after the decisions have been taken. At this late stage the proposals cannot be reversed so the public naturally asks, why bother with the debate at that late stage?

The third example of how frustrated people can feel has arisen over the issue of speed cameras. The present government decided to base its road safety policy entirely on controlling speed. This was a very odd decision. Independent research showed that speed is a contributory factor or the main factor in fewer than one in ten of all accidents. Most accidents occur at junctions in controlled-speed areas, and involve vehicles not exceeding the speed limit. The combination of driver error and bad road and junction design causes far more accidents than speed.

The government then decided that basing its policy on speed would enable it to automate the detection of the offence. Instead of recruiting more traffic officers to patrol the highways and to make intelligent judgements about whether speed was dangerous or not, and excessive or not, they decided to litter the highway with thousands of cameras capable of logging vehicles that were exceeding the stated speed limit. These proved to be extremely good revenue generators for the state. The police ran a successful campaign to say that they wished to have the proceeds of the fines for their own budgetary purposes. As a result, the government decided to establish a series of quangos round the country called Camera Partnerships, which could then spend the money from the fines on more cameras and more speed enforcement measures.

This policy has proved extremely unpopular with motorists. Cameras have often been used to enforce speed limits that motorists feel are unrealistically low. Why should there be speed limits of only

40 or 50 mph on dual and treble carriageways into London, where traffic is properly segregated from other traffic and where pedestrians are segregated from all vehicles? Why should there be a 20 mph speed control outside a school on days when the school is not functioning and there is no danger to children? Drivers tend to adjust their speed to the conditions and make a judgement. Sometimes their judgement is in conflict with the official speed limits on the road. When these speed limits are then enforced in a robotic way by the camera managers, motorists feel they have been unfairly treated. Their sense of injustice is compounded if the camera is concealed from view. Motorists argue that if the aim of the policy is to get them to slow down, then surely the camera should be as visible as possible to make the point to them that they are not going to get away with a higher speed.

As a result of Britain switching its successful road safety strategy of the 1990s to the all-camera-based strategy of the present century, we now have a far less satisfactory performance in reducing road deaths and injuries than our Continental counterparts. Better driving, better road and junction design, segregation of pedestrians, cyclists and motor vehicles from each other, and segregation of traffic travelling in different directions at junctions are all important ways of improving road safety. Having a proper police crackdown on so-called joyriders, people driving stolen cars, and driving without insurance and without a licence would do much more than the Camera Partnerships to improve the safety of our roads. A large proportion of accidents are caused by the uninsured, the unlicensed and the unruly.

It is very difficult for the public again to have any influence over this. They can try taking the matter up with the local councillor. He will often say that he cannot control the actions and activities of the local Camera Partnership. The public may try to take the matter up with the police, who will also say that the Camera Partnership has some independent action. The government, appreciating the unpopularity of the policy, is now making some signs that it wishes to rein back but it has created a self-perpetuating system that intends to carry on its merry way.

As someone who does try to obey the law on speeding, I regret the way in which the speed camera regime is causing tensions between largely law-abiding members of the public and the police. I regret the way in which it is not tackling the problem of road safety as vigorously and as sensibly as I would like. It is yet another example of how power can get out of control when it passes into diffuse and unelected hands.

The frustrations of the British public are entirely understandable when you look at the ramshackle, overgrown, expensive, over-mighty and unaccountable structure that is government in Britain today. Much of it comes from Brussels. More of it comes from quangos than from elected officials. The role of the councillor has been downgraded, the MP is more commentator than executive member of the government, and government ministers have found dozens of ways of hiding behind other bodies or avoiding strong and open public debate about their laws and executive decisions. It is very difficult now to get the dragon of government by the tail without being fried by its breath. Anyone who comes to government from outside as a result of having to run a campaign to save their home or improve their lives is amazed at how complex it is, how it seems to malfunction so much of the time, how difficult it is to get a straight answer from anybody. The frustration is compounded when you realise just how much of your income you are paying to employ so many officials and elected people in roles where they themselves feel they are impotent, or where they are unable to help.

4

Globalisation

I WANT TO MAKE A DIFFERENCE

I want to help tackle global poverty
Trade works better than aid:

- Change your shopping basket: buy fair-trade produce, watch the origin labels on the garments you buy, read the packaging on the food you buy – favour the poorest countries
- Campaign for an end to the Common Agricultural Policy. The CAP puts barriers up against food producers from poor countries
- Campaign for the EU to spend our aid in its budgets on the poorest countries – today it spends substantial sums on the not so poor
- Campaign against EU restrictions on importing trainers, shoes and textile products from low-income countries
- Campaign for effective spending of UK national aid programmes – don't let any of the money be spent on dictators' cars, civil wars and arms
- Encourage links with people who can make a difference in poor countries
- Support people being educated here who can return to their home countries to be a force for the good
- Offer a welcome to people from poor countries who come to learn
- Visit the countries you are most concerned about
- Spend some of your money on your visit – it helps create jobs
- See for yourself what a difference you might make

We live in a global village. News travels round the world in a few seconds, thanks to the speed of television and data communications. Images of what is going wrong in the Middle East or the Far East can be on television screens in London or Washington instantaneously. The poor world presses its nose against the window pane of the fabulously rich West, catching glimpses of the products, brands and lifestyles for which the West is famous. The great global corporations bring with them the promise of jobs and riches and the lure of their branded products.

It is one of the paradoxes in the rapidly globalising world that the more news, entertainment, communications, products and services are supplied on a global basis, the more many people, especially in the rich West, think locally. Indeed, modern British, American and continental European people think locally more than they think globally. If we take two of the predominant preoccupations of people in the richer part of the world, their health and the environment they live in, we see the paradoxes in full flow. There is more than a hint of hypochondria in many American and British hearts. Newspapers, magazines, television and radio features pander to the growing fear that tomorrow we may be ill and the day after we may be dead. All the evidence abounds that thanks to diet, lifestyle, central heating and some of medicine's advances, we are on average going to live a very long time. But too many of our fellow citizens have palpitations day by day that they may be the unlucky one, that they may be the one who dies early despite the average.

If we believed all we read in newspapers about allergies, the danger from our air or water, and the hidden menace within so many of the foods we eat, we would not give ourselves much chance of surviving long. We are now told it is dangerous to drink sugary fizzy drinks, to eat too many sweets, chocolates or potato crisps, too much red meat, too many dairy products, too much carbohydrate. Apparently we might survive on carefully cleaned water and the odd lettuce leaf supplemented by a little carrot soup. But even then we have to be careful how the lettuces have been washed and how the carrots have been grown in case they have the wrong chemical composition. If you are worried about fats giving you too much cholesterol, sugars giving you diabetes and animal proteins gumming up your system, you would be hard pressed to eat enough calories during the average day to keep the body ticking over.

The preoccupations with keeping healthy are both very local and individual and extraordinarily global. One day the national press may be gripped by the fear that we're all in imminent danger of dying of a new killer influenza that's sweeping the world before the chemical doctors and the pharmaceutical companies can get to grips with the new malevolent strain. The next day we might be told that death is going to be visited upon us from that extra packet of potato crisps we were planning to consume, or from sitting too long in front of the television instead of going for a run. Sometimes we are led to believe that good health does lie in our own control, something to be worked out by proper diet and proper exercise. Other times we are told we are impotent, given the forces unleashed by global food enterprises, by chemical-based farming, and by the incredible ingenuity of global viruses to thwart human invention.

I WANT TO MAKE A DIFFERENCE

I want to eat food that is good for me and the environment
Buy from local farmers' markets or farms
Buy produce which is in season
Buy free range or organic produce
Buy from suppliers who look after animals well
Eat more fresh fruit and vegetables
Don't buy canned tuna unless it is dolphin friendly
Campaign against industrial fishing which damages the seabed and catches too many sea creatures and endangered species that we should not be catching
Grow your own vegetables and fruit
Don't buy foods which contain too many preservatives, salt and sugar
Aim for a balanced diet – fatty or sugary foods are OK in moderation for most of us
Spend time planning different and balanced menus

The politics of food has become almost all-consuming in Britain. Jamie Oliver gripped the short attention span of the nation with his attack upon school dinners. Schools over several years have done their best to grapple with tiny budgets for the food component of the meal, allied to the known passion of children to eat all the things that experts think are bad for them and to spurn all the things that experts think are good. At the same time, some parents led children to believe that it is dangerous to walk the streets after dark and felt that childcare is best taken sitting down in front of the television. The nation got into a panic about a new generation of obese, unexercised, flabby children, hastening to their deathbed before their parents, largely because of inadequate school dinners. So dramatic was Oliver's impact upon the public debate that government ministers had to be brought to account both in the House of Commons and in the high court of the media to answer for their sins. More money had to be found from the public purse to beef up the menus or, perhaps more appropriately, to lettuce-leaf-and-carrot up the menus in order to reassure the experts and the newly nervous parents.

The politics of food also encompasses the Friends of the Earth and related campaigns aimed against any company experimenting with genetically modified food in general, and against Monsanto quietly amassing a new seed library for the world in particular. Through the pages of the *Daily Mail*, campaigners against GM foods dubbed them 'Frankenstein foods' and conjured up images of triffid plants that would mass across the countryside before doing our stomachs untold damage, leading to our ultimate ruin. Some were worried about GM companies' business practices, fearing they had discovered a way of patenting nature to the detriment of the Third World, desperately in need of seeds to get itself out of poverty. Others were more concerned about the impact nearer to home, worrying that organic products from their local farm were going to be waylaid and mutated by contagion from the adjacent fields full of GM products.

A new Labour government, led by people who either are scientists or friends of scientists, tried to keep the balance. It recognised the force of popular reaction against the GM product but wanted to keep the large science-based companies happy. Lord Sainsbury, the science minister, kept up pressure for Britain to be a home friendly to GM crops. Margaret Beckett, a scientist herself by training but also an astute politician, kept telling us GM introduction had to be based on the science and decided upon a very cautious path of only gentle progress for the harbingers of new generations of GM crops. Ministers often hid behind EU policy, finding it convenient to evade responsibility.

Some people pondered that GM crops were very similar to what had been happening over many centuries, as we moved from rudimentary farming to more intensive farming. After all, hadn't the eighteenth- and nineteenth-century advances been based upon selective breeding, both of animals and of plants, until the plants and the animals had the characteristics that made most economic sense and the best taste? Others felt that in the GM laboratories things had been taken further than simple cross-breeding. The idea of gene manipulation led them to fear that the whole experiment would get out of control. What if someone unleashed from the laboratory a killer plant that nothing could halt in time?

The politics of global and local can become a little giddy. One day the politician is expected to be an expert on the dinner menu in a local primary school in a corner of his constituency. He's expected to have a view on whether chips should be served once a month or, more dangerously and racily, once a week. Another day he's expected to have profound views on the science of GM crops worldwide, and the morality of Monsanto's trading position. In neither case can a national politician or a national parliament have a great deal of influence. It would be extremely heavy handed for people at Westminster to legislate in such a way that the caterers and dinner ladies of any particular primary school had to conform to a national menu, or seek the agreement of the Secretary of State for Education, before deciding to venture beyond pasta and salad. These are decisions surely that are better made locally, either by the school itself or conceivably with the help and advice of the local education authority.

At the other end of the spectrum, an honest member of a national parliament outside the United States would have to accept that there are limits to what national legislation and regulation can achieve, to tackle the problems of the spread of Asian flu or of GM crops. When it comes to global killer viruses, all that national governments can do is try and create conditions in which local scientists and the companies they work for have the best possible chance to provide the counter quickly. In the case of GM crops it may be possible for the national legislature to ban them entirely but this can only be done within the frameworks of international law and international trade agreements and, in Britain's case, under the influential eye of the European Union. Most country legislators cannot stop the spread of GM crops across their land frontiers if their neighbours take a different view. Whilst the mainland of Britain has more control, there is little we could do to control the spread of GM seed on the wind across the UK's land border with the Republic of Ireland.

The results of the move of capitalism to global ambitions have created in many a sense of powerlessness. What can we or our elected representatives at national level do about the ubiquitous Microsoft software, the phenomenal success of Coca- and Pepsi-Cola drinks, or the universal appeal of all the leading consumer brands? Don't the companies that produce and market these have more power than many national governments? How can we have any influence on what they do? Doesn't it mean that a great deal of national and local politics is without purpose because these corporations are off the leash and will do as they wish?

It is this very sense which lies in part behind the intensity of the moves towards localism in many people's political sensibilities. We may not be able to tackle global warming or the power of the American corporations, they argue to themselves implicitly or explicitly, but maybe we can stop a new rubbish tip being placed down the road. Or maybe if we kick up enough fuss we can influence the menu in our local primary school, or have an impact on the speed limit on the road through our village.

In order to understand the background to this attitude towards politics, it is important to ask ourselves some questions about the process of globalisation itself. How new is globalisation? How far has it come and how far might it go? Is it something we should welcome or fear? Is it a process which can be regulated, accelerated or retarded by decisions in any given country or area? Are its critics right that it represents exploitation and the immorality of naked capitalism? Or are its proponents right that it offers mankind the best hope of a brighter tomorrow? One of the biggest divides in global, national and local politics today is the divide between those who broadly welcome globalisation and the jobs, products and brands it brings, and those who broadly oppose it because they do not like the free enterprise process itself.

The critics of globalisation have been clever at getting a lot of their prejudices into the public debate in Britain, especially through the BBC and the way it treats business stories, its attitude towards the USA, and the priorities it sees for global politics. In the view of the Western critics of globalisation, it is a process of creating an economic and trade empire for the American corporations. They see it as backed by the power of American weaponry, and by the American interventions in the Middle East in support of the flow of oil to the big Western corporations. If you listen to or watch a representative sample of BBC political commentary, analysis and news, you will soon learn that America, especially under a Republican President, is the origin of so many of the world's ills. We rarely get informed and good programmes on the high levels of unemployment in Germany or the riots, social divisions and ethnic dislocations in France. Even when Paris was experiencing night after night of bloodshed and torch, there was surprisingly little coverage and little follow-up. Lesser problems in New Orleans following the flood created a barrage of comment and discussion over whether New Orleans showed the unacceptable divisions of American society and revealed the true faults of American capitalism.

Many European commentators were reluctant to point out that New Orleans, if translated to Europe, would be one of the richest and finest cities in our continent despite being one of the poorest in the USA. The poor in New Orleans may not have new cars but nor do the poor in the suburbs of Paris or the East End of London, let alone in most of Africa and parts of Asia. The poor in New Orleans did have larger homes than the Europeans. They had colour televisions, clean water, and access to a plentiful supply of food at good prices. It was not poverty as a Ugandan or Namibian family would understand it.

The critics of the USA believe that the American corporations, from Microsoft to Coca-Cola, from General Electric to Boeing, from IBM to Google, are too powerful, too successful, and have, as a result, become exploitative. Their case is based on an innate hatred of competition and the profit motive. They believe that American corporations and other multinationals from countries such as Britain profit at the expense of locals when they set up factories or trading companies in developing countries. Isn't Wal-Mart wrong, they ask, to buy produce from African farmers at a much lower price than they would pay for the equivalent American produce? Aren't American and British pharmaceutical companies wrong to expect African governments and health services to pay first-world prices for the medicines Western companies have developed, patented and are selling on the global market? Isn't it obscene for multinationals to be making money out of selling food to the starving or drugs to the dying? Isn't there a better way?

Some who take this line are genuinely affronted morally by the fact that a multinational corporation will pay workers in the developing world a small fraction of what it pays similar workers in the advanced world. They would be satisfied if the multinationals put the pay up in the developing countries. Others are worried because they are protectionists who would like to see the multinationals creating and preserving more jobs in the first world, and do not wish to see the jobs exported to the developing world, where the work can be done more cheaply. These two positions can be part of the same coalition against multinationals but they are completely incompatible.

Some object strongly to the way the large multinationals such as oil and mining companies go into the developing world to exploit the natural resources that are found in some parts of it in abundance. Why should Shell, Exxon, BP be allowed to exploit the oil resources of the developing world, they ask. Don't they simply despoil the countryside and extract with the natural resource some of the profit that should belong to the country that is fortunately endowed with it? Aren't the multinationals of the world guilty of extracting too much oil, cutting down too many rainforests, consuming too many natural resources, charging too high a price for what they produce?

Sometimes the critics of globalisation blame the multinationals for the inequalities that are all too obvious in the world around us. They move from observing that an African worker is paid a lot less than a British worker to apparently believing that that in some way is the fault of the British or the American multinational, rather than the result of the different economic policies followed by the rich West and the African states. They are reluctant to see that the poverty of some African countries owes a great deal to civil wars conducted by the political classes in those countries, to droughts often made worse by the water policies pursued by the state-run enterprises in those countries, and to the failure of the public health authorities to take the most elementary precautions to control the spread of infection.

So what are we to make of this case? The critics are right that large parts of the world are dirtier than they should be and that the environment is not being looked after as we in the West would like. They are right that too much of the rainforest is being cut down, right that water is not being collected, cleaned and properly used in many places. They are correct that pay rates are many times higher in the West than they are in the poorest countries, and they are right that the famines, pestilences and civil wars which characterise life in the worst-governed countries on our planet are mercifully missing in the privileged West.

However, it is difficult to see how you can blame multinational companies or the global enterprise system for these problems. If it were true that the multinational oil corporations took both the oil and all the profit from countries that happened to be endowed with oil, then why would those countries allow those corporations in to do it? Many developing countries have now become shrewd drivers of tough bargains with the large mineral companies that have the technology, know-how and access to markets to exploit their natural resources for them. The multinational oil companies bring to the developing country an exciting package. They offer it the technical ability to find the oil in the first place. They offer it the capital investment and technical ability to extract the oil, to refine, market and transport the oil, and the ability to find end user customers, especially in the advanced world, who will pay high prices for the resulting products. If the developing country tried to do all this for itself and keep it internal to itself, it would find it very difficult to locate the oil, make the investment, refine the oil, and even more difficult to find a sufficiently large market internally to pay good prices for the oil, to create the amount of activity, jobs and enterprise that the multinationals produce. That is why developing country after developing country welcomes the multinational oil companies with open arms, especially if they come before the oil has been located offering a contract which ensures that the developing country's state will collect a lot of the profits in the form of taxation. Locals will also benefit from the creation of more jobs.

The case is even clearer to see with manufacturing and service companies. India and China, the two largest developing countries in the world, are now living through periods of explosive growth. One of the main motors of their economic success is their open-door policy to the multinationals, who can bring the intellectual property, the ideas, the product designs and the access to Western markets that Chinese- and Indian-based enterprise requires. It is true that in both India and China talented people have set up local businesses selling to local people. It is also true that a lot of the extra growth accelerating the pace of creating better jobs and higher incomes has come with technology provided by Western multinationals, and from business plans and business investment brought to those countries by the successful companies of the West.

Today the Chinese and American economies are locked in a mutually beneficial trading arrangement. American companies help the Chinese generate the ideas and make the investment in producing the goods and services. The hugely rich and affluent American market buys many of the products the Chinese succeed in making. The profits on the sale of the manufactures to the USA are often saved by the Chinese, who then lend the money back to the Americans to go on buying their goods. It is good for both societies and is the prime force moving the successful Chinese lift-off. The first good that globalisation brings is the technical and managerial ability of the West to create the jobs and to provide the access to the rich Western markets that so many developing countries need to improve their prosperity.

Western technology is needed not just to help people create successful factories or ways of delivering good services but also to solve many of the problems that beset developing countries as they tackle poverty, disease, drought, and social dislocation. Let us take the hotly disputed area of treating disease. Western, chemical-based medicine has had considerable success in tackling some of the great killers of the world. Smallpox, diphtheria, poliomyelitis, tetanus and malaria no longer stalk Western countries, even where the climatic and environmental conditions pose a potential threat. Programmes of vaccination, preventative medicine and powerful drugs to treat the conditions should they ever break out have between them succeeded in removing our fear of these killers. But they still stalk many parts of the developing world.

Globalisation's critics argue with forked tongues. They imply that they do not like the intrusion or interference of Western companies in developing countries, yet they are desperate for Western companies to share their know-how or to provide their medicines to tackle these problems in African and Asian states who are in need. One of the great positives of global enterprise capitalism is that some of its leading corporations are capable of finding the scientific means of controlling or eradicating these diseases. There are rightly arguments over the basis on which this technology is shared with the developing countries. Of course, the enterprise companies of the West want a good return on the money they have spent on inventing, testing, proving and marketing their products. Of course, the poor countries and consumers of the developing world find it difficult to pay the prices that the West can afford. This does not mean that the multinationals are wrong or that they should be told they have to supply everything free into the developing world. Indeed if they did so, there would soon be people abusing the free product in the developing country and running it over to the rich Western countries, where they could sell it at great profit themselves and at considerable loss to the multinational that had supplied it. Sensible governments and the United Nations understand that a way has to be found to reward the companies fairly, and at the same time to ensure enough buying power in the developing world so that they can enjoy the benefits of such breakthroughs.

The same is going to be true of environmental technology. Critics of globalisation imply that it is globalisation itself that is despoiling the planet, creating global warming and belching out carbon dioxide into the atmosphere. After all, they argue, isn't it in the rich West, sustained by the large corporations, that most cars are driven, most fridges are used, and where people are profligate with the electricity they burn in their homes and the heating they turn up in the winter? It is true that people in rich Western societies use much more energy per head than people in poorer societies. That does not mean that the right answer to these inequalities is to stop people in the West from keeping warm or keeping clean by using hot water, or driving to work to keep their job. On the contrary, it means that we need to redouble our efforts to develop the technology that allows us to keep clean, to keep warm, to get to work, without producing so much waste product which could be damaging to the global environment.

The sad truth in the present situation is that it is India and China that are now adding the largest amounts to the pollution problem of the world. They are bound to do so because they have many times the number of people living in those two countries than there are living in the EU and the USA combined. Those people rightly aspire to get closer to Western standards of living, including Western levels of burning fuel in their homes, in their offices, in their factories and in their cars. It is also true that in the early stages of industrialisation, countries adapt and adopt much more energy-intensive ways of making things and providing services than the richer countries they are seeking to compete against. We will not solve the world's environmental problem by trying to take heat, light and transport away from the West. We might solve the world's environmental problem by accelerating the development of technical answers in the West and exporting them rapidly, and on favourable terms, to the developing countries of the East.

Western technology has already eliminated practically all of the harmful emissions from the back of a car. Lead has gone from petrol, and emissions of nitrogen dioxide, sulphur dioxide and particulates from the rear of passenger cars are now tiny. Today the emphasis is on controlling carbon dioxide. The latest generations of hybrid technology engines and diesels churn out far less carbon dioxide than their predecessors of just a few years ago. We need to spread these gentler technologies rapidly and quickly to the developing world.

The global companies at the forefront of design and technology are not the problem but the solution.

Nor is it fair to say that globalisation is the source of inequality in the world. We in the West could stay pretty rich just trading with one another. The USA and the EU between them still have almost half the world's output and income, although they are earned and consumed by less than a tenth of the world's population. If we were no longer able to trade with the rest of the world, we would rapidly have to develop substitutes for the raw materials and food we get from there. But I'm sure after some years of transition we would still be many times richer than the struggling developing countries. What is more, they would lose out far more than the rich West from any attempt to reduce or remove trade and investment between the two blocs. Given a little transitional time, Tesco could get people to grow beans in western Europe instead of buying them in Africa. We could put up enough nuclear power stations, renewable energy centres and shale oil conversion plants to solve our energy and petrochemical feedstock problems, and life would then carry on as before. Pity the poor African states no longer receiving any of the technology, know-how, advice, investment and access to Western markets that multinationals can bring, or do bring, already. What would China do if she were barred from the American market as a way of selling her extremely good-value manufactures?

The great success of Hong Kong and Singapore in Asia shows that it is possible for one-time developing countries to use the advice and investment of the multinationals and access to Western markets to develop and grow to Western levels of income themselves. China and India are now attempting something similar as extremely large countries. They certainly both value their access to Western markets, and China was keen to establish herself as a full participating member of the world trading system. But, of course, access to world trade does not remove inequalities overnight. The inequalities only reduce if governments, people and companies in the developing countries do the right things and are able to compete successfully. The world now shows that it is quite possible to do this with a number of success stories. There are no known success stories of countries getting out of poverty and getting closer to Western living standards by turning themselves inwards, resisting the approaches of Western multi-nationals and saying no to the international trading system. Even the protagonists of tackling global poverty have been campaigning for freer as well as what they call fairer trade worldwide, acknowledging that access to Western markets is an important part of tackling poverty.

If access to world trade were bad news rather than good we would expect more developing countries to be refusing such access or to be taking their countries out of the world trading system. In recent years the opposite has been true. There has been a queue of countries seeking full admission to the Western trading club, with no queue of countries seeking to go the other way. You have to remember that all the countries that join the World Trade Organization are volunteers. The West does not make them do it, and if they ever decide it is no longer for them, they are at liberty to leave as quickly as they wish. No-one forces the developing countries to accept investments from overseas multinational companies, and no-one forces them to accept the loans and grants which the West regularly gives them. Critics of the system say the West is clever in hooking them in. The offer of a grant or loan one day entails contractual and moral commitments which they argue may not be in the countries' interest. Most of us believe that these contracts and commitments are very much in the countries' interest, and that they have entered into them freely and sensibly. If we are wrong it is still open to those countries to pull out of all these arrangements by unilateral action, and on the understanding that if they did so they would not be welcomed back having spurned the banking agreements, the contracts and the supply arrangements that they had freely entered into.

Indeed, the West goes further than this. The West does accept that in some cases developing countries have been badly governed, and those governments have taken on debts and contractual obligations which turned out to be too heavy for them. Instead of insisting on its pound of flesh, requiring that every dollar of interest and capital be repaid, the West has had an ambitious programme of cancelling debts and allowing long periods of interest rate holiday, without exacting penalties on the developing countries concerned. All too often there have been cases of aid, grants and loans going to developing countries for good purposes, only for the donor or lender to discover that in the hands of the receiving government the project has either been badly implemented or the funds have not been used in the intended way at all.

It is extremely difficult to get out of poverty if a country is in a state of ethnic feud and civil war. It is very difficult to create a successful enterprise economy if there is no properly upheld law of contract, if theft, graft and corruption are not kept to a minimum, and if people cannot be assured that they can earn the fruits of their labour in relative peace and stability. That is why the West has structured its free enterprise association with the developing world with a series of global institutions, which give the developing countries voice, but also a sense of a disciplined framework which will help them create enterprise economies as successful as those in the West which they seek to emulate.

There are conflicting views on how good the International Monetary Fund's economic advice has been. There are different views on how suitable the lending policies of the World Bank have been, and whether all of the conditions have been properly judged. There have been fashions in the remedies offered and there have been clear examples of policies pursued by the international body that have not enjoyed the success they planned. However, I am quite sure that the intention behind those bodies and the policies they were pursuing were entirely honourable. The people making those loans or offering their economic advice did wish to see the state they were advising prosper and do better. Sometimes it may not have worked because the advice was ill conceived, as history subsequently revealed. On many other occasions it did not work because the implementing state, the developing country, failed to deliver the basics that were required to allow enterprise to flourish.

Globalisation is gathering pace. Its prime engine now is the phenomenal pace of growth in both India and China. When the world's two most populous countries, with a combined population of 2,500 million – five times that of the USA and the EU combined – start to get their act together they create enormous economic waves around the world. It is Chinese and Indian demand that is keeping up the oil price and the prices of steel, aluminium, copper and the other basic raw materials. It is the output of the Chinese and other Asian factories which is driving the world price down of t-shirts, trainers, computer hardware and vehicle components. It is China and India who are now every bit as big exponents of globalisation, and active practitioners, as the USA.

If you look to what people do rather than what they say, you will see that in practice most of us in Western society are fans of the American multinational corporation. There may be people who don't like drinking Coca-Cola, who don't wish to eat a McDonald's hamburger. They may buttress their moral outrage at the way the beef is raised to go in the sandwich with a genuine distaste for the bubbly liquid. All too often, however, those same people are using the American Google search engine to put together their political campaigns against the American multinationals, and are busily sending their e-mails to their political friends on Microsoft software. They may well be using IBM, Honeywell, Hewlett Packard or Sun computers. They may be driving Fords or Vauxhalls produced by an American car corporation, and they would doubtless fly on many a Boeing plane as they seek to make their campaigns more global in reach. Some years ago in Britain a television sitcom, ironically called *The Good Life*, showed how difficult it was to cut yourself off from the global corporation and lead any kind of sensible life in an advanced Western suburb. It showed how often in order to survive the individuals concerned did have to depend on the neighbours, and indirectly through them on the multinationals which sustained the whole life system. There was nothing very good about the peasant life in Europe before the Black Death even though it was mercifully free, as globalisation's critics would see it, of global American corporations with motor vehicles or pharmaceuticals and GM foods.

You only have to remember the look of excitement in the eyes of eastern Europeans when the Berlin Wall was torn down, and they realised that for the first time Western brands and Western products were theirs for the taking. They soaked up not only the West's belief in freedom and democracy but also CDs, trainers, cars and fridges. They had been starved of consumer durables and good brands under the long years of communism, which had diverted a very high proportion of low state income into defence. They welcomed the

West's belief in clean water and clean air, something they had also been starved of by the military-industrial complex that kept the Soviet Union going. Many poor Africans near starvation in their villages would like a good meal as the West enjoys. They too aspire to the televisions, the radios, the clothes, the football merchandise that are the birthright of the Western family.

The global marketplace teems with opportunity. People from the poorest of societies may individually find their way through the commercial jungle. An African athlete who can run fast, an African soccer player who can mix it with the best in the world, an Indian film maker who can hit it in Bollywood, can all use the rich and easily accessible markets of the West to gain access to Western fame and lifestyle to transform their lives.

Is it any bad thing that people in the poor ghettos of the world's largest cities or in the poor villages of the world's countryside can dream their dreams and sometimes see beyond them? Whilst we would rather their societies and countries as a whole go forward together with us, at least there is some hope that individuals might succeed, if they glimpse the opportunity on a television set or meet talent scouts from the West who can show them a different life.

Which brings us back to Western politics. The same television, communication and data technology that is beginning to show, not just to the leaders but also to the people of the world, that there is another way is also showing people of the rich and sophisticated West that billions of people worldwide are still deprived of things we regard as routine. Many people in the world lack access to supplies of clean water, do not have power at the touch of a button in their home, and cannot afford three meals a day. This is an affront to the West's conscience and is becoming a big political issue in its own right. We will see in Chapter 5 just how this is affecting politics in Britain. A part of the debate in Britain is trying to recreate the old argument between communists on the one hand and capitalists on the other. There are still some in Western societies who do not accept the judgement of history and the judgement of the eastern European and Russian people, that communism definitely failed to deliver a good quality of life. They use the same tired old arguments against globalisation that they once used in favour of the Soviet system. They still want there to be a planned answer. They still wish to see the USA as the West's Satan and the multinationals as the satanic mill. The evidence points in the other direction. When people are given the chance anywhere in the world they want the Western goods and products. When they get a chance to elect a government in Africa or Asia they nearly always choose a government which welcomes in the multinationals.

The exception to this rule is the world of Islam. The USA is up against a cruel dilemma. She felt she was doing the right thing taking her version of democracy and freedom to the oppressed people of Iraq. She felt she was doing the right thing freeing the people of Afghanistan from the repression of the Taliban. She is now discovering that if you give people the vote in Islamic societies, they may not vote for parties and leaders who welcome Western multinational companies, who see the Americans as their friends and allies, and who want to ape Western lifestyles. The Islamic way of life is different from the American, Western enterprise way of life, having different values and serving a different religion. The moral, political and ideological argument now in the world is between the USA's democratic enterprise system and the Islamic fundamentalists. Elsewhere in the world Western ideas of prosperity and liberty have made enormous progress. Now the debate is about how to see them through and to implement them rather than about their desirability.

The USA's problems in the Middle East are considerable. She is the principal and natural ally of Israel. Many Arabs deeply resent the Israeli pattern of settlements in Palestine and beyond Israel's borders. No-one has yet been able to find a negotiated peace based on the principle of two states – a democratic Israel and a democratic Palestine. All the time this huge issue remains unresolved we live in danger of hotter conflict breaking out and more countries being pulled in to take sides.

But perhaps this is no longer the major problem that the USA faces. Although it is an important element in the bubbling cauldron of Middle Eastern politics, in some ways the bigger issue now is what the USA does as the liberation of countries by American weaponry fails to produce stable democracies that she can live with comfortably. What should she do if it turns out that the invasion of Iraq has removed an important counter-weight to Iran? What if Iranian society is happy being led by people who not only dislike the state of Israel but have a strong loathing of the whole American way of life and the American value system? What if Iran defies the world authorities and decides to arm herself with nuclear weapons or worse regardless? What if the results of the election in Iraq do not produce stable, democratic government for the whole country but intensify forces that wish to split her into at least three parts? How long can American forces stay in both Iraq and Afghanistan if there is no stable, moderate civilian authority seeking American assistance to maintain the peace?

Unlike many, I think President Bush went in at least in part for good motives. I think he did have a vision of how regime change would transform these societies, not just to make them better allies of the USA or to keep the oil flowing but to enrich the lives and spirits of their people and to free the subject peoples of Iraq from the tyranny that had definitely done damage to many millions of her citizens. Maybe some in the American regime were concerned about the oil supply and others concerned about the threat Saddam Hussein represented to the region. But maybe as well there were many noble crusaders in the USA who did take the cause of all those who had been locked up, tortured or had their loved ones murdered by a barbaric regime. There were those in the USA who understood that the Kurds could never be happy under Saddam's tyranny.

Whatever the reasons for the invasion, critics and friends of the President alike have to understand that now we live in a difficult and uncertain world. The President could rightly point out we lived in a very difficult and uncertain world before the intervention. The problem is that now the difficulties and uncertainties arise in part from American action, as well as from the intrinsic instability and problems in the Middle East itself. There is no easy or obvious way out. Boeing, Microsoft and Google cannot ride to the rescue as it is a different kind of problem. Tesco cannot arrive waving contracts in the way that it can in an African village, offering jobs and hope. American diplomacy can work away behind the scenes, trying to find an agreement between Israel and the moderate Palestinians. The USA does have some leverage with Israel and Israel might make further strategic retreats in the hope that they will result in the moderate forces in the Arab world establishing a peace around a sensible Palestinian state. Even if that miracle were to happen, we would still have the unresolved problems of how to stabilise Afghanistan and Iraq, how to secure the withdrawal of Western forces, and how relations between Iraq and Iran would then develop. Many in the US administration now see an arc of evil through the Middle East, linked by terrorists who wish to destroy Israel.

The USA is already wrestling with the dilemma of Saudi Arabia. Saudi Arabia has been one of the USA's best friends in the Middle East over the last fifty years. The USA has given her every military support and Saudi Arabia has been a moderating influence in world politics, often turning on her oil taps to avoid even higher prices and substantial dislocation of the Western economic system. The USA has turned a blind eye to the way Saudi Arabia is governed, accepting that she is not going to be a liberal, multiparty democracy on Western lines. President Bush's relationship with Saudi Arabia today shows that he himself is not such an ideologue as many of his critics portray him. His relationship with Saudi Arabia and the Gulf states is pragmatic, recognising that democracy and liberty on Western lines cannot be introduced all in a hurry in every Middle Eastern state in one go. Much work remains to be done in the two countries he has invaded in the wake of the terrible attacks on New York and Washington.

The darkness of Middle Eastern politics serves only to highlight the very different hues of globalising politics in the rest of Asia as the enterprise system works its magic, pricing people into jobs, creating opportunities for whole communities, and allowing more countries to join the Western family of enterprise nations. Globalisation is not the problem. The clash of opposites, the conflict of religions and ideologies, the machinations over geo-political interests of the great powers in the Middle East are the things we should worry about. People in the West should recognise that they have done well out of globalisation, including its critics, and should recognise that just as the multinationals have served us well, so they can serve the developing world well in their turn. Of course, there must be a framework of law. Of course, monopolies must be broken or regulated. Of course, developing countries must have advice and advocates to make sure that the terms of the deal they do with the incoming corporations are fair and just. Of course, all people of goodwill want to see free trade and fair exchange, not exploitation. Those of us who believe in the free enterprise system have to remind people time and again that profits are not evil but the lifeblood of enterprise. It is profit which pays the risk taker and makes it worthwhile for someone to venture their capital. It is profit which buys the machinery to keep the factory working. It is profit which pays for the research and development that produces the new products. It is profit which might find a new drug and profit which might create the next factory opening in another developing country.

It is also important that the friends of free enterprise constantly remind people that you cannot make the poor rich by making the rich poor. None of us likes to see extremes of inequality but inequality is much less terrifying if the people at the bottom of the pack enjoy an American-style life than if they are starving. The true enemies are not inequalities and profits but famine, civil war, barbarism and disease. If we try to limit the freedom of those with money to invest and to spend we may merely destroy jobs in the very places we wish to help. If we spend all our time running down the multinationals who find the new drugs and develop the new technologies, we could end up living in a meaner, crueller, dirtier world rather than a more successful one. It is to the problem of poverty that we should now turn.

5

The assault on poverty

I WANT TO MAKE A DIFFERENCE

How can I help people less well off than myself?
Charity begins with your own family
Does anyone in your wider family need temporary accommodation whilst they sort themselves out? Do you have a spare room?
Is someone in your family desperate to buy a house but unable to afford the deposit?
Can you help them, with a gift or by buying a share of the property to get them started?
Is someone in your family unemployed? Can you help rebuild their confidence, suggest ways of finding a job, introduce them to people who might help?
Has someone lost a loved one, or been through a difficult marital split? Can you give them a home for a few weeks to help them get over it?

Helping your neighbour
Is one of your neighbours elderly and lonely?
Can you spare a little time to talk or to help?
Can you help with the shopping, or give them a lift occasionally when you are going into town anyway?

Are some people in your district down on their luck?
Can you pay them to do some work for you?
Can you introduce them to someone who might want to employ them?

Do you have spare accommodation you could rent out?

Are you involved in a relevant charity to help local people in need?
Could you help fundraise for good causes?
Could you give some of your time as a volunteer to help people in difficulties?
Could you be a Citizens Advice Bureau adviser?

In a rich Western country poverty is an attitude of mind more than a state of being. The single most important thing we need to do to help people out of poverty is to give them an attitude of 'can do'. The same is true internationally. The single most important reason some countries remain in poverty and others climb out of it is that those who lead the countries that stay poor fail to raise the capability of their nations. If people believe they can get on in the world, they are more likely to do so. If they believe the struggle is necessary, reversal is inevitable, that the chances of success are reasonable, they will put in that extra effort, go that extra mile and be more likely to succeed.

Successful societies where most people lift themselves out of poverty encourage responsibility in individuals and to each other. Successful societies recognise obligations of kith and kinship. Parents help children. In their turn children help parents when they grow old. One family member who succeeds recognises obligations to family members who have not yet succeeded. There is a mutual understanding, a mutual respect, a mutual sense of shared journeying and obligation. In unsuccessful societies these ties of kith and kin break down. Society fragments and atomises. Parents do not give children a helping hand, children recognise no obligations to ageing parents, and extended families fall apart.

As our current Prime Minister has rightly said, successful and good societies encourage respect generally. Whilst the immediate obligation is to do all that one can to look after oneself and then to look after one's family, there is a wider obligation to respect, help and encourage others who live in the same community and society. Successful, prosperous societies encourage good neighbourliness as well as self-help.

If we could inculcate these values and virtues in struggling communities within our own country, we would soon make more progress in lifting people out of relative deprivation. If we could encourage these virtues amongst those who lead the struggling countries of the world, there would be many more success stories on our hands.

In a rich Western country such as the United Kingdom the good news is that for many poverty is a temporary state rather than a permanent condition. Figures showing social injustice and deprivation capture a snapshot at any given time. Yes, it is true that too many people at any given time are on a low income or no income. Yes, it is true that too many people are without a job, often the single biggest reason why they are relatively poor. Yes, it is true that there are still too many people in our community who own no property and have no savings. They are dependent day by day on the revenues from their daily labours and have nothing to fall back on. If we roll the camera forward and look at the picture a few years later, we may still see too many people in all those categories, but in many cases they will be different people.

The most depressing and serious kind of poverty within our country is where families and communities get stuck in very long periods of unemployment, low income, no savings and no ownership. There are such places and such pockets of poverty but they are not the whole story captured by the unemployment figures, the savings figures and the ownership figures. The neighbourhoods may stay poor but often the people who make their way out of poverty will have left the neighbourhood as part of that process. The poor neighbourhoods in Britain are those where all the housing is socialised. Of course, as soon as anyone starts to succeed, gets a job or a better job, they move to a neighbourhood where they can buy a flat of their own. Of course, when someone in a poor neighbourhood decides to establish their own business they are attracted to establish the business in a richer neighbourhood nearby, where there is more custom and where there may be less violence, burglary and theft.

In a rich country, poverty is always with us because the definition of poverty is constantly rising. I was brought up in a relatively low-income working household with no colour television, no central heating, no telephone and no car. Thirty years ago the colour television, the central heating, the car and the telephone were the luxuries of the better off, not the birthright of the many. Today you would be classed as poor if you had no colour television, and Labour now think that deprivation includes missing out on a phone. You can still lead a perfectly good life without either a TV or a telephone but you may be deemed to be in poverty by some if you try to do so.

In Britain today poverty means depending on benefit payments from the state, which take care of the basic needs of accommodation, heating and food. To be poor in Britain is to be rich by the standards of more than half the rest of the world. For poverty is an attitude of mind. It still hurts to be poor in Britain, as your poverty is judged by what others have in the society around you. The politics of poverty is allied to the politics of jealousy by those who think the answer to making the poor rich is to first make the rich poor. All too often people believe that if the tax on the rich was just increased a bit, enough money would be available to cascade through the system to solve all problems of poverty. The problem of poverty will never be solved, because it is a relative problem and it is an attitude of mind.

This does not mean that we should take poverty lying down or we should pretend there is no real problem. Of course it hurts to be poor, and in a rich society the level of income and physical comfort at which you feel poor is considerably higher than in a poor one. Politicians of all parties regard poverty as something to be blackballed and treated. The issue between us is not whether politicians should do what they can to help lift people out of poverty at home and abroad but what might be done that can make the biggest contribution to achieving this worthwhile end.

If we wish to tackle poverty at home and abroad we have to do so by encouraging the 'can do' approach. For an individual this can encourage a sense of helplessness about the magnitude of the task. How can one of my constituents tackle the problems of urban deprivation in downtown Liverpool, let alone the crisis in Zimbabwe? The Christian's answer to 'What can I give him, poor as I am?' is to 'give my heart'. This remains good advice 2,000 years later. If you have fire in your belly to tackle the problem of poverty, then take an interest in your local school, and enthuse and motivate some of the pupils that come from the lowest-income households in your neighbourhood. If there is a family living in your community afflicted by loneliness, ill health, run-down spirits, then take an interest and see if you can help build them bridges to a more prosperous and enjoyable world. If your village or town is frustrated by the lack of global success in tackling African poverty, then why not adopt an African village and see if your money, care and attention can make a difference?

Today many people in the rich West have their conscience stricken by the poverty, famine and dreadful conditions that blight so many people elsewhere in the world. Modern telecommunications can bring us horrific images of civil war in Darfur or famine in the Horn of Africa instantaneously. The vivid contrast with the full shelves of the local supermarket can move most of us to a sense of great injustice. This has led to an explosion of political action by many in Britain. Real concern was voiced by thousands about the aftermath of the tsunami that hit the shores of many Asian countries just after Christmas 2004, and many have been moved by images of Africa through recent crises. They have written in their thousands to MPs, demanding that governments take more action to tackle the problems of poverty.

Governments can make a difference, as we will see. We should look to governments in those countries to establish a rule of law, to keep the peace and to adopt policies favourable to enterprise and prosperity. But we all need to look to ourselves in our different ways to make a contribution to tackling the problem of attitudes. As tourists and teachers, as neighbours and employers, we rub shoulders with many of our fellow citizens of the world from the poorer countries. In our daily dealings we can encourage that change of attitudes which could make the difference.

The politics of poverty have been explosive in Britain all my lifetime. Those on the left think that the rich and successful should provide for the others through collective taxation and government programmes. They often also seem to believe that the rich and successful are to blame for the poverty and the lack of achievement of others. There is an inverted sense of responsibility on the part of the left. They seem to regard people as being responsible for every-one save themselves or their own family. We need to explore these attitudes to understand why the politics of poverty is so complicated, and how the left have been successful in dominating the terms of debate in much of the fashionable media. They do so by appealing to an innate selfishness in many, offering them simple solutions to com-plex problems and offering them solutions that require the minimum of effort by themselves.

In the left's demonology, if a person competes successfully and earns a high income then he, and it is usually a man, is responsible for so many of the ills of the modern world. The rich man would doubtless drive a large car. He is regarded almost single-handedly as being the cause of pollution on the planet. Attention is always focused on the large-car driver rather than the inefficient domestic boiler or the coal-fired electricity plant. He probably works for a large company which in the eyes of the left is itself busily destroying the planet and at the same time creating global inequalities. Doubtless the rich man is consuming too many of the earth's resources in the selfish pursuit of his own lifestyle without a care for others who have to share the planet with him.

In contrast, if that successful man's old school friend has failed to pursue a successful career, he or she may well be the victim of injustice. She may have been discriminated against at work for being a woman. He may have come from the wrong ethnic background, suffered from the wrong upbringing or had the misfortune to choose the wrong parents. The left so often assumes that if you went to the wrong school, if you dropped out of school, if you came from a broken household or if your parents had very little income, it was somehow God given that you were bound to fail. In the left's victim culture, if a person from the wrong background is not earning sufficient income to look after themselves properly or earning no income at all, it is proof positive that discrimination lives and sufficient reason for the state to take care and provide.

The New Labour government is currently agonising over the problem of disability. Like the Conservatives, New Labour believe that if someone is unable to get a decent job because they are blind, deaf or maimed, the rest of us should pay them an income so that they can lead a decent life. None of us begrudge such payments, made in part because of our sense of fairness and in part because we are so grateful that we do not suffer those afflictions ourselves. But today we have the problem that some people who claim disability show no visible distinctions from those of us who make our own way in the world. There are many people now claiming disability benefit because they say they are depressed. There are others who tell us their back is very painful but doctors can find no proof on the X-ray of a slipped disc or a broken vertebra. The parties have come together in believing that true disability deserves our care and our cash, and are puzzling over what we do about the invisibly disabled and those who claim mental impairment which they think justifies a state pension.

Labour are also puzzling over another difficulty that has afflicted poorer communities in our society in recent years. Where once working-class communities offered each other neighbourly support and showed some pride and respect, venerating work and appreciating the need to toil for your income, today in some dysfunctional communities attitudes are very different. In the lowest-income districts in Britain all too often the poor burgle the poor, gangs assault each other and terrorise each other's younger relatives. In fully socialised communities where public housing makes up maybe more than 90 per cent of the total stock, there are no private spaces and little sense of dignity or respect.

Yet even within those communities there are welcome signs that all is not lost. High on the balconies and walkways of the inhuman vertical villages of the inner cities you'll come to flats with meticulously tended window boxes, as people desperately attempt to bring something natural into the inhuman concrete surroundings and show that by energy and care they can create something more beautiful in a world of ugliness. From those same council estates someone can emerge as a talented footballer who goes on to earn millions, or an entrepreneur with a business idea who will move out as he moves up.

In working-class communities in the 1950s and 1960s different attitudes prevailed. Neither my maternal nor my paternal grandparents ever owned their own home, bought their own car or had their own telephone. One of my grandfathers worked all his life as a labourer, the other as a carpenter. They were not generously paid but they and their wives managed the money in such a way that they could feed and shelter the family. They felt very strongly that they should never accept charity, which included means-tested benefits from the state. In retirement they lived on their state pension, which they felt was theirs because they had paid their stamp over their adult years in employment. They were true sons and daughters of the Beveridge settlement, believing in only drawing out from the national insurance system their entitlements when sickness and old age dictated.

Today it is much more common to find in poor districts the view that you should maximise your income from the state by acquainting yourself with all the enormous complexities of the means-tested benefit system, so that you can apply for and receive your maximum entitlement – housing benefit, council tax benefit, disability living allowance and income support. Some in those communities go further and believe that you should play the system to your own advantage, exploiting any weaknesses or mistakes that government officials may make. The left have created a dependency culture where many look to the state as their prime source of income and assume that their communities will not support a more active work-based lifestyle. It is this problem above all others which Gordon Brown has worried away at with endless interventions in both the labour market and the benefit system. Still he has not found his silver bullet to crack the problem.

The attitudes in post-war, working-class Britain were very different. People brought up on the discipline of the forces were inculcated with a sense of self-respect and pride. 'You might be poor,' you would be told as a child, 'but you're not going out looking like that.' Cleanliness was next to godliness, tidiness was important, taking some pride in your appearance reflected a pride in yourself. The whole system encouraged people to believe that you could be better off tomorrow than today, and you could be so by your own efforts. Today there are so many places where attitudes encourage the opposite view. People are told that tomorrow will be no better than today and maybe worse. They're told that tomorrow could only be better if government were persuaded to do something more. People are not told to smarten themselves up but are told if all else fails to take political action.

This attitude that people are not responsible for themselves or their own family has spread like wildfire throughout our whole community. One of the interesting areas where many people feel that governments of both Labour and Conservative persuasion have been wrong is the approach towards care for the elderly. Both the Conservatives and Labour in office have held the line when it comes to paying for care for an elderly person in a residential or nursing home at the end of their life. The government has said that if the elderly person has money then that money should be used to pay the fees of the care home concerned. If an elderly person is dependent upon the state pension then part of that should be a contribution to those fees, as the elderly person is getting all their accommodation and food paid for within the nursing home package. If the elderly person has insufficient income to pay the fees but has moved into the nursing home from a property of their own, then that property should be sold or mortgaged in order to meet the bills.

There has been endless pressure from many of the children of elderly people that this is unfair and unjust. This is surprising, as the policy includes all the safeguards you would wish to see. If the elderly person going into the nursing home still has a living partner who wishes to remain in the matrimonial home then, of course, they are entitled to do so and the home does not have to be sold. If the elderly person has children who are desperate to inherit that particular home, then it is open to the children to pay the fees for the elderly person so that the home is left untouched. But the children of such elderly relatives often argue a different case. They claim to be defending the interests of their elderly relative. They say that it is unreasonable that the elderly relative's home should be sold and the proceeds applied as far as is necessary to paying the fees. They claim that the elderly person has paid taxes all their life and therefore deserves a free place in a nursing home, as part of the National Health Service settlement. If you counter-argue and say that, of course, the elderly person will continue to get all their medical care free, just as they would if they were still living in their home, but that does not extend to providing them with free board and lodging, the children get very upset and claim that that is uncaring and unreasonable.

What the children are saying is that the responsibility for the food and lodging of the elderly person is no longer that person's, nor is it the responsibility of his or her children or spouse and family. They think it has automatically become the responsibility of the state because the elderly person has reached an age where he or she needs to live in a nursing home or residential care home. Some may genuinely believe this to be a responsibility of the state but others seem to be motivated by the selfish impulse that they wish to inherit the house unencumbered, even though they have a house of their own. It would usually be tactless to discuss with them alternative ways of financing the inheritance of the house, although there may well be a route to do this. Unfortunately elderly people committed to nursing and residential care homes do not on average survive for a very long time. They rarely survive long enough to spend all of the money that would accrue from the sale of a decent house in the south of England, given that the sale proceeds would presumably be placed in an income-bearing investment to pay the bills. The financial loss to the children might be quite modest if the money were properly invested, given the average length of survival of an elderly relative. If they are desperate to inherit that particular house, then it would be far more sensible to come to an agreement with the elderly relative about occupying the house when the elderly relative goes into the care home, selling their own house, and paying a rental to the elderly person during his or her remaining years of life, which could be used to pay the nursing home fees.

It is a sign of how socialised thinking in Britain has become that many people who have shown all the attitudes of self-help in their own careers and lives think it right that they should ask the neighbours to pay for their elderly relatives in nursing homes and residential care homes, so that they can have a capital windfall when their relatives die. Similarly, many people now no longer believe that they have some responsibility for their wider family, if a member of that family goes through some type of financial crisis. When a member of my family lost his job, his marriage and his house all at the same time in one of those collapses that can be quite common these days, given the way that divorce laws and redundancy work, my wife and I naturally offered him a room in our home for as long as it took to find another job and a place to live on his own. All too often people who come to MPs' surgeries are apparently without any family. Young people turn up and say they have nowhere to live. You ask them why they can't stay with their parents, aunts, uncles. They look sheepish and say their relationships are not good or they're not in contact, or their parents don't want to help. Much has been written in sociology about the breakdown of the wider family. Aunts and uncles, nephews and nieces, cousins in varying degrees of proximity no longer figure prominently in many people's lives. Things seem to be getting worse than that. In many cases there is little communication or sense of mutual obligation between parents and children, and a growing pattern for fathers to be uninvolved in their children's financial upkeep or their general wellbeing, unless the state intervenes and requires the father to make a payment.

It is good in this society of ours, despite the growing tide of state involvement in all our relationships and the increasing offers of cash by the state for all sorts of mini-crises within our lives, that there are many people who still recognise the traditional responsibilities. There are many caring parents who accept long-term responsibility to their children. They help them with the university fees, the purchase of the first car, and even the purchase of the first home. They give them encouragement and support using their friends and contacts to ensure their children have a good start in life. There are also still children who accept responsibilities for their ageing parents, helping them financially or ensuring comfortable and good provision should they need long-term care in their dying days.

There is, however, a creeping socialisation of all our relationships and a growing sense that we should all at some points in our lives be pensioners of the state. Many mothers are now married to the state, looking to the government to provide them with a home and an income for themselves and their children. School pupils are now becoming employees of the state, being offered an income to stay on at school to improve their qualifications. Many elderly are now in the care of the state, and even those in work are now becoming state pensioners through the growing range of income top-up benefits, paid by a government more worried about income and inequality than the lack of an enterprise society.

This approach, with the state taking on so many of our individual responsibilities of yesteryear, has long since taken over in many areas where people used to feel obligations to others who are not part of their own family. If in this new world some parents do not accept obligations to their children, it is not surprising many more people no longer accept obligations to those living in the wider community.

Some years ago people in my constituency campaigned that we had a problem of rough sleeping in Wokingham. They naturally thought the answer to this problem was to build more subsidised houses and to make these available at low rental or no rent to the individuals concerned. I myself was suspicious of this. I went out at night to try and find the homeless sleeping on the streets that I had been told about. Fortunately I encountered none. What struck me as interesting was that some of the campaigners lived in large houses with several spare rooms. If you suggested they could help tackle this crisis that they perceived to exist, by offering their rooms at attractive rents or rent free, they did not seem to think that was a sensible answer.

We are also witnessing the nationalisation of neighbourliness. Because families are so split and so atomised, people often don't bother about their neighbours either. Where old working-class com-munities relied on mutual self-help, with people constantly popping into each other's houses to borrow things or to assist with the DIY, today the natural reaction is to stay in your own little place and to ring the council. People often come to see MPs or clergymen or the Citizens Advice Bureaux because they are lonely. They dash in and out of their own homes in the middle of busy working lives and spend the evening doing the chores and glued to the television rather than taking an interest in the human drama next door. We live in a world where things on television have greater reality than reality itself. Someone may be living in the midst of a community more fascinating than *EastEnders* but they wouldn't notice it because they are so busy watching *EastEnders*.

So what can be done to turn the tide or resist the pressures? Some of the things that need doing do not require the expenditure of any additional money. Tony Blair's 'respect agenda' is working away at this truth. If through the schools we can inculcate a sense in young people that they live in a community and have ties and obligations to their neighbours, we would start to make progress. If we could use the community that surrounds each secondary and primary school to start to recreate some of those ties of neighbourliness and friendship that characterise successful communities, that too would help. There are times when I am out and about talking to my constituents on their doorsteps that I literally have to introduce neighbour to neighbour, to try and resolve a problem which they have naturally escalated up to the council or the MP. For some people now it is more normal to involve government in their problems than to sit down with neighbours to sort it out for themselves.

Other things require changes in government policy. Successful communities are mixed and balanced communities. If a community is made up of 90 per cent social housing it will lack the entrepreneurs, the community leaders, the people with business and professional expertise that a balanced community requires. Successful working-class communities did not see the doctor, the lawyer or the managing director of the local factory as a threat or a class enemy but as a necessary part of the society. In the case of the doctor he was a valued confidant and adviser when confronting life's difficulties. People would look to their employers as a source of good advice and support when a suitable issue arose, and to the professional people in the local community to provide the lead when it was necessary for them to do so.

In schools serving poorer communities we need to break out of the cycle of poverty of ambition. If education authorities and teachers expect less of children because of the background they come from, they are unlikely to be disappointed. There is no intrinsic reason why the child of an unemployed labourer should do less well than the child of a solicitor. To those who say that because the solicitor may offer more parental support his child is bound to do better, I say: do not despair and do not deprive the child from the less advantaged background because of who their parents are. It could be that the child of the rich family gets all too little emotional support and encouragement because the parents are so busy. It could be that the child of the unemployed labourer gets a great deal of emotional support at home. Even if it isn't true, it's even more reason why that person should be shown a better way, a pathway out of poverty, something to aspire to, something worthwhile for them to do.

As with people, so with nations. The left are busily demonising successful countries just as surely as they demonise successful people. Because the United States has led the world with her technology and economic growth during the last hundred years, it is America that is at the centre of their ire. It is strange, for it is to America we should look to see how most people can be got out of poverty most quickly. It is in America where the average experience is a lifestyle beyond the dreams of more than half the people of the world. Living in relatively rich Europe many people do not realise just how much more successful the USA has been. The leading western European countries would struggle to be in the bottom ten of the poorest states of the United States of America, enjoying average incomes of under one-half of the richest states or the District of Columbia. People in the USA on average live in homes with twice the floor area of British or German homes. They are more likely to have a car, a dishwasher, a washing machine, a colour television, a telephone and all the other consumer durables of the modern world, and have considerably more spending power for things other than the necessities.

For this success America is pilloried as the capitalist Satan, the country that consumes too much of the world's resources, and even as the country that does too little to tackle poverty. Her critics ignore the fact that America gives more aid than any other country, retires more debt than any other country, offers more inward investment into poor countries than any other country, and transfers more technology than any other country. They ignore the fact that to be poor in America is to be rich anywhere else outside the advanced West.

To the left, nations who remain mired in poverty are the victims of the global system, misled by the USA. America's investment in developing countries is seen as exploitation rather than helpful business support. American advice on how a country's economic policy should be run, retailed through global bodies such as the International Monetary Fund and the World Bank, is regarded as harsh and unhelpful, even though evidence abounds that countries that accept monetary and fiscal discipline do considerably better than those that don't. If America takes military action to intervene because the government of a given country is doing damage to the freedoms and economic prosperity of its citizens, then she is condemned for flexing her muscles. If the USA fails to intervene in a delinquent state, then sometimes she can be blamed for that as well.

There is still a collective guilt that hangs over the West about Africa. The uprising of goodwill towards the very diverse countries of Africa that we witnessed in Britain in the second half of 2005 is part of this overhang. All of us felt it would be good if our government, leading the G8 group of nations and the European Union, could energise the rich countries of the world to find more positive ways to assist the poor and oppressed of Africa. It is curious how long this collective guilt has survived. It is half a century now since the Western colonialists began packing up shop and pulling out of the remaining African countries. More than two generations have passed. People now leading those African states were either not born when they were under colonial government or were very young. African countries have now educated two generations of children under their own control. Those same countries have received very large volumes of financial aid from the West, considerable technical expertise and the transfer of technology, and large loans both to the governments and to the private sectors. There has been no lack of goodwill on the part of the former colonial powers when it comes to encouraging and helping the development of African economies.

So why then has it been so unsuccessful in so many cases? Is it right that we should still feel so guilty or even responsible? The poor of Africa should now be looking to the rich and the powerful of their own countries for a way out of their difficulty.

There are many theories about what it takes to trigger successful and rapid development of a poor country. Having studied this for many years and advised in several countries, there are five things above all else which I think are needed to make it happen:

- The first is that the countries themselves need to impose their own rule of law. It is impossible to build an enterprise economy if theft and violence are the norm, if contracts are dishonoured, and if the state is corrupt.

- The second important requirement is peace. Civil war and international war are destructive of enterprise and prosperity, as well as of life and freedom. If African countries are determined to fight amongst themselves or to fight their own peoples, it will make it difficult if not impossible to stimulate the jobs and commerce they need.

- The third is that stable governments at peace need to follow policies that are favourable to enterprise. If a country taxes too much it will put people off from setting up business there. If governments regulate and boss people around too much, people will take their business ideas elsewhere.

- The fourth thing that is needed is motivated people. We're usually told that what is needed is education. This is true as long as it is education of the right kind. Of course, it is difficult to run an enterprise economy if people cannot read, write and add up. But it is also difficult to run an enterprise economy if all the brightest and best people have been taught to a higher standard, to believe that they should work for the government and that answers have to come from the state. Education has to equip people not only with the basic skills it needs to run an enterprise economy but also with the self-belief that people can do things for themselves, and that enterprise will deliver most of the solutions.

- Finally, a successful, developing country needs investment from outside as well as from within. Local savings would flow into investments if the other four things happened. If contracts are respected, if money keeps its value, if the country is at peace, and if there are motivated people to employ, then local savings will naturally flow into local investment. So also will money and ideas come in from abroad. A stable, motivated, outward-looking economy which respects property rights and allows people to repatriate their capital or pay themselves dividends if they are successful will naturally attract money from around the world. With the money will come the ideas, the technology, the organisational skills which the infant economy requires. The successful developing economy does not see the Wal–Mart purchasing manager or the Microsoft salesman as a threat but as part of the process of growing up.

If we look at the state of African countries, we will see that those that remain deepest in poverty have managed to achieve none of these five central propositions to equip themselves to grow and expand.

Poor African countries come out very badly in the rankings of the *Index of Economic Freedom*, produced jointly every year by the Heritage Foundation and the *Wall Street Journal*. There is a high correlation between a country having a low score in its tables, showing it is a very free country, and doing well economically. There is also a high correlation between having a high score, showing that countries are largely unfree, and doing very badly economically. In the most recent tables, Equatorial Guinea is 136th, Sierra Leone 137th, Angola 139th, Nigeria 146th and Zimbabwe 154th out of 161 countries ranked, meaning these are some of the most oppressed countries in the world. Within the 161, Sudan and the Democratic Republic of the Congo do not provide enough information even to gain a ranking but are doubtless well down at the bottom of the table. Most of the countries fail to deliver on at least four of the five points that are central to economic success.

If we take the case of Sudan, we see the damage that a continuous civil war can do to a struggling economy. The long civil war between the Islamist government in Khartoum and the Christian liberation movement has disrupted Sudanese life for many decades. Despite the peace agreement in January 2005 and the attempt by a new government to introduce stability, violence continues in the Darfur region, where the government is supporting Arab–Muslim militia groups, organised as the Jingaweed, who are killing black African Muslims in the locality. There have been many hundreds of thousands of deaths and refugees as a result of the conflict. Although the country has oil resources, it is difficult to exploit them against the background of continuous bloodshed and damage to investment.

Just as Sudan has been hindered by war, so the Iraqi economy has been damaged by international war. The Iraqi economy was disrupted by the invasion of Kuwait and the war that ensued to restore Kuwait to independence, and more recently by the American overthrow of the evil regime of Saddam Hussein, which had failed to develop and maintain the oil installations.

War has done even more damage in the Democratic Republic of the Congo. As the *Index of Economic Freedom* describes:

> The country has been disrupted by the 1997 rebellion led by Laurent Kabila, and the subsequent challenge to the new government by rebels backed by Rwanda and Uganda. Much of the Democratic Republic of Congo is only nominally under government control, and instability continues, especially in the eastern part of the country. Economic activity is largely informal, barter transactions are common, and corruption remains endemic. Most people are engaged in subsistence agriculture. The infrastructure is in disrepair and practically non-existent in many parts of the country.

Even worse is the plight of Zimbabwe. President Robert Mugabe has continued in power, using violence and corrupt means to stay in office through a series of rigged elections. Anyone who declares for the opposition to Mugabe can find themselves on the wrong end of the violence of government supporters. They often lose their land and their livelihoods and sometimes their lives. Mugabe's dreadful mismanagement of the economy and the society has turned a successful country which could feed itself into an overregulated, lawless place that requires food assistance to keep going. Unemployment is extremely high and much economic activity has to be done through barter and informal arrangements. Mugabe's recent evictions have left at least 300,000 people homeless and the regime is now characterised by its thuggish conduct, misappropriating property when it wishes.

The result of these devastatingly bad governments can be seen in the income per head figures. The Democratic Republic of the Congo is estimated to have a per capita income of $87 a year only, Zimbabwe $351 and the Sudan $433. There are no available figures to tell how low Iraqi per capita income has fallen, despite the huge reserves of oil.

We see the same pattern of the damage that repressive regimes can do in Asia. There, in a continent where countries such as Hong Kong and Singapore have done stunningly well, and where China and India are now emerging from poverty, Laos still has a GDP per capita languishing at $352. There a one-party communist state continues to do damage to economic freedom and centralises all the crucial decisions. Burma too, with a GDP per capita of only $154, has suffered from the bad policies followed by its ruling military junta in past years. Evidence abounds that the main reason for the poor performance of all too many poor African and Asian economies is bad government in those countries themselves. The left continue with their view that the problems can be solved by a change in attitudes and behaviour by the Western countries. They argue four particular points designed to paint the West in a bad light, suggesting that if only the West changed its attitude and its polices, suddenly the problems in Sudan or the Congo or Burma or Laos would be magicked away.

First of all, the left argue that the burden of Western debt is one of the main causes of poverty in developing countries. The argument is sometimes developed by people saying that it is not fair that a new regime in a given country should have to pay the debts of the outgoing regime that incurred them. There is eternal optimism that a new military junta or communist clique will somehow be more benign and better judges of investment than the outgoing military junta or communist clique, and that they should start with a clean slate. If only elected, democratic governments coming into power in a Western state could start with a clean slate it would make life much easier. But, of course, international commerce and trade rests upon the assumption that an incoming country government will recognise the obligations of the outgoing one, and continue to pay the interest. I am all in favour of cancelling debt for the poorest states but only where the new regime there will be serious about creating conditions for economic success.

The second argument is that the West has offered insufficient aid. There is apparently nothing wrong with the Zimbabwean economy which the payment of a bit more Western conscience money could not provide. The wide belief in the power of aid continues despite the abundant evidence that the countries that have received most aid have been the least successful. As with money lent to countries, so with aid money it needs to be spent on projects that improve the capital stock, and allow the country to make progress in building a better economic structure for itself. All too often aid money has been swallowed up in unnecessary government expenditure, in armaments, in new Mercedes cars and jet travel for the ruling junta, or in showy economic projects that did not work on the ground.

The third argument is that the West is too exploitative in its approach to these developing economies. The man from Tesco is driving too tough a bargain when negotiating to buy agricultural produce from an African state, or the American multinational, seeking to exploit the oil, is repatriating too much profit to Wall Street, and not leaving enough money in the domestic economy. It is difficult to see what these critics expect and want of the Western companies concerned. Surely they can see that it would be far worse for poor countries if Tesco decided to source all its agricultural produce from western Europe, rather than buying from African states. I'm sure they drive a tough bargain but the answer is not to make it more difficult for Tesco to buy their beans in a west African country but to make it easier for other Western companies to buy their beans in Africa. Healthy competition would drive the prices up. Nor would it be sensible to say that American multinationals are no longer able to exploit oil in African countries. They bring technology, expertise and the ability to get the job done. They do spend large sums of money locally. The challenge for the local economy is to get better at supplying the people and the products the American multinational needs to get the job done. The skill for the host government is to drive a tough enough bargain so that they get their fair share of the royalties and revenues.

The fourth criticism of the West is that it recommends policies and ideas that harm the fragile African or Asian economies. In particular, the left are worried that privatisation will be used in sensitive areas like water, where state organisation has so signally failed to provide a clean supply of drinking water for everybody's household over the last fifty years. It is claimed that privatisation would put prices up and supply less water to fewer people. This seems extremely unlikely, as the sole purpose of introducing private capital into the water industry in an African state would be to expand the network and to supply more.

The truth is that, even if the left had their way and all these things were remedied, it would not improve the lot of the people in Sudan or Zimbabwe or the Democratic Republic of the Congo, or the other tough cases in Asia and Africa. Tesco could double the prices offered for beans, Exxon could double the royalties it paid on the oil, and the West could agree to no more privatisation of services in any African state. It would not suddenly solve the problems of civil war, famine, bad government and corruption. Similarly, the West could cancel all of the outstanding debt and double the aid but past experience shows that where this has been tried, the countries at the bottom would remain on the bottom, if they continue with their current government and current policies.

The left face a paradox in the way they treat the West's relationships with the developing world. On the one hand they are rightly very concerned that the West should not become a new colonial power. On the other hand, when the West fails to intervene and solve the problems, they are full of condemnation that it has not done enough. The sad truth of life is that, in a world where we have rightly backed independence for all these countries, we have to expect the main impetus for change and improvement to come from the countries themselves. There is no point in tipping ever more cash in if a country is fighting a civil war or if it is run by a dictatorship, which will spend the foreign aid on aggrandising itself and on repressing its people. The West can offer advice and help, and it can back the advice and help up with cash if the country concerned decides to take sensible action. There is no point in kidding ourselves that Zimbabwe or Sudan is suddenly going to come right if we cancel debts, spend more money and turn a blind eye to the obvious brutalities and errors of their domestic governments.

Should the West intervene militarily where countries are treating their people so badly? Recent experiences show that left and right are becoming more circumspect. Intervention in Iraq to throw out a dictator who had destroyed his country's freedoms, damaged its economy and done far worse by terrorising and killing many of its people has proved to be extremely controversial. The West has discovered that it is difficult to stabilise the country once the war has been won. Evicting the dictator is the relatively easy part of the task. The West rightly called for free elections and then expected domestic politicians to get on with the job of forming a government and stabilising the country. Unfortunately, it has not proved that easy, with local politicians struggling to gain control against the background of no tradition of a stable rule of law and democratic government. Again, there is only so much the West can do. The West is keeping its troops there at the behest of the civil power but if the civil power does not get a grip and does not radiate a natural authority, the Western troops will be unable to help it keep order. The experience of Iraq seems to militate against the idea of invading Zimbabwe or Sudan with a view to creating a new and stable democratic government. Instead we sit and watch as evil regimes do untold damage.

The belief that more foreign aid will solve the problem is the same as the belief that more regional transfers of cash and grant will solve the problem of relative depravation within a rich, Western country. All my lifetime Liverpool and parts of Scotland and Wales have been receiving large sums of money from the United Kingdom government, with a view to narrowing the gap between those local economies and the United Kingdom average. Even larger sums of money have continuously been being pushed into Northern Ireland, where the main problem has been the disruption caused to the domestic economy over many years by the terrorist campaigns of the 1970s, 1980s and 1990s. Despite all this money, these parts of the United Kingdom remain the poorest today, as they were thirty years ago. It seems to prove the point that expenditure of extra money alone does not solve the problem. State-directed cash going into state-approved projects does not trigger the enterprise success that we need to create a more prosperous and free society.

The EU has fallen prey to exactly the same foolish doctrine. It has been setting up complex and expensive mechanisms to shift money from the rich and successful parts of the Union to the poor and unsuccessful parts. It will be another wasted opportunity, as it does not tackle the underlying causes of relative poverty in different parts of the Union.

Poverty is an attitude of mind. It cannot be solved by pressures from without. Exaltation and cash on their own will not do the job. Taking the local government of a fading region over or invading a country whose government is doing the wrong thing may create many more problems than it solves. Overcoming poverty has to come from within. It is a battle that has to be fought in the hearts and minds of the individuals living in poverty. It is a battle which has to be fought and won in the hearts and minds of those leading the poor communities in the rich countries and the poor nations of the world. Just as you cannot make the poor rich by making the rich poor, so you cannot make the poor rich by getting the rich to run their lives. Successful people and successful countries could be a role model, they could be a source of inspiration, they could be a source of ideas, techniques and advice. They cannot do the job for people and countries, and whenever they try to do so they usually make things worse. Foreign aid is so often misplaced conscience money, paid to the government of the poor country that is the problem and not the solution. Turning a blind eye to the gross errors in self-governance or in government for individuals and countries is not the way to make the world a happier place.

The problem in some ways is far more intractable than the left believe. The problem is winning the battle of individual hearts and minds. In other ways it is much easier. It can be solved by lighting that spark, creating that flame, in people and countries who come to believe that they can do it for themselves.

The phenomenal success and energy of China has been released not by more foreign aid or by American invasion but by the dynamism and energy of the Chinese people, themselves suddenly released by the advent of a government that believes in economic freedom in selected areas, even though it does not yet believe in wider freedom. The success of people living on a barren rock in Hong Kong, in the middle of a relatively poor continent, has come from individual sparks of enterprise within the hearts of every one of them, and from the low taxes and light regulation of the colonial and now of the Chinese regimes that govern them.

The success of the American people comes from their belief in the American dream. People in the USA do believe that anyone can become a Hollywood star, a baseball ace or a business millionaire if they put their mind to it. America has a free enough society to allow the human spirit to flourish, and enough verve to tell people it can. It is the spirit of enterprise and the priceless gift of freedom that will bring prosperity to the poor and enfranchisement to those with nothing. Do not look to governments and to more transfer payments to solve the problem. Look instead to individuals and to inspired leaders.

6

All change for climate change?

I want to help save the planet from global warming
I can change my life so I cut the carbon emissions it takes to keep me going

Travel
Can I walk instead of drive for short journeys?
Can I get a lift from a friend or give a friend a lift?
Could I take a bus or train and would it make sense to do so?
Can I change my car for one which burns less?
Can I lobby my local bus company to buy more fuel-efficient buses?

Home
Can I put in a condenser boiler to raise the fuel efficiency of my heating system?
Can I turn the heating down or off when I am out?
Have I set the thermostat at a sensible level?
Can I wear a jumper at home more often and reduce the background heating a little?
Have I fitted fuel-efficient light bulbs?
Am I running the washing machine on full load?
If I have the cooker on, am I cooking all I need to cook at the same time?

Do I use the hot water I heat up, or am I heating it up only to let it cool down again?
Can I plant some trees and shrubs to mop up some surplus carbon?

Work
Do I switch the lights off when I leave a room empty as I would at home?
Have I put forward any fuel-saving ideas to my boss?
Do I switch my PC off when I am not using it?
Do I keep a TV on all day without needing to?
Can I cut down on my use of office paper and supplies?

Government
Have I told my local councillor that I expect the council to cut its emissions?
Have I put forward any energy-saving ideas to the council?
Have I lobbied my MP to help cut the national government's fuel waste?

Experts tell us that climate change heralds disaster for millions of people in the world. They forecast a rapid warming as a result of man's inhumanity to man. They see in every car exhaust and every boiler flue another contribution to a process which is going to drown the low-lying cities of the world, as the ice caps melt, and turn large tracts of habitable land into desert. Some say it is already too late to reverse the process because of the very large quantities of carbon dioxide already emitted into the atmosphere. Others say that if mankind could curb its appetite for fossil fuels the damage could be limited.

Although opinions, surveys and casual observation tell us that most people accept the global warming theory, there is absolutely no evidence in their daily way of life that they take it seriously. The vast majority of people in Britain are happy to condemn President George W. Bush for expressing scepticism about the idea of global warming as a result of mankind's behaviour. If we look at the daily conduct of most of our fellow citizens, they carry on as it if were nothing to do with them. Indeed, it's not just most people who ignore the doom-laden warnings of the global warming theorists but the governments themselves that retail the doctrine as established fact.

Recently I attended a conference on sustainability organised by the Anglo-German Forum in London. Held in the magnificent Locarno Rooms of the Foreign Office, it brought together business and political leaders from both the United Kingdom and Germany. A German government minister talked to us about the need for the West to do so much more to control emissions. The British govern-ment was represented by a senior official from the Department of Trade and Industry who reinforced the same message. It would all have been so much more convincing if the conference organisers had lived the message as well as providing a platform for it to be represented.

Instead the German ministers spoke on a bright sunny day with six curtains drawn across to keep the sunlight out, with almost 200 light bulbs blazing at full intensity from the chandeliers and wall lights in the magnificent Foreign Office room. It was only after I pointed out that the sustainable thing to do was to draw back the curtains and switch off the lights that we achieved that modest progress.

I was unable to persuade them to get control of their heating system. As it was a very well-attended conference the room soon became far too hot. The Foreign Office's answer to this problem was to fling wide open the windows at each end of the room, so that the taxpayer could have the pleasure of paying to heat the centre of London. Officials looked perplexed when I suggested that they needed individual room-heating controls with thermostats and on–off switches, so that they could start saving some of the fuel they were burning so wantonly.

Doubtless many of the people coming to the conference had flown in by jet aircraft from Germany, and had been whisked from Heathrow Airport to the centre of Westminster in chauffeur-driven, large-engined cars. To compound their trouble and error, the conference organisers laid on vehicles to take the conference attendees the short distance from the Foreign Office to the Department of Trade and Industry for the afternoon session, thus avoiding the need for a seven-minute walk instead. It is very difficult to take seriously people preaching that we all need to change our conduct to avoid global chaos, when the people in charge behave like that.

The British government has been particularly bad at offering any kind of example to the rest of us on how to control emissions and to limit waste. Night after night lights are left blazing in office buildings long since vacated by all or most of their staff. Night after night and weekend after weekend office buildings remain heated to high standards, and in the summer many of them now have air conditioning trying to cool them down to a temperature lower than what they are heated to in winter or to something very similar. In the government Cabinet ministers have been offered the choice of a large-engined Jaguar or an environmentally friendly Toyota Prius, which does 60 miles to the gallon. There were very few volunteers for the Prius other than the transport minister and the Chancellor of the Exchequer, who have wiser political heads, or who realised their own vulnerability should they choose the less energy-intensive vehicle. Even the environment secretary was photographed getting in and out of an older, fuel-hungry Jaguar instead of choosing to buy the cheaper and more fuel-efficient vehicle.

Earlier in the life of the Labour government the deputy Prime Minister, with responsibility for environmental and transport matters, demonstrated the advantages of using the train for a number of camera crews and press reporters. The impact of his leadership was somewhat dented when the true story was revealed. He only took the train a short distance up the line, and once he thought the media had completed their filming he got off the train to get back into the chauffeur-driven ministerial limousine.

The Conservative Party, under its new leader, David Cameron, has seen the need to offer leadership in this important area. It is no good lecturing others on the need to change lifestyles, if those giving the lectures cannot change their own. Greenness begins with every one of us. A successful green strategy is the result of hundreds of choices by each individual in a given society, seeking to do more with less fuel in a variety of ways.

It may well be that we are living through a period when the world is warming up. Any student of Earth's history or meteorology will tell you this is nothing new. Over the estimated five billion years of the world's existence so far, there have been long periods of global warming followed by long periods of global cooling. In the early 1970s expert opinion came to the conclusion that we were living through another global cooling period. Scientists told us to worry that our warm water ports in the northern latitudes would freeze in winter, our plants and foodstuffs requiring equable climates would perish in the cold, and many elderly people in northern latitudes such as Britain's would die, suffering from the impact of climate change.

Some years later most expert opinion is equally sure that the opposite is happening. We are warned of melting ice caps. Pleasant Mediterranean climates will turn to tropical deserts. Temperate climates, like those in Britain, will be transformed into Mediterranean ones.

From the British point of view, global warming is clearly preferable to global cooling, as we are offered the spectre of a better climate with more opportunity to grow Mediterranean-type products including vines. This reminds us that the English climate was like that 2,000 years ago, when the Romans grew grapes in many parts of England to satisfy their wish for the comforts of home whilst stationed overseas on imperial duty.

None of us want to see ice caps melting, destroying whole cities and low-lying countries. Of course, we would prefer it if we could stabilise the world climate at today's levels of temperature, as our current pattern of settlement reflects the existing coastline and topography of deserts, tropics and good crop-growing lands. Today's climate may be bad news for large tracts of Africa but, from the Western point of view, it is a climate pattern we can manage. Our settlements and prosperity are based upon the recent pattern of climate. Western governments say they're concerned about Africa but not to the point of wishing to manage world climate with its interests in mind. A warmer world might shift trade winds with their rain-bearing properties. It might green the deserts in some parts of Africa as it turned the soil further north and south into arid landscapes. I've not seen anybody argue that we should deliberately engineer a given quantity of climate change to solve the African problem. This is probably realistic, given the lack of control mankind has over the whole issue.

Any student of the earth's history will tell you that its climate has been subject to ceaseless change, long before man arrived on the scene. The pattern of the oceans was mightily different in the age of the dinosaurs from what it is today, we believe. Most scientists think the dinosaurs were wiped out by global warming. The fossil evidence does not suggest that they had overdone the 4x4s or failed to let the train take the strain.

Modern science also advocates the theory of continental drift, where huge forces push land masses together in some places and pull them apart in others. You only have to witness the power of a volcano or a tsunami to realise that there are natural forces greatly superior to man's ability to make and mould the landscape which will continue to dominate. Even modern man with all his powers is unable to stop a tidal wave for one minute. He cannot plug a volcano or even channel its lava in a harmless direction. If mankind could stop its contribution to global warming it would still have no power to prevent some natural calamity doing the same, perhaps more quickly and more powerfully.

There is in much global warming theory breathtaking arrogance about the importance of man, and about man's ability to control and mould the planet he lives on. Fatalists would say, what will be will be. Whatever mankind might do by way of polluting the air and seas, the future of the earth might be decided elsewhere through the movements of the comets, changes in the sun, or through the mighty and terrifying movements of the continents as they bang into each other on the surface of the globe. The shifting of the plates in California could wipe out huge American cities in a few hours. Another tsunami in the Pacific region could wreak more havoc than the last one.

I am not a fatalist. I do think it makes good sense for mankind to curb the pollution it pumps out into the atmosphere and does what it can to look after the planet where it holds the lease. Most sensible people in the debate agree that business and individuals should cut their pollution. Most agree that it makes sense to reduce carbon emissions as well as the emissions of more harmful substances such as lead or nitrous oxide. The fact that random, natural events may swamp our impact on the planet does not give us a licence to abuse the earth.

We can agree with the Greens that a civilised and rich society can make a much bigger contribution to curbing pollutants of all kinds than a poor or developing one. We can agree that maximum effort by all of us should now be given to minimising the impact we have upon the environment we have inherited, especially because there are now so many people living on the world that our combined impact is so much greater. Indeed, the greenest policy of all would be one favouring smaller families around the world, curbing poverty and pollution at the same time. With every mouth to feed and pair of hands to work that a new birth brings comes an individual who will emit much carbon dioxide and create much waste over his or her lifetime.

There have been campaigns, regulatory pressures and technological breakthroughs that have made a signal contribution to cleaning up our act. In the United Kingdom, a government decision to lower tax on unleaded petrol to encourage people to switch was very successful. Most people soon used the unleaded fuel, making it possible to ban leaded petrol altogether.

The decision to privatise the electricity industry was the greenest decision taken in the post-war period by a British government. It triggered a change of power source from coal to gas. Combined-cycle gas generation is considerably more fuel efficient than coal generation and the fuel is somewhat cleaner in other ways. The new combined-cycle gas power stations hit 55 per cent fuel efficiency compared with 33–35 per cent for the coal stations they replaced. This made the vital contribution to hitting the UK's Kyoto targets and to reducing the unpleasant emissions, as well as the carbon emissions, into our atmosphere from power generation. Neither of these moves inconvenienced anybody, neither damaged our way of life, both contributed to cleanliness and greater prosperity. It shows that it is possible to clean up our act whilst not damaging business or our standard of living.

The typical analysis of the present British position is based on the idea that road transport is the principal villain of the piece. The government based its whole policy from 1997 to 2000 on the proposition that it could persuade, by regulatory action and other means, a sufficient number of people and businesses to switch from private road transport to public road transport or rail. It did this in the name of tackling carbon emission and global warming.

At no point did a minister carry out a proper audit of the relative contributions of private road transport, public road transport, rail transport, air and sea transport, and non-transport activities to carbon emissions. Nor did policy makers succeed in finding a way of persuading people to leave the car at home and use some other means of getting about. They were equally unable to stimulate enough rail freight to make a significant difference to the amount of lorry traffic on our roads. They decided instead to pitch themselves against human nature. Most people want to have flexible, personal transport in both their private and their business lives. People do not use trains for many of their journeys if there are no trains going where and when they want, or when the complications of getting to and from the stations with their belongings are too great.

My car, van or lorry is always available when I want it. It is there where I am, ready to go when I wish. It is never late for me but I can be late for it. It can take me to more or less any address in the country without requiring me to change cars or vans, and without having to tie in with somebody else's timetable. I can load the car or van at one end and unload it at the other. It gives me a protection against the rain, wind, snow and hail. The car or van usually functions even when we have the wrong kind of snow or leaves on the road. That's why around 85 per cent of all our journeys are carried out by private road vehicle.

The contribution of transport to the carbon dioxide problem is important but far from dominant. In 1990, 18 per cent of our CO_2 emissions came from transport. This rose to 21.3 per cent by 2005. Government figures suggest some further upward increase in the relative share but remaining below a quarter over the rest of this decade. Within that figure, cars are the main source of CO_2 emissions because there are so many of them but buses and heavy goods vehicles produce far more carbon dioxide per vehicle than the average family car. The position on other unpleasant emissions shows that more progress has been made with cleaning up cars than other vehicles. In the case of nitrogen oxides, cars account for 17 per cent of the national output as do heavy goods vehicles. Buses account for a significant 3 per cent on the relatively small base of the number of vehicles, with the railway contributing a further 1 per cent. In the case of particulate matter cars account for only 5 per cent of the amount emitted to the atmosphere as do heavy goods vehicles, with buses contributing another 1 per cent.

As a result of a successful ban on leaded petrol, all transport now accounts for only 2 per cent of the total lead emitted to the atmosphere. Improvements in exhaust handling and tight regulatory standards also mean that transport now only accounts for 3 per cent of the sulphur dioxide emitted into the atmosphere. These figures show just how much progress has been made in controlling the pollution from transport vehicles, given that 36 per cent of all the energy used in Britain is consumed in transport machinery.

In recent years the fuel efficiency of the average car sold has improved considerably. There has been a reduction of one quarter in the amount of fuel burned by the weighted average new car in 2004, compared with 1978. Today very big strides are being made in a further substantial reduction in fuel burn, through the substitution of diesel cars for petrol cars. The average new diesel vehicle can go 40 miles for each gallon consumed compared with the 30-mile average for each petrol vehicle. Most fleet buyers now purchase diesel vehicles and the private individual is now catching up, given the very strong incentive to do so from the sharp upward movement in taxes and prices of fuel.

If road transport accounts for only around a fifth of our CO_2 emissions and all transport under a quarter, where should we look for the main part of the problem? The two main sources of carbon dioxide are business and residential. Within the business sector power generation is the single largest source of difficult emissions. It is in this sector that great progress was made in the 1990s with the dash for gas but where problems lie ahead, given the lack of a clear government energy policy over the last nine years. Today around a fifth of all our power is generated from nuclear power stations. These produce very few unpleasant emissions, although, of course, there is the question of handling of radioactive waste, especially at the end of the useful life of the power station concerned. The government has been in a dilemma over whether to replace nuclear stations with more nuclear to prevent there being any growth in CO_2 and other polluting emissions, or whether to start replacing these nuclear stations with the fossil fuel-burning ones, which means that Britain's contribution to global warming would increase again. The government seems to have come down in favour of replacing nuclear with nuclear, recognising the damage it would do to its global environmental reputation if it had to admit to the world community that in future Britain's CO_2 emissions would be rising because of a substantial shift to fossil fuel power generation within the UK.

The residential sector accounts for about a quarter of all CO_2 emissions, more than cars do in aggregate. The single biggest contributor in the typical household is the combined water heating and central heating boiler. Whereas the regulators and politicians have been keen to tighten the standards on new cars and to pressurise people into switching from old vehicles to new ones, there has been no comparable pressure on people to do the same for their domestic heating boiler. We are now in the paradoxical position where most people are bigger polluters because of the age of their domestic boiler than they are because they drive their car.

According to the UK government a typical, heavy, old boiler is only 55 per cent fuel efficient. A lighter, old boiler is typically 65 per cent efficient whereas a new condensing boiler is 88 per cent efficient. It is possible now to buy a new condensing boiler which is 97 per cent fuel efficient, a huge advance on the typical, old, heavy boiler the government describes. The government believes in 2006 that a householder could cut his or her bill by more than a third for heating his or her house or flat by switching from an old boiler to one of the new, far more fuel-efficient varieties. If people could be persuaded to renew their boilers over the next decade, and if the government would ensure renewal in all government-owned properties, the impact on our carbon emissions would be very substantial. We could now make a bigger impact on our contribution to global warming by concentrating on the domestic heating boiler than by further restrictions on the motor car.

Within the transport sector, we need to analyse the green impact of different types of transport more carefully before sounding off about policy. All is not as it might seem. The general view of the government and others is that switching people from car to train is one of the most important ways of reducing our pollution. It is clearly true that if an express train carries a full 460 people between two cities, they will each burn considerably less diesel or electric fuel than if they went by private car. In this case we need to examine carefully how likely this is, and we also need to understand what other emissions are made when people undertake their journeys by train rather than by private automobile.

Very few of the 460 people travelling on a full train live at or near the station and walk to it. We should include in our account the amount of carbon given off as our train travellers drive to the station or take a taxi or bus to get there. The train service has had a sub-stantial adverse impact upon on all the other people trying to undertake journeys by other means. In order to try and make trains safe, no other form of transport is allowed on or near the railway lines as trains cannot stop in time and cannot steer away from an obstacle. Rail travel makes a contribution to traffic congestion. At level crossings cars queue patiently, often with their engines running, awaiting the passing train. There is also a lot of concealed extra pollution. Many other motor vehicles are delayed by urban congestion because there are very few bridging points over the railway lines, jamming vehicles onto too few routes.

Our idealised train carrying its full complement of 460 passengers is not typical. In order to offer people a reasonable service, a train company needs to offer a frequent choice of train to persuade people to give up the complete timetable flexibility of the private motor vehicle. A larger number of trains travel around the country with very few passengers on. Whilst a train has a big advantage over the motor vehicle, offering far less friction between wheel and rail than between rubber and road, it has the disadvantage that it is much heavier. A typical 460-seater train is 350 tons or more in weight, requiring considerable power on slippery rails to start the vehicle up and to get the train moving. Our 460 people travelling by train may need three trains, not one, to take them all at times more suited to their needs.

Most modern trains are fully air conditioned. Because their windows do not open they run the air conditioning all the time. Whilst an increasing number of private cars also have air conditioning, people tend to only run the air conditioning on hot days, as they are very conscious of the fuel impact from running it.

I live 10 miles from the principal railway station of Reading. If I wish to travel from my home to a meeting in Birmingham at peak periods, it can take me around an hour to drive into Reading through the very congested streets, park at the station, walk to the ticket office, queue for a ticket, get to the platform and await the train. Quite a lot of that hour would have been spent in a motor car with the engine running very inefficiently, at low speeds or no speed. When I get to Birmingham, I would then need a taxi to drive me through the fairly congested streets of Birmingham to my meeting. Whilst I would have burnt less fuel by sitting as a passenger on the Reading to Birmingham train rather than driving on my own on the motorway, it may not be the case that I've helped the environment overall. To go from my home to a meeting in Birmingham is a two-hour drive at sensible speeds on the motorway. For most of the journey the car is working very efficiently, averaging more than 40 miles to the gallon. The journey by car is not only quicker than the journey by train but it also avoids polluting Reading.

Older vehicles are dirtier vehicles. A bus clearly pollutes less per passenger mile than people going by car if the bus has a large number of passengers on it. However, the average bus in Britain has very few passengers on it – an estimated nine only. In addition, the average bus in Britain is around nine years old, built well before the latest high standards came in to control engine pollution. Switching people from modern fuel-efficient cars on to buses that are old with few passengers will increase the amount of carbon emission and other pollution going into the atmosphere from the journey. Again we need to know exactly what the impact is before proposing a particular remedy.

Common sense tells us that switching people from private to public transport can make a favourable impact upon environmental pollution when certain conditions are met. The first is that public transport vehicles should be fairly new, just as most private cars are fairly new, so that modern technology can take care of their fuel efficiency and their emission rate. The second is that the public transport vehicles should benefit from high occupancy. This means that public transport is a sensible alternative on busy and congested routes at busy times of day but is unlikely to be a green answer at unpopular times of day and on less densely populated routes. Trains are ideal for commuting at the morning and evening peak when you can get maximum utilisation and offer a frequent service, making them more attractive to people. Buses are best in large conurbations like London, where again potential popularity of the service enables a frequent service to be laid on, increasing its desirability to the potential user.

Transport policy should understand that people have tasted the fruits of flexible, private transport and they're not going to wish to switch back. We need to tame, green and clean the private vehicle, rather than thinking we can get people to abandon its flexibility. Indeed, we've come a long way in doing just that. Successive rounds of emission regulation have succeeded in getting rid of practically all of the noxious fumes from the back of the modern car. All that remains is to curb the CO_2 emissions, where progress is now being made.

Joint electric and petrol engines already double fuel efficiency. The new range of hybrids offer people cars that do 60 miles to the gallon compared with the 30 miles to the gallon average for modern petrol vehicles. The next development may well be diesel hybrids. There is no technical impediment to twinning an electric engine with a diesel engine in the same way that current petrol hybrids twin a petrol engine with an electric one. This could then produce a new generation of cars offering 80 miles to the gallon, drawing on the more fuel efficient diesel technology.

There could also be a development of all-electric vehicles, which would be emission free if they could recharge their batteries from electricity generated from renewable sources. The running bills would be well down as it costs about 1p a mile to run a car on electricity compared with about 10p for petrol, according to Energy Saving Trust figures.

Work is underway on bio-fuel vehicles. Plants, municipal waste and agricultural residues can produce organic compounds to fuel an engine. Bio-diesel, often derived from rape seed oil in the United Kingdom, can be used as a direct substitute for diesel fuel. Currently the way forward is thought to be to blend this with conventional diesel. Others believe that hydrogen is the coming fuel. Hydrogen has to be produced from water or natural gas. It can then be liquefied or compressed so that it can be stored into the road vehicle. If the hydrogen is produced from renewable sources then it can provide a carbon-free and sustainable option.

Work is also underway investigating fuel cell vehicles, where devices convert the energy stored in a fuel cell directly into electricity. Fuel cells convert chemical energy into electricity efficiently like a battery. According to the Energy Saving Trust, the most commonly used fuel cell technology for vehicles is the proton exchange membrane fuel cell. Demonstration vehicles have been produced.

The government's strategy of switching people from road to rail has not been successful. In 1952 18 per cent of all passenger miles travelled were undertaken by rail compared with 27 per cent by car, van and taxi; 42 per cent went by bus and coach. By 1997, when the present government took over, only 6 per cent of passenger miles were covered by bus and coach and 6 per cent by rail, with a massive 86 per cent by private vehicle. The latest figures show no change in the percentages undertaken by rail or bus at 6 per cent each, with motorcycles gaining at the expense of cars and vans, up from 4 per cent to 6 per cent, and cars and vans down from 86 per cent to 85 per cent. There has been some increase in the number of passenger journeys undertaken by train and a massive investment in expanding and improving the capacity of the network. This, however, has been sufficient only to prevent further reduction in rail's market share.

Under nationalisation, there was a steady fall in the number of passenger journeys undertaken by train. On the main rail network in 1950 1,010,000 passenger journeys were undertaken. This fell steadily to only 740,000 in 1993/4, at the time of the privatisation, a fall of more than a quarter despite central planning and large government subsidies. Since privatisation the railway has more than replaced the lost journeys under nationalisation, with the figure reaching 1,088,000 in the year 2004/5. The system is now up against severe capacity restraints and will be unable to increase its share of the overall travel market if growth continues generally.

The biggest growth in public transport from a low base has come in the most fuel-intensive method, aviation. In 1950 there were hardly any passengers on domestic flights. In 1997 there were fifteen million journeys by air and in 2004/5 twenty-two million. Journeys by bus, trolleybus or tram continued in freefall throughout the nationalised era. In 1950 they were running at the level of 16,445 million and last year had declined to only 4,613 million.

People spend a lot on transport. In 2003/4 the average household spent £51.90 a week on motoring and bicycle costs and a further £8.80 a week on public transport fares. Around 14.5 per cent of total household expenditure was spent on getting around. A further £10.40 a week was spent on average on motor vehicle insurance and taxation on top of the petrol taxes included within the general figure. Investment in infrastructure is skewed in favour of the railways. In 2003/4 £5,186 million was spent on the rail infrastructure and only £4,231 million on the road infrastructure.

The change in the position of freight has been equally dramatic when looking at the balance between road and rail. In 1953 37 billion tonne kilometres moved by rail against 32 billion tonne kilometres by road. The rail figure plunged throughout the era of nationalisation, largely a reflection of the reluctance of the nationalised industry to allow single-wagon marshalling, requiring any user to fill a whole train with its freight. This strategy took the amount of freight moved by rail down to a low of only 13 billion tonne kilometres in 1994 at the time of privatisation. Over the same time period, road freight surged to 144 billion tonne kilometres. Since privatisation rail freight carriage has increased by 50 per cent, rising to 21 billion tonne kilometres whilst road continued to grow at a more modest rate, reaching 160 billion tonne kilometres in 2004. Today the bulk of petroleum products is moved by water, the bulk of coal and coke by rail, and everything else predominantly by road. The railways have recently lost the Post Office contract for mail.

We need to be more adventurous in our search for public transport solutions that are customer friendly and green. It should be automatic that more rigorous standards should be set for reducing harmful emission from trains and buses We should also look at combi vehicles to try and overcome some of the defects of railway routings. Technology has been perfected which allows a lorry or coach to run on rubber tyres on the road system, in order to get to the railhead, and then to lower steel wheels to run on the railway with less friction and more fuel efficiency. Vehicles to collect both freight and passengers could be designed that could either run independently on the tracks or be assembled into train loads at suitable interchange points. The combi vehicles could also solve some of the problems of current defective railway technology. If tarmac was put down the sides of the tracks along the railway bed, the combi vehicles could then lower their rubber tyres and put some of the weight upon the rubber-tyre axles where conditions were preventing good or full traction on the steel wheels. In the autumn, when there were leaves on the line, or in the winter, when there was snow and ice, the extra flexibility of being able to put some of the weight and pressure onto rubber tyres would enable the vehicle to get sufficient traction so that services were not impeded or slowed down unduly. This system of dual rubber and steel is used on the Paris Metro on the lines of that underground railway where the gradients are too steep to permit normal running on slippery steel wheels.

The main reason we lack capacity on the commuter railway is the large distances we have to allow between different trains running during the morning peak, owing to the poor braking and acceleration of trains using all-steel wheels on steel tracks. Steel rails and steel wheels are best suited to very long-distance, high-speed travel on straight, flat track. As soon as you introduce gradients and curves you greatly increase the dangers of the train detaching itself from the track, and you make acceleration more difficult if the gradient is too steep. The commuter railway needs maximum ability for the trains both to accelerate quickly and to brake quickly, as the journeys are characterised by a large number of stops over a short distance to pick up and drop people off at the busy times in the morning and evening. To do this, it would be more suitable to have an element of rubber to provide the extra adhesion necessary. It might be possible to double the capacity of the commuter railway by increasing the grip of the train's wheels to the landscape. At the moment the railway has to resort to sandboxes to try and provide some friction in the largely friction-free environment of polished steel wheel against polished steel rail. It would be a good idea to experiment with these combi vehicles on track that is otherwise going to be closed. The government is currently reviewing the numerous lines around the country where passenger and freight volumes do not justify the maintenance of the track to the expensive high standard required to guarantee reasonable levels of safety. These tracks still represent important routes and could probably make a suitable experimental bed for combi vehicles, giving both public transport operators and freight transport operators an added flexibility. It would also be important to find ways of linking the resulting combi vehicles into the main rail network, preferably in train loads so that it did not damage the main rail network and disrupt timetables.

Business generally needs to make a bigger contribution to curbing its fuel burn and its emissions. Britain's ability to hit its Kyoto targets in recent years has resulted in part from the sad process of exporting energy-intensive industries elsewhere. The relatively high price of gas now charged in the British marketplace to industrial users is a good recruiting sergeant for leading overseas countries to persuade process industry to relocate. The most recent big investment by Corus, the former British Steel, is going to be in the Netherlands owing to the great price advantage of gas there compared to the United Kingdom. Industries such as glass, ceramics, steel, cement and brick making all require large quantities of heat and power, and are sensitive to the price environment in different producing centres around the world. It is important that Britain maintains a competitive environment so that we do not succeed in exporting process business from Britain, where things are relatively clean, to dirtier parts of the world, where regulations are less stringent and labour a lot cheaper. Nor should we regard it as progress if we reduce our carbon dioxide emissions by exporting steel plant to first-world competitors like the Netherlands. Proper accounting would still attribute to us the CO_2 emissions needed to produce the steel which we intend to consume.

There are businesses in Britain that could do themselves a favour and help the global position by investing in heat-saving, heat-retaining and heat-reducing processes. Waste materials from industrial processes from plastic to wood can be used to fuel more efficient boilers, and heat can be recycled through a factory building rather than vented to the atmosphere. Sometimes new plant results in dramatic reductions in the length of time something has to be fired or heated. The drive for higher quality can eliminate waste. Getting things right first time saves fuel. That means everything we make is of high quality and we do not have to burn fuel making things that are rejected and then make their replacements. Modern production techniques can be much less fuel intensive. When I was responsible for one of Britain's large ceramic tile-making plants, new investment dramatically reduced the kiln transit times we needed, slashing the amount of fuel required for each tile produced. Modern technology can be used in the service of fuel economy.

Let us suppose that Britain continues to reduce its carbon emissions successfully, as it did in the earlier 1990s. To do so will require considerably more effort than at present. It will require a new energy policy, placing the emphasis on renewables and decentralised energy whilst thinking about bringing in clean coal. It will require more initiatives to tackle too many emissions from both the business and the residential sectors, as well as continuing progress in curbing the emissions from vehicles. But even if all went extremely well and we did cut our carbon emissions, we have to remember we are but one small country of sixty million people, less than 1 per cent of the world's population. Our effort is about to be swamped by the impact of India and China. Some 1.3 billion people in China and 1.2 billion people in India, 2.5 billion in total, are now getting their economic act together. As they get more prosperous so they will consume far more fuel. Many Indian and Chinese homes currently lack central heating and proper boilers to heat enough water for normal family use. This will be altered as the people get better jobs and the incomes that go with them. Most Indian and Chinese homes lack a car in the garage but many are now seeking to fulfil their dream of car owner-ship. Most Chinese and Indian homes are without air conditioning and lack many of the labour-saving but energy-using devices common in Western homes, from dishwashers through washing machines to large fridge-freezers. As these consumer goods spread more widely amongst the billions of people in teeming Asia so the demand for energy will surge.

We have already seen the impact of strong Chinese and Indian demand upon the world energy supply. Oil prices have gone to new high levels in 2005/6 as a result of strong buying from Asia. These pressures are going to intensify immensely as the Asian homes and garages fill with energy-using products. India and China are both in a dirty phase of growth, needing far more energy for every extra unit of output than the USA or the UK. They are putting in a lot of basic industrial plant and not always going for the most modern and fuel-efficient technology.

We desperately need technological answers to the problems of carbon emission and other pollutants. We need to sell or share with India and China our best technologies for transport, industrial process and domestic purposes, so that they can immediately benefit from the huge strides we have already made. We need to work with them on how they can generate their electrical power in much cleaner ways with less carbon emission.

India and China are embarking upon huge programmes of power station building to meet the surge in demand for domestic and industrial electricity. We need to consider the expansion of nuclear technology, encouraging them to put in more nuclear generation. We need to share with them our knowledge of renewables, so that some of their power can be generated in much more planet-friendly ways. We need to develop rapidly the idea of putting carbon back into the ground in carbon sinks, and we need to discuss on an international level how we can maintain and increase the spread of forests, so that the trees can absorb the carbon dioxide and produce some more oxygen. We need to develop decentralised energy.

India, China and the USA have all been unwilling to sign the Kyoto protocol. America alone has borne the brunt of criticism from around the world for this failure but if you believe in the Kyoto target-driven process, then you should be equally alarmed by the refusal of China and India to join in. As soon as you introduce the Indian and Chinese dimension, you see the limitations of the target-driven approach. Whilst it may be possible to say to a rich Western country that it has to make do with emitting less carbon dioxide next year than this as its sacrifice to help the planet, it is impossible to say that to a country emitting relatively little carbon dioxide but whose emissions are growing as a result of rapid economic growth. India and China rightly say to the West, 'Why should we restrict ourselves when our current levels of emission per person are lower than yours?' If we do not manage to find a way of harnessing China and India to the process, whatever is achieved under Kyoto and its successors will not be sufficient, as world output of pollution of all kinds, and especially CO_2, will continue to rise at alarming rates.

In the rest of the West there is a great deal of humbug in the approach to Kyoto. Several countries have signed the protocol in order to clothe themselves in moral dignity, only to fail to hit the targets that have been set for them. It seems strange that there should be so much more moral indignation about the USA, which refused to sign on the grounds that it might not be able to hit the targets, than about countries that did sign and promptly did exactly what they were condemning the USA for doing openly. The UK will hit its Kyoto targets because of the privatisation of energy and the dash for gas in the early 1990s. However, it is very unlikely to hit the more exacting targets imposed by the new Labour government when it swept to power in 1997, given the chaos and confusion over energy and transport policy and the reluctance to tackle the energy-profligate residential sector.

In order to succeed we need policies based upon technological breakthroughs that go with the grain of human nature. We're not going to wean people off flexible, personal transport. We need to design a new generation of flexible, personal transport that is green and clean. The technologies are already available to transform the carbon output from our cars and vans. If government is serious about this it should offer leadership, both by buying the more environmentally friendly products and by offering tax breaks and other encouragements for their extended use. Why not, for example, abolish all VAT on purchase of any new vehicle which meets specified environmental objectives? Why not offer a tax break to those who are prepared to scrap an old car and replace it with one which is at least 50 per cent more efficient?

We need to tackle the domestic sector. The government has done something by setting higher standards, and is using the building regulations to ensure much higher thermal insulation standards and better fuel efficiency in boilers in new build. Unfortunately, the proportion of new build to existing stock will remain tiny, and it will take many decades for this to flow through to a substantial reduction in energy use in the residential market.

If Britain can demonstrate that she can maintain and improve her standard of living whilst becoming considerably greener, she will then gain the moral and commercial opportunity to spread this technology more widely in the most populated parts of the world.

It is in the West's interest that the poor should become richer. If Britain wishes to be truly green she should first demonstrate she can do it at home, and then show how that technology could be spread more quickly to the developing parts of the world, so that they can grow rich and clean at the same time. The poor of the world are going to want personal, flexible transport just as most in the West already have it. They are going to want higher standards of home heating and domestic appliances. They will want to use much more energy. This requires a new urgency in the initiatives worldwide to generate much more power from green sources, and to use it in far more efficient machines, engines and vehicles.

7

All politics is local

I WANT TO MAKE A DIFFERENCE

I want to improve my local environment
Identify what needs doing (road and pavement maintenance, better public spaces, more sensitive development, noise reduction etc.)
Talk to the neighbours – see if they agree
Write to the local paper
Talk to local radio
Form a group to campaign for what you want
Discuss with local councillors
Write to the chief executive of the council setting out the vision
See if you can do some of the things by voluntary effort:

- Have a weekend team to go in and decorate the school hall (with permission!)
- Have a litter squad to clean up dirty areas
- Shame the council into cutting the grass or planting the flower beds by doing some of it to show them how much better it can look
- Launch a sponsorship scheme for better flower beds and hanging baskets

Or stand for the council yourself and put things right

People may say they are interested in the problems of world poverty and global climate change but nothing motivates them like a threat to their own street, village or town. When 40 per cent no longer vote in general elections, when only twenty or thirty may turn up to an open public meeting to discuss public issues in the round, any suggestion that half a dozen houses may be built near them is likely to produce a protest meeting of over a hundred, and a proposal for a large housing estate will easily fill a hall with 200 or 300. In Wokingham, a meeting to discuss Britain's future in the European Union, organised by the local branch of the United Kingdom Independence Party, marshalled all of fifty-one people, compared with nearly three times as many to hear the local conservation officer talk about the future of a small stream called the Embrook in a public meeting. Most of them had come to complain about a district council policy to cut the grass less often in a local meadow.

In local elections now, in marginal wards the campaigners who really wish to win differentiate their literature street by street, as people expect comments relevant to them in their daily lives as they poke their head outside their front door. The more incomprehensible and beyond their grasp the big issues seem to be, the more people concentrate on the local, the particular and the specific. It is these attitudes and interests which are increasingly turning each general election into a series of by-elections.

People expect their local MP to take a great interest in what the local authority does, to write to it and lobby it whenever they wish, and to seek to change its policy and outlook. Some of them believe that the MP, as the senior elected person on the patch, does have the power to override the local authority. Others, better versed in British constitutional practice, just wish that the MP did have that power or believe that in some mysterious way through the party system, if the MP shares the same party as the ruling group in the council, then he will be able to sort them out. Few recognise or want to understand the sad truth that councils are largely out of political control at the local level across the country, whichever ruling group may nominally be in charge.

The failure of local democracy is even more stark than the weakening of national. Turnout in local elections is often down to around 30 per cent. This means that a ruling group may have only attracted one in seven of all the adult voters who could have voted for it. Six out of seven either positively disagreed with it or abstained. As the collapse of democracy is more advanced in local government than national, it is important to study it to understand what might happen next to national democratic accountability.

The gradual decline of local government has been continuing for many years. There has been an acceleration in the lack of interest in local government proper in recent years. This is surprising given the growing interest that so many people have in their neighbourhood, their street, and the immediate environmental issues around them in their daily lives. It is this paradox which we must seek to understand. How can it be that as people get more interested in the very areas of life that local government can direct and control, they remain uninterested or become even less interested in the elected people that should be directing it?

Politicians tend to see the argument in very political terms. Parties in opposition always blame the party in government for over-centralising. Parties in government always claim they have a good reason for overriding local government or seeking to make it more homogenous. Under the Conservatives in the 1980s there was growing public unrest about the very high levels of rates imposed by some councils, and the very rapid pace of increase in those rates that they imposed. The Conservatives responded with a rate-capping scheme which gave people in every area a guarantee that the increases would not be unreasonable. Under Labour the wish to centralise has broadened still further. Swept to power promising to get rid of rate capping and a whole range of other central controls over local government, they have instead kept rate capping in place and gone on to impose a variety of performance tests and quality standards across the range of public service provision, nominally under the auspices of local councils.

Ministers claim that they will be held responsible if the schools do not work properly. There is after all a Secretary of State for Education, and he or she has found it increasingly frustrating in the Labour government to have to take the blame for the very wide range of provisions and the very differing quality of achievement school by school, district by district, county by county. Ministers responsible for transport and the environment have worked out that it is difficult to have a coherent national strategy for either if all local roads, public transport and local planning decisions are under the control of councils who may not agree with the government. A welter of circulars, laws, statutory instruments and guidance notes have showered down from Whitehall onto the environment and highways departments of local councils. Social services and housing can have an important impact on the lives of those who are least well off. The Chancellor's crusade to deal with what he calls 'child poverty' comes into conflict with local autonomy. In many cases local autonomy has to buckle beneath the weight of government direction.

It is this government which has introduced comprehensive performance analysis and review. Not only does the government set a whole series of indicators which it wishes local councils to monitor but it also carries out frequent inspections, publishes league tables, and demands improvement in the performance of those councils which it feels are not meeting its requirements. The total cost of the overhead imposed on central government is estimated at around £1 billion. That's £1 billion spent on people compiling figures, people putting the figures into league tables, and people investigating and inspecting to understand why some do better and some do worse on the measurements set by the central government. It was Conservative policy at the general election of 2005 to abolish all of this number crunching, to spare local government the trouble of compiling all these statistics and conforming to all these blueprints from Whitehall. Labour were unrepentant and decided they wished to continue with them all when re-elected, so that their heavy footprint from the centre would be seen on every council.

Some might argue that there is nothing undemocratic in the senior elected body, Parliament, overruling the junior elected bodies or councils in this way. After all, the public do have the opportunity to get rid of the government if they do not like the blueprints being imposed from the centre on so many councils. Just as the Conservatives can say they had a good case for rate capping in the days of extreme left-wing councils who were driving the rates up by double-figure percentage increases year after year, so Labour can say that they have good cause to require certain standards and ways of doing things in order to implement their environmental, educational or social service policies. The public have certainly taken the message. As far as they are concerned, it means there's no point in voting in local elections because they have this feeling that the strings are pulled from elsewhere.

The truth is that the strings are pulled in a rather different way from the way you might think. It is impossible to understand what is going on in local government today unless you understand the career structures of local government officers, and their interplay with the big army of consultants that are now so influential throughout the public sector.

Because this government has defined politics as being an activity primarily undertaken between the politicians and the media, it has been all too negligent in the detail of government itself. To most Labour senior figures politics is the daily battle of the airwaves. It is the result of the clash of spin doctors with producers and journalists. A good day's work at the office is to deliver good headlines in one newspaper and stop another newspaper publishing an unhelpful story. A better day's work at the office is to secure the minister concerned prime time on television and radio to put out the government's vacuous sound bites. The daily grind of the business of government, writing the statutory instruments, drafting the orders, producing the guidance notes, tweaking the policies, setting out the framework, even composing the White Papers, is left to civil servants, who in turn delegate a great deal to expensive consultants. The old idea that the minister should provide the lead and be the voice of common sense in all discussions of policy, new regulation and new directions for the government seems to have gone out of the window in the 24/7 media age, as Mr Blair would call it. Preventing a minister going on television or radio is treated as some kind of punishment, rather than as a welcome relief from the tedious duty of having to answer the same question endlessly to someone who doesn't really want to know the answer or, worse still, is quite sure the answer is other than you know it to be. Ministers on gardening leave from media duties could revel in the opportunity it gave them to do more work behind the scenes to have a real influence. This group of ministers sees no coverage as failure, for it appears that most of them are completely out of the loop when it comes to the day-to-day detail of government policy, which matters to the governed far more than the sound bites on the airwaves.

In local government, officers are so often more at the centre of politics than the politicians themselves. The councillors are at a great disadvantage. They are part time. Most of them of working age have to do a full-time job elsewhere to pay the family bills. They do not themselves receive most of the letters or e-mails, they never sign a contract, negotiate a deal, or execute anything they want to happen. Most of them are amateurs in a world of professionals. They are usually seen as temporary birds of passage by the officers concerned. Some majority groups undermine their position further through the interplay of the leader and the leading spokespeople in the group. Now that we have so-called 'Cabinet government' in local government the officers can strengthen their grip wherever the leader believes in regular reshuffles, interrupting the continuity and the understanding of individual councillors over individual departments. Politics often becomes a way of diverting the attention of the elected officials towards the media and away from actually running the council, or it becomes a way of undermining the councillors who might be effective at controlling the executive, through diverting them into unproductive, political dogfights with each other. The councils have started copying some of the worst characteristics of national politics, with councillors increasingly worried by the stories in local newspapers rather than by the experiences of their voters day by day as they seek to interact with the council.

One of the ironies of politics as public relations is that even in this field the elected officials do not seek to become professionals themselves. The fascination with what the *Anytown Times* might say tomorrow is all embracing. However, MPs and councillors increasingly believe that, in order to have a chance of competing successfully with one another and with the journalists of the *Anytown Times*, they need to employ a growing army of PR consultants, media advisers and spin doctors, to help chart their way through the rough oceans of press coverage. In its turn, the press plays up to and panders to this new world of political vanity. The press is less inclined to take someone seriously if he or she is unsupported by an army of press officers and official briefers. The story may not run at all if it is given to a local newspaper by an individual councillor or to a national newspaper by an MP. If, however, the same issue is 'briefed out' by the Prime Minister or the Chancellor's people then the story 'has legs' and doubtless 'bottom'. Politics and politicians are busily digging their own grave with the media. The more seriously they take the media the more ridiculous they appear to the media. The more their efforts are concentrated on securing the favourable good story, the more likely it is that they will be alarmed by the headlines and by the direction of the media's interest.

Local government's growing fascination with local newspapers has gone on whilst the decline of the local newspaper and the change in its nature seems to have been unremarked by the politicians prepared to do ever sillier tricks to pander to the newspaper's interest. Local newspapers are now struggling badly. The rise of online advertising to handle property sales has hit the amount of revenue from property advertisements. In 2005 the recruitment industry started taking online and website advertisement more seriously, and this is now making substantial inroads into the revenue from classified job advertisements. Reduction in the cohesion of local communities, the influx of a large number of new people in many places, and new patterns of living based on all adults in the household having a full-time job are all hitting circulation figures for local titles. Local newspapers are in a squeeze and they know it.

As a result, local newspapers are changing their formats and competing in new ways for the dwindling audience. Just like their sister titles on the national stage, they are becoming more magazine-like and less the retailers of news. Like the national press they are downgrading political stories. Like the national press they are desperately seeking more and more features on clothing, make-up, leisure, house decoration and other lifestyle issues. Above all they are in hock to celebrity, both local and national.

A successful formula for a local newspaper rests heavily upon making local celebrities out of as many people as possible each week, to encourage their friends and family to buy the newspaper. There can be the Christmas carol concert and nativity play supplements, where as many children as possible from each local school are generously photographed with credits. There are the summer fêtes, the carnivals, the sales of work and the markets, which again allow a very large number of people to be photographed. A good edition would include photographs of a royal visit and the opening of a local shop or supermarket by a well-known star of the small or large screen. The mayor or council chairman is likely to get in each week with a friendly colour picture, wearing his or her chain, but most councillors have struggled to get any recognition for themselves or their work. They would be wise not to wish to become famous as it usually means publicity born of notoriety. The councillors we hear about are the ones who have been caught in sexual or financial sleaze, or because the political rows have got so out of hand they have been reported to the Standards Board as part of the political dogfight.

Meanwhile the business of the council carries on under the guidance of the executives. They are very attentive to Whitehall guidance and requirements. They understand that their career pattern will span several councils. They know that they will be assessed and reviewed in relation to all those government targets. They wish to keep themselves out of harm's way, free from the grip of judicial review and aggressive lawsuits. They argue to themselves that the best way to do this is to follow slavishly the guidance coming from Whitehall which protects the most vulnerable officer flank.

This means that any council trying to go in a different direction from the one laid down by the government will find it extremely difficult or impossible. If, for example, a council is elected which wishes to be friendly to motorists, it soon discovers that its executives do not reflect the spirit of the policy in what they do. They will still be bombarding councillors with proposals for bus lanes, cycle ways, humps, chicanes, speed cameras and restricted junctions. Even where councillors insist on making junction improvements with a view to increasing the flow, the executives will counter with designs and schemes for the junctions that try to offset the beneficial intended effects. In my own district of Wokingham, councillors managed to interest their highways department in a new link road to deal with traffic chaos in the town centre, which stemmed from a lack of road capacity. Officers immediately countered with a proposal to close the central road if and when the new link road was introduced. The nervousness of officers when asked to distance themselves from government guidance, or to go in a different direction from that which the government favours, has been increased by the hollowing out of the professions on council payrolls. The time was when the highways department of a local council employed professional highways engineers and surveyors with enough self-confidence to design road schemes for the council. Today it is much more likely that the highways department staff will put the work out to private sector consultants. This has the advantage for them of giving them someone else to blame should a mistake be made, and allows them to give the remit to the private sector consultants so they must follow government guidance at all times. This limits innovation, differentiation and common sense in the design of highways around the country.

Central control and involvement is even more obvious in the planning area. People feel passionate about how much development there should be in their local community and of what kind and where. It is the one area above all others where they would like their local councillors to have real control, and reflect their views. There is never any problem filling a meeting about a planning issue. People are willing to form protest groups, raise money, hire lawyers and planning consultants, and attend any number of meetings in order to get their case across. Their frustration is enormous at the lack of responsiveness and flexibility within the system.

My local authority is run by a controlling group who are strongly against more large-scale development in the district. They have campaigned on this before and after elections. They have made it clear it is the council's policy. Yet in so many cases the policy strings are pulled from above, from the regional government and from Whitehall. There have been two large areas of disagreement between the two layers of government. The first is over brownfield development. Both major parties in central government have favoured brownfield development over greenfield development wherever possible. Both have required that local councils have a supply of land available with planning permission for new house building. Both have required councils to bring forward as much brown land as possible to meet the overall housing land requirement in the planning permissions they grant. So far so good.

However, this New Labour government has decided to redefine 'brownfield'. Brownfield always used to mean land which had been used for a development purpose in the past. The idea was to tidy up derelict factory sites, to pull down redundant industrial and commercial buildings, and to redevelop where other uses were still visible on the land in question. This government has now decided to define people's back gardens as brownfield sites.

Most of the public do not agree with this interpretation. Most people's back gardens have never been industrial or commercial sites in the past. Most of them have never seen rows of bricks piled on top of each other or succumbed to any concrete other than the garden path. Nonetheless they are now lumped with redundant factories, old timber yards, closed oil depots and redundant power stations as brownfield sites suitable for housing development.

The politics of this is extremely explosive. In any given neighbourhood there may be three or four people who think it would be an excellent idea to club together, to sell half their gardens to developers, to sell one of the properties so that it can be demolished to provide a road through to the new development, and to put in for planning permission. Councils have been well versed over the years in the need to reject back land development. Building behind the existing building line is intrusive, noisy and unpleasant for those who live on the existing road alignment. Demolishing a house or two in order to provide a new road through greatly intensifies the traffic on the existing residential road, which has to accept the additional houses in the back gardens. Neighbours who are not part of the scheme, and will not be benefiting from the substantial capital gain, are naturally very put out by the neighbours who do wish to make a quick buck.

In the past all has been well because central government has broadly supported local government and resisted such developments. Today the councils know that they are very likely to lose such a planning application on appeal if they decide to turn it down. Local communities shake their heads in disbelief at the thought that the government can want this to happen.

Protestors soon discover they are dealing with two layers of government and that the one that matters is the national. They may succeed in organising their protest well. They marshal their arguments, they may retain professional help, they may appoint a professional spokesperson to attend the council committee meeting on their behalf to present the case. They may prove successful and the local council may in the first instance turn the planning application down. Far from being an end to the matter, our protestors discover that this is the beginning of a very long process. The neighbours who are seeking the development decide to put in an appeal in conjunction with the developer who wishes to buy the site and build the houses. The protestors have to organise their arguments again and have to make written representations to the independent inspector appointed by the secretary of state, whose task it is to implement the secretary of state's own policy. All too often now local councils lose on appeal over this very issue of so-called 'brownfield' development. This encourages cynicism and a defeatism amongst local communities, who cannot believe that when they, their elected councillors and even the council officials all seem to agree on something, the answer has to be the opposite of what they wanted.

It is often worse with large-scale development. Councillors are required to make sure there are enough planning permissions in their locality for there to be a five-year supply of land for house-building purposes. Five-year supply is based on the government's own requirements or forecasts of the number of new houses that should be built in any given area. In the south of England these forecasts are normally well in excess of what successful and prosperous communities would like to see. They are an endless bone of contention between energetic local councillors and a centre determined to control the issue.

Very often house builders or development companies acquire greenfield sites adjacent to existing settlements in heavily congested parts of the South-East. They then put in a planning application for several hundred homes on these green fields, using the argument that the council has to grant the planning permission in order to make sure it is maintaining its five-year supply of land. Quite often the local developers choose to acquire greenfield sites in places where the council has publicly consulted in the past about whether that site would be a suitable one in order to meet its five-year target. The fact that council officers have identified the site themselves, only to see it rejected following consultation, often weakens the hand of the council in trying to defend that particular site from development.

In these situations officers often are in disagreement with the councillors above them. The councillors will continue to argue that the local development is unnecessary and undesirable. They will reflect local people's views that they do not wish to see the settlement expanded in a material way. They recognise the pressure it will create on water supplies, on school places, on hospital capacity, and above all on heavily congested roads. They say enough is enough, there has to be some limit, and they object to the idea of further major development.

Council officers get nervous. They see the strong pressure coming from the centre to permit more development. They fear the lawyers and the forceful techniques being used by the development companies and house builders. They constantly urge their councillors to do a deal. Their hand is strengthened by the presence of Section 106 agreements, contracts voluntarily entered into between the house builder and the local council over sharing some of the planning gain. In the south of England, agricultural land which may be worth £6,000 an acre as farmland is often worth more than £1 million an acre as development land for house building. If the developer has acquired the land at or close to agricultural land prices, he clearly has plenty of scope to offer to share the profits with the council, which has the power to grant planning permission. A Section 106 agreement basically takes the form of a free gift of money by the developer to the council in return for the development permission. Sometimes the money is clearly linked to a particular local project or projects which the developer and the council officers think the local community may want. For example, the local community may want a swimming pool or a new road link or recreational facilities. The developer promises to pay for these. Sometimes the contract is specific and the developer agrees not only to pay for the local facility but also to put it in. This is quite common in the case of road links, where council officers might seek not only the necessary road infrastructure to service the new local development but also some improvement in the existing road infrastructure to take the extra traffic. In other cases, the developer says that he is giving money for a swimming pool but it remains up to the council to decide how to spend the money, which is paid into its general funds.

Councillors will be told by the officers keen to do a deal that the developer will make a certain offer if the planning permission is granted in the first instance. If the council turns the developer down and the matter has to go to appeal, then the opportunity for the council to get a benefit out of the development gain is often lost. The secretary of state's inspector will judge the issue in relation to stated government planning policy, and will not make an order instructing the developer at the same time to share the gain. Some councillors are persuaded. They take the view that they are very likely to lose the development on appeal, and so they see the officer's point that it would make sense to pocket some money for the council whilst bowing to the inevitable. Others understand how the public see this kind of transaction. It is one of the types of decision of local government that does the most to undermine its reputation in the eyes of the public. Very few members of the public say, 'What a wonderful idea, we are very grateful to the developer.' They do not value the public good on offer sufficiently to counter the negative impact that they anticipate from the new development.

Indeed, some of the public facilities that are purchased through Section 106 agreements are almost as unpopular themselves as the housing developments that spawned them. For example, a number of councils think it a good idea to require a developer to provide play facilities on common ground or to make money available for recreational facilities adjacent to the housing. These play facilities can become a cause of considerable nuisance to householders. All too often young children's play facilities are taken over by older children, and all too often they become meeting places for drug takers and others at night which can cause nuisance and disturbance to people living in the vicinity. Similarly, extra road development may mean more traffic and noise, and can certainly be very disruptive when the roadworks are being undertaken. This explains why all too often the Section 106 goodies that councillors and council officers have alighted upon are far from popular.

Some members of the public go further. They seem to think there is something corrupt in the whole process of Section 106 agreements. Effectively, it means planning permissions are up for sale and people think there is something very distasteful about the whole process. Because they do not value the facilities very highly that are going to be bought with the public money they have a preference for the council doing what they wanted to do, turning the development down and taking their chance on appeal.

A surprising number of people think developers and house builders have too much power, and are suspicious of the ways in which planning permission is obtained. People often remark on what a different approach the council seems to offer to the developer, backed by substantial money, going into meetings with a bevy of planning consultants and lawyers at his right hand, compared to the reception an ordinary householder gets when trying to undertake a modest extension or improvement to his or her home. There often seems to be a presumption in congested areas against the householder seeking a modest improvement, whilst all too often there seems to be a presumption in favour of the large-scale developer for fear of his retaliation.

The frustration of local communities spills over all too readily on planning issues. It sums up all that is wrong in government for them. They may involve their local MP but he usually is unable to do anything to change the position. The MP has no direct power in the first instance. All he can do is lobby the planning committee like the rest of his constituents and hope that it reflects local opinion rather than officer intention. When it comes to the planning enquiry, the MP can make both written and oral submissions but all too often inspectors resent the MP's interference and may make it clear in their judgment that they have not been swayed by it. The strength of public feeling against a development is not a legitimate planning consideration anyway. All the MP can do if he wishes to help his community win is to assist them in marshalling the planning arguments related to highways, traffic flows, water supplies, faulty flood plains, densities, and the inevitable argument over the five-year supply of land and the numbers that back it up.

The government's enthusiasm for running house-building policy has intensified in recent years. This reflects a growing difficulty for young people in gaining the first foothold on the property ladder. When Labour came to power in 1997, the average age for a first time purchase of a property was thirty-one. Today it is thirty-four and rising. It means a whole generation of young people in their twenties and early thirties now either have to make do with renting pinched and expensive accommodation in the private sector, or stay living at home with parents until they have saved enough for the large deposit now required to purchase a property. The Labour government has recognised that home ownership is a strong aspiration by the many, and understands it cannot put the clock back to a world in which the natural expectation of blue-collar workers was to rent a home from the council. Around half the people currently in rented accommodation would desperately love to own their home. The same cannot be said the other way round, where people are, of course, at any time free to sell their home and move into rented accommodation if they really wanted to.

The government commissioned a study by Kate Barker to find out why house prices were so high, and why young people were finding it so difficult to get going in the property market. Barker is an intelligent woman who could have produced a good report. Unfortunately, she and her committee chose to produce an extremely partial and fundamentally flawed review of the problems. It is strange that they thought they could discuss house prices without analysing in detail the mortgage market and the attitude of lenders. They ignored the way in which house and flat prices have been bid up, through the decision of lenders to take into account both partners' earnings in a two-adult household and to provide a higher multiple to work out how much can be lent. The main reason house prices are so much higher today than they were ten years ago is that banks and building societies have decided that they should lend ever higher multiples of people's incomes. They now calculate 'affordability' by comparing interest costs at low interest rates with net pay. There are clearly limits to how much further this multiple expansion can run. When banks and building societies decide they have reached the natural limit of how many times income they can lend, so there will be a natural slowing in the rate of house price growth. When we reach that point, house price growth will then be proportionate to income growth rather than exceeding it.

Barker and her team decided instead to look almost entirely at the supply and demand for housing. On the supply side she made the assumption that if there could be an increase in the supply of houses, then there would be a reduction in the price or a reduction in the rate of increase in the price. This clearly works in a marketplace supplying disposable items. Practically everything we buy for the home these days is disposable. There is no active market in secondhand fridges, freezers, washing machines, spin dryers and other capital equipment for the home, and obviously no secondhand market in food, clothing and furnishings. If new suppliers come into the marketplace, as they have done recently from China and India, and expand the supply then the price does fall. If the European Union succeeds in imposing quota restrictions, anti-dumping devices and tariffs on the new supply from outside Europe then the price will go up again, as supply will be restricted.

The market in housing is very different because the secondhand market is the dominant marketplace. People tend to move house on average every seven years. This means that in any given year more than 10 per cent of the existing stock of houses can be up for sale, compared with the 1 per cent added to the stock by new build. In a market where secondhand stock is more than ten times as important as new build, we need to have a clearer understanding than Barker did of the drivers behind pricing and supply of secondhand houses, rather than concentrating attention on the supply of new ones. If Barker's review succeeded in persuading the government to adopt policies which would increase the supply of new houses by as much 50 per cent, it would still have a very small marginal impact on the total supply of houses in the marketplace, given the predominance of secondhand houses.

Barker had no surer a touch on the demand side either. She and her committee retold the general point that more and more people are living on their own following marriage break-up, or following the end of unmarried partnerships. Busy people pursuing their own careers have less time and need for the stability of marriage. Marriage was a crucial institution up to the middle of the twentieth century because most women did not go out to work and developed relationships with men based on a mutual dependency, where the man supplied the income and the woman looked after the home.

Barker and her committee are right that this model has changed and it does mean some greater demand for single-person accommodation. It is not, however, true to say that because more marriages break up it means that all those people wish to live separately in a home of their own. Very often marriages break up because either the husband or the wife favours a different partner. What then happens it leads to a series of property transactions, so that the two different people who wish to live together can end up living together in a different property, rather than all the people involved in the marriage break-up wishing to live on their own.

Nor is it true to say that the prime reason for the extra demand for housing comes from marriage break-up. The single most important reason why there is a bigger demand for properties of all kinds with each successive year is the high rate of net migration into the country which this government has allowed or encouraged. According to Migration Watch, based on government figures, more than 200,000 additional people come to stay in our country every year. This figure is the difference between two very large figures, the numbers of those emigrating or temporarily leaving the country taken away from the numbers of people coming in on a permanent or temporary basis. Two hundred thousand people every year is a very large number of people that need housing. It means that to keep up Britain has to create the equivalent of a couple of towns the size of Reading every year to match the demand.

It is a pity that the Barker review missed an opportunity to write something definitive on this important and complex subject. It is correct that if we wish to continue with very high levels of migration then we do need to build more homes, or to adapt existing units to take more people. It is not true to say that this automatically forces prices up, as that depends entirely on the willingness of banks and building societies to lend and the multiples of income they are prepared to lend. This is an independent process which is governed partly by regulation and partly by general monetary and interest rate policy. It would be possible to create conditions in which more people came into the country but there was no rise in house prices because the finance was not available to push prices up. People would not be so well housed, as less money would be available for extensions and new build. It would also be possible to have much less migration into the country but still have rising house prices, if the lenders still had surplus funds and were increasing the multiples of earnings they were advancing.

One other trend which we have to recognise is the growing wish of many people to have more space to live in. Some amongst the government and its friends seem to think this is a new kind of evil against the planet. They should instead realise that it is a welcome sign of growing affluence. Why shouldn't people spend more of their income on extending and embellishing their living accommodation? Why should people have to live in very small spaces when our towns and cities make it possible to expand the living space available?

In the United States the average house is 1,800 square feet in size. Here in the United Kingdom the average house is half that at just over 900 square feet. As I go about my own constituency, I notice the growing tendency for people to want more space and in some cases to be able to afford it. Houses being built today for the so-called executive market will have a bigger principal reception room, a bigger kitchen, and an extra bathroom and garage compared with the executive homes built thirty years ago. Many people, put off by high stamp duty and other transaction costs from moving to bigger accommodation, are busily applying for planning permission to build an extra room over the garage, or to extend the principal reception room or to build a room into the loft. Governments and planners need to understand this dynamic.

So how then can we reconcile the apparently irreconcilable gap between what the public wants individually – better houses, more space and sometimes bigger gardens – and what the public wants collectively – no more building in their community or near their homes? There are several ways that can bring things into better balance.

The first thing that people would like to see is a more understanding approach by many councils to the wish to enlarge or extend an individual property in a pleasant residential area. The easy answer to meet people's aspirations is to allow them to build the extra room where they currently live which does less to disrupt the neighbourhood than building a new housing estate on the back garden. The second is to allow larger-scale new house building in places where local communities would welcome it. One of the tragedies of modern Britain under Labour is that, whilst the south is seeing homes crammed into every available green corner and spare space, in some of the northern cities whole terraces and streets of houses are being ripped down for want of buyers or tenants. The imbalance in prosperity and development around the country has, if anything, got worse under Labour, a tragedy for a government dedicated to greater social justice and equality. It means that they have political problems at both ends – despair in the community demolishing the homes and anger in the community accepting more homes than it wishes.

During the twentieth century a number of ways were adopted to allow new homes to be built in large numbers. Practically every village and town in the country was expected to take some new housing. English towns are characterised by waves of development going out along the arterial roads, much of this ribbon development taking place in the 1920s, the 1930s and the 1950s. In the 1970s and 1980s a lot of infill estate development was permitted in the fields between the principal arterial roads into and out of the main towns and cities. The second planning departure was the creation of new communities. A ring of new towns grew up some 30 to 50 miles outside London. Places such as Bracknell, Milton Keynes and Hatfield were transformed by the new towns policy, which required relatively small settlements or villages to be transformed into cities or major urban locations. The third policy that has been tried is substantial redevelopment of formerly industrial and commercial areas in large cities, with a mixture of commercial and residential accommodation. The most notable large scale example of this is in Docklands in the East End of London, where the Conservative government of the 1980s initiated a project which first attracted Labour hostility but has subsequently attracted the praise and support of the present Labour government.

At least two of these three policies are still welcome avenues for future progress in supplying the homes that people want. There is still substantial brownfield development potential in many of the large cities of Britain. This is not a process which need be concentrated entirely in the south. Leeds, Manchester and Birmingham are all thriving and vibrant cities where there is huge scope to redeploy more of the wasted acres that can be freed for development, by a combination of demolition and reclamation. The conversion of old mill and factory buildings can make attractive residential accommodation. Large areas can be freed for industrial parks and office accommodation as well as for domestic development.

There could also be scope for more new town- and city-style development. I favour an exciting and bold new city settlement in the eastern Thames corridor beyond Docklands, on the way to the Medway towns. This would mainly take reclaimed land but it would make some intrusions into the adjacent green fields. Extra space could be created by reclaiming land from the sea along the river estuaries and the north Kent coast, incorporating better sea defences into the structure. Whilst there would be some local resistance, I would favour generous compensation to individual householders where they were close to the new developments, so that they could have the choice of whether to stay or to move somewhere else. Milton Keynes would be happy to expand, according to its elected representatives. It has fast mainline train communication to London and the north, and a generous street plan based on the needs of the modern motor vehicle, which make it a suitable candidate for substantial additions. The Labour government also wishes to expand the Cambridge area and Ashford. These are far more contentious locally but show the Labour government trying to square the circle of its immigration policy with its land planning policy, in a very traditional way of concentrating the problem in certain main settlements. Intelligent development of these types of policy will allow the government to abandon its very unpopular town cramming, garden development policy which is tearing local communities apart and pitching neighbour against neighbour as some go for the money and others wish to maintain the property they originally bought.

The growing frustration locally with the failure to deliver spills over from too much housing to the things that seem to come with it.

People are frustrated by how busy and congested the roads are and by the incessant noise if they live on one. They are coming to see more and more of the problems that overdevelopment creates. The south of England has in 2006 been plunged into water shortage. In March people were told that they could not run their hose-pipes at all throughout the summer, condemning their bedding plants to an early grave in the event of a few dry weeks. People in one of the richest parts of the world in the south of England are being told that they should shower less often, abandon the bath, and drive around in dirty cars in the interest of conserving water.

How has this come about? It's come about for two main reasons. The first is that water was organised as a nationalised industry for most of the twentieth century. This industry failed to invest in its infrastructure, meaning that today the privatised industry still is the proud owner of many a leaky pipe and inadequate water main. Huge quantities of water regularly burst out of the pavements in London to the despair of all who watch. Many roads are now being dug up throughout the south as the privatised industry desperately tries to catch up with the huge backlog of inadequate maintenance. Meanwhile estimates suggest as much as a third of the water is lost between reservoir and tap as a result of poor pipes. In Scotland, where the industry is still nationalised, leakage continues at a substantially higher rate than in England.

The second main reason is that no planning permission has been forthcoming from the government for the reservoirs necessary to ensure adequate supplies. Thames Water, a very large monopoly supplier of much of the Thames valley, including London, has long had on the drawing board a plan for a huge reservoir at Abingdon which it thinks is necessary to guarantee supply. The project, some ten years after its original proposal, still awaits planning permission. Similarly, Thames Water is fighting the mayor of London over its proposal to have a desalination plant at Beckton, in east London, to top up supply during times of shortage. The mayor objects to the desalination plant on environmental grounds. It is the price of overdevelopment. It's all those hundreds of thousands of new homes built over the last decade throughout the south of England that have boosted water demand out of all proportion to the available supply.

If we are going to carry on building large numbers of new properties in the south, as the government requires, then the government at the very least should also require and permit the construction of the reservoir facilities necessary to keep pace. It should also ask a company like Thames Water to investigate the feasibility and economic viability of a pipe link between the rivers Severn and Thames, so that more water can be shipped across from one river basin to another to the areas of highest demand.

Overdevelopment similarly produces pressures and tensions within the school system. Many parents would like more choice of school within the state framework. Most parents cannot afford the choice they would like by paying the fees to send their son or daughter to a public school. They are forced to rely upon the monopoly state provider, which takes their taxes and is meant to supply a good education for their children. As more and more homes are crowded in so more and more people seek places at the better schools in any given neighbourhood. Councils react by narrowing the catchment areas, making it extremely difficult for people to get in the schools unless they live very close to them, and by narrowing criteria in other ways where a school is very popular. Many parents are frustrated. Their local council, and even now the government, says they have a right to choice but in practice they have no choice at all because the one or two most popular schools in their area are very over-subscribed, in part because of the advent of large numbers of new settlers into the new housing estates recently constructed. As councils expand the number of places at popular schools, as sensible councils do, so they find that these places in turn are taken up by the arrival of new families in new homes.

The most obvious consequence of overdevelopment is more traffic congestion. Every settlement in the South-East now suffers from a shortage of transport capacity of all kinds. It is not possible to tip more people onto the railways as the trains are full at peak hours, and the line capacity does not permit the train company to run more trains. The train companies are already investigating the possibility of lengthening platforms to have longer trains or raising bridges to accommodate double-decker trains. The available technology of steel wheels on steel track with current signalling techniques does not permit more trains to be run per hour, limiting the numbers that can go by train. Most people for a variery of reasons have to go by car or bus, requiring road space.

Some 85 per cent of all the transport miles travelled are travelled in motor vehicles. Very little new road space has been provided in the last ten years anywhere in the south of England. More and more families have two cars: as most women now go out to work they need a car to get there. It is no longer possible for a family to locate itself close to its place of employment as its members have two places of employment, usually separated by quite a few miles. The family concerned about travel and the environmental impact of their jobs will choose to locate itself in a home midway between the two, meaning that both the husband and the wife need a car to get to work. Young people when they pass their driving test immediately clamour for a car. Many a driveway now sports a third older vehicle for the son or daughter. Each of these cars needs road space when people are out and about and in some cases needs road space to park. Many of the homes in southern communities were designed for no car or one car at best. Now that many of the households are two- or three-car households, the parked cars spill over onto the public highway, further restricting the available space for driving. In London the problem is particularly severe as very few houses have garages. Even the most expensive housing in the fine terraces of Belgravia or Chelsea has no garage space. Residents' parking schemes attempt to solve the problem with on-street parking but all too often this is insufficient as well, and cars spill over onto other parts of the highway in the evening and at the weekend.

Delays at hospitals can also be related to the rate of new migration and house building. Health capacity has not expanded sufficiently rapidly in fast-growing parts of the country such as Berkshire or Hampshire. Once again the public sector, keen to force houses onto communities, has failed to keep pace with the need to provide more public facility to go alongside the extra people.

These problems, caused fundamentally by planning difficulties, become the daily life of an active MP in a fast-growing community. People are desperate for a little bit of peace and quiet and see the new planning application as a noisy nightmare, meaning builders' disruption for many months followed by new neighbours who may simply be too close so that normal living disturbs. People are worried as they see more and more cars pressing onto the roads, both because it means more traffic late at night, when they would like to sleep in peaceful surroundings, and because it means when they want to get out and about in their car they must endure the battle of the traffic jam. New trains have meant more noise and disruption as the new train services have come with very noisy warning horns, sounded at every whistle board and on the approach to most stations, to the detriment of the lives of those who live within a mile radius of the tracks. Many MPs of all political persuasions have campaigned long and loud to try and cut the noise of the offending horns, or to direct it specifically up and down the tracks away from the houses to either side. Local communities once again have been frustrated. They can see that their elected representatives entirely agree with them. Ministers have sat on the sidelines or expressed sympathy. The consultants and the experts have taken over, insisting that there are fundamental health and safety reasons why horns have to be as loud as the new ones are, and insisting that there are technical problems with any attempt to direct or baffle the sound in a way which protects the householder. We've yet to find a professional consultant or expert who lives close enough to a whistle board to really want to solve the problem, although new instructions have reduced the use of horns when approaching stations.

Some people say that the decline of interest in local government is related to the absence of personality. In a celebrity-driven age, where people seem more excited to know the contents of a politician's breakfast bowl or his fridge or his interests outside normal working hours than to know his views, these reformers wish to put the personality back into local government. They think the way to do it is to create an elected mayor in each area, combining political power with public visibility. They see that local papers and regional media coverage concentrate on the elected, official representatives of each council – the mayor or the chairman. They see that in their mini-royal capacity – opening fêtes, distributing prizes, visiting local charities – they do attract some attention. Wouldn't it be possible, the reformers argue, to harness this modest degree of media interest to a much bigger degree, by allying the public presentational roles with real power to make decisions? Thus was born the movement to create elected mayors throughout the country.

The biggest and best known of the genre is the elected mayor of London, Ken Livingstone. He has certainly succeeded in attracting a great deal of publicity to himself. By making a series of aggressive comments aimed against people he seems to dislike, he has created a fire-storm of publicity about himself. By backing high-profile, potentially very unpopular projects such as charging people £8 every day they wish to drive into the centre of London, he has shown that he can use the power of his office to make substantial changes in the way London is governed. They are in themselves also extremely newsworthy because they interfere with the daily lives of so many Londoners and people coming into London from outside. Livingstone's attack on the motorist and the taxi driver was good copy. The low level of participation in London elections, reflecting the general cynicism about politicians, helped Livingstone win the first time and win again, despite his actions designed to make it more difficult to get around the centre in a vehicle. Livingstone seemed to be proving the point that notoriety and publicity are common bedfellows, and that this combination certainly made London politics intelligible in a celebrity age. London was the one city that would accept a congestion charge because only a minority of inner London residents rely on their car to get about.

However, it does not seem to have changed the underlying problem. In Livingstone's second election there was no great increase in turnout to reflect either the enthusiasm for the well-known man, or the despair and anger at what he was doing. Livingstone's principal opponent, Steve Norris, managed to poll less well in the mayoral election than the Conservative candidates for the London Assembly on the same day, based on the same electorate. When voters were asked either why they didn't vote at all or why they voted in the way they did, most of them implied they did not think it was a terribly important election. Whilst they could see that the mayor had been instrumental in putting through the congestion charge, it was difficult to see what else he had done that made any difference. If you look at the press clippings many relate to things Livingstone has said about foreign policy, an area well outside his sphere of direct control or influence. The rest of the publicity is mainly related to his mini-royalty roles – attending concerts, launching firework displays and supervising circuses, drawing on the old Roman colonial tradition by offering at least half of their 'bread and circuses' programme.

Elsewhere the presence of elected mayors has similarly failed to dent the general apathy concerning local government elections. Most elected mayors are better known than council leaders. This is partly because they have noisier and more expensive campaigns to become elected mayor in the first place, and partly because they combine the two roles of the old mayor and the old council leader. It is still difficult, even in elected mayoralties, to get informed journalism analysing how much impact a mayor has, what his or her policies might be, what analysis they are based on, and whether they are actually working for the greater good. Without this it is difficult to see that the elected mayoral experiment is working in rekindling proper democratic engagement by people in their local government.

Part of the reason elected mayors are not going to solve the problem is that this government has no more fundamental belief in elected mayors than it does in any other form of elected, democratically accountable power. I think the government does see mayors in the way it sees politics generally. Mayors are there to entertain, amuse and to feed the media. Mayors are there to provide a continuous stream of favourable news stories if they happen to be Labour mayors, or a continuous stream of mistakes and bad life choices if they belong to any other political party, to help Labour usher them to the exit. Elected mayors have not been given powers materially stronger than those currently residing in councils without them. Elected mayors encourage exactly the same amount of cynicism about their ability to get things done as elected councils under strong majority group control, for very similar reasons.

If the government is determined to set out in great detail how traffic is to be managed, whether roads can be built or not, how people are to be switched to public transport, how many homes are to be built in any given area, how individual junctions and estate roads are to be designed, how many homes have to be placed on each hectare, not to mention the 101 different ways that social services and education have to be administered and assessed, it is no wonder that people are cynical about what local government can achieve and whether voting matters. If they really understood the interaction between the professional officers, the outside consultants and advisers, and government civil servants, they would realise that most of this system is completely outside proper, democratic control of the old-fashioned kind. Ministers and councillors are very limited in what they can achieve or do, and are constantly being threatened with advice that if they try to do what they wish to do they will fall foul of legal requirements, health and safety requirements or EU requirements of one form or another.

The EU is gradually intruding itself into all of this. Its railways policy now places restraints on how railways can be expanded and developed. Its planning policy is making incursions into the map of England, demarking Sites of Special Scientific Interest, which can no longer be developed in any way. This makes the government's task that much more difficult to find where it's going to cram all the houses it wishes to fit in. The EU is increasingly intruding on transport policy. It has issued many environmental directives, some of which impinge on decision making in English local government.

No wonder the local communities of England are increasingly frustrated and fed up with the whole business. They look to their elected ministers and their elected councillors to protect all that is fine, to give them a right to light and peace and quiet, to provide good-quality schools, and to ensure that there is water on tap and hospital accommodation if they need it. Instead they find a convoluted and expensive system. To get results they so often have to resort to forming pressure groups themselves, hiring in legal and other professional expertise, and undertaking direct action to gain publicity. They are learning that this government is only interested in managing the headlines, and discovering that this government's media obsession extends down to the *Anytown Times* as well as up to the national *Times*. 'Hit them in the headlines' is good advice when trying to influence this government. It's unlikely to respond to the well-written or the clearly spoken expression of local opinion in council chamber or Parliament. It may well respond if it has more than one day's bad headlines, even in little-known and little-read local publications. Get something on regional television and you will get ministerial interest of a heightened kind.

The local government experience is just a further advanced form of the decay of democratic elected politics at national level. Turnout at local elections is now tiny. People are cynical about the ability of their elected politicians to achieve anything, for understandable reasons. They have understood that they need to escalate disputes and problems up to national level. They have grasped that the way to be effective these days is to campaign in a media-savvy and friendly way, backed up by good lawyers and other professional advisers. The public too is beginning to play the bureaucrats' game. In sophisticated communities planning lawyer engages with planning lawyer, planning consultant with planning consultant, and PR expert with PR expert. We are professionalising our politics as we take it out of the normal elected routines and pass it instead to a mixture of pressure groups, journalists, officials and consultants. It is probably the consultants who not only make the most money out of the system but have the most influence. We are now governed by little-known men, who have privatised themselves out of government or have been recruited direct into the private sector for services, who now tell us which roads to build, where to place our houses, what densities they should be at, and how we can comply with EU law. As the politicians spend more and more time briefing the media about the contents of their fridges and the details of their expense claims the real power has decisively shifted elsewhere, carefully concealed from the daylight of public inspection. That is why people are so disenchanted with local government and why the rot is now spreading to the centre.

8

They're after your money

I WANT TO MAKE A DIFFERENCE

I want a lower council tax bill
Have you written to your councillors to tell them this?
Have you proposed any reductions in spending that would help them deliver a lower tax?
Have you phoned the local BBC, written to the newspaper or published your view in any other way?

Have you thought of establishing a taxpayers' group locally to campaign for lower council taxes?
Could you work up a series of proposals with friends and helpers that could cut costs without reducing important services?
Does your local council need so many officers. or could the numbers be cut as people leave?
Is your council controlling its own energy bill properly?
Are all the road changes necessary or could the council save some money on those?
Do the street lights need to stay on for as many hours as at present?
Does the council need all the land and buildings it currently owns or leases?

Have you thought of organising a petition against higher council tax?
Could you persuade someone who knows the council budget well to stand for election to the council with a view to getting better value for money?

In my eighteen years as a member of Parliament so far I have never once had a letter from a constituent complaining about a shortage of hotel rooms. Constituents wanting to take holidays in different parts of the world, people requiring hotel rooms when travelling on business in the United Kingdom, and families wanting hotel rooms for functions or celebrations have never once reported to me any difficulty in finding what they need. The reader would wonder why I mention this fact as it would never occur to him or her that a shortage of hotel rooms was at all likely. Yet throughout the last eighteen years I have regularly had reports of a shortage of hospital bedrooms, both locally in the Thames valley and more generally throughout the United Kingdom. There have been periods when the shortage has been more acute and periods when it has been a bit easier. There have been times when people may have to wait eighteen months for a vacant hospital bed and times when celebration breaks out that they can get in within three months. Very few of my constituents expect or get a room of their own in the local hospital when need arises. They accept the idea that their bed should be in a room shared with half a dozen people. Until recently they accepted the possibility that they might have to share their bedroom with members of the opposite sex, although this is now very rare following a mini-riot about the practice. In the local hotels people are offered rooms of their own and a wide choice of menus. They can select the breakfast or the lunch they want. In the local hospital the meal choice is either very constrained or non-existent.

Nor over my eighteen years as a member of Parliament have I ever had anyone writing to me to complain that there aren't enough cars in the marketplace, should they wish to buy one. Casual observation in the local paper tells me that a huge range of different types, sizes, styles, ages and prices of car are available day by day in my local community. Observation as I go from house to house visiting tells me that people have very wide-ranging tastes and pockets when buying cars which enable the overwhelming majority of my constituents to own at least one. The market delivers a flexible and easy choice. When someone wants a car they can usually find it, try it and buy it all on the same day. I have, however, had many letters complaining about the shortage of road space when people try and use their vehicles. My constituents regularly complain about being caught in huge traffic jams at popular times of the day, should they wish to drop their children to school or get to work for normal office hours.

I have had no complaints over the years about a shortage of solicitors or accountants. Anyone who needs a lawyer to act for them or an accountant to put in their tax return is able to get one. I do, however, under the present government, regularly get complaints that people cannot get access to an NHS dentist. There is a shortage, meaning that some people have to go to a private sector dentist and others have to travel long distances to exercise their right to an NHS one.

The more I have thought about the areas of life that cause my constituents most difficulties, the more I've come to the obvious conclusion that they are all created by government monopoly or by government regulation. The marketplace does a very good job of delivering us the cars we want, the hotel beds and restaurant meals we want and the professional services we may need from time to time. The government makes a complete hash of supplying the transport capacity we need, of supplying the physical buildings in the National Health Service that the professionals need to do their jobs, and maintaining and motivating a sufficiently large workforce of dedicated professionals in some parts of the public service to supply everyone who requires the service.

Socialists might respond at this point that the private sector avoids difficulties in the supply of cars or hotel bed spaces by using the price mechanism. They say the reason we have problems with road space or NHS dentists or hospital beds is that we supply them free. If only the socialists could tax people more they could break through and supply enough public service free at the point of use, to deal with the apparent problem of the unsatisfactory and limited supply of the public good. Contrast this, they say, with the injustice of the marketplace, which means that you can only get the good or service if you can afford to pay the bill.

This is not a satisfactory explanation of the reasons for the difference we experience between the surplus of hotel beds and the shortage of hospital beds. There are examples in the private sector of people supplying a more than adequate number of items free at the point of use. There is absolutely no shortage of free news-sheets in the areas that have them. The free news-sheet providers ensure that everyone in the local area receives one. They need to do so in order to make a success of the operation, based as it is upon the advertising revenue they collect from other users of the news-sheets. There is no shortage of ITV programmes provided free at the point of use to all those with a television. We never see on our screens 'your next ITV news is going to be three months late owing to a financial squeeze', nor do we read about the need for massive budget cuts at ITN resulting in the main news of the day being reduced in length. The private sector is quite capable of running services free at the point of use very successfully.

It is a myth sometimes put round by socialists that free public services are somehow provided without us, the consumers, paying indirectly for them. They conjure up the idea that there is something called the public sector ethos which motivates public sector workers in an entirely different way from that in which private sector workers are motivated. Apparently those of us who work in the public sector do so only for the best of reasons, and regard the weekly or monthly pay cheque as coincidental or an unnecessary addition. As most people will realise, life is not like that, as most of us public sector workers, like our private sector counterparts, do need the money we get paid. Of course, many of us are proud to do the public sector jobs we do and do them to the best of our ability. It is difficult to say that our motivation is wholly different from those in the private sector, who serve their customers well because they wish to be paid at the end of the month.

The truth is that we all pay huge sums of money to join the queue for the hospital bed when we need it or to make the long journey to find the NHS dentist to have our teeth checked. Nor are these services entirely free from direct charges on the users. Labour in government shortly after the Second World War sold the pass on a National Health Service entirely free at the point of use when they introduced prescription charges. An increasing number of items in my local NHS GP surgery are priced. If I want an injection before travel I will pay. If I need pills I will pay again. If I go to an NHS dentist and manage to find one, there will still be a substantial bill for whatever the dentist decides needs doing. If I go out on the roads I've already paid for as a taxpayer, in London I have to pay £8 a day for the privilege of using them in addition to the substantial vehicle excise duty I have to pay as a poll tax on owning a car. I also pay huge sums every week when I put petrol in my tank, as a result of three-quarters of the pump price going straight to the Chancellor of the Exchequer.

The reason we are short of hospital beds and road space and NHS dentists is that all three are badly organised, government monopolies. Monopolists behave in a very different way from all those competing in the marketplace. Monopolists can afford to close early and tell people to come back the next day. Monopolists can afford to charge you anything they like. There is no alternative down the road you can go to instead. Monopolists can worsen the quality of the service and, again, there is little redress. Monopolists can put their own convenience above that of their customers or clients and frequently do. Monopolists can make you, the potential client, jump through hoops before supplying you with what you're seeking. A public sector monopolist has one advantage even over a private sector monopolist. The public sector monopolist can not only charge you what he likes through the tax system but does so backed up by the threat of imprisonment, if you should ever dare to say that you don't think it's worth it and refuse to pay.

There are parts of the public service which are kept honest by the introduction of some forms of competition. Any MP wishing to survive for longer than four years in their job recognises that they are working in a very competitive environment indeed. General elections keep MPs honest and attentive to their constituents' wishes because they know that constituents and the media could get their revenge if standards of service fell. In well-populated areas any individual school has to recognise that parents might choose to go to the other schools in the district, leaving it struggling to fill all its places. Whilst the local education authority might come to its aid and insist that some people go to that particular school, it can nonetheless be uncomfortable if one school falls a long way behind and parents spend a lot of time and trouble trying to avoid sending their children to it. If the public monopoly Highways Authority makes a real mess of one of its roads, then all of us motorists will soon get the message and divert to another.

The problem of the public monopolist is that it is difficult to pin down just how wasteful and how bad a deal any given part of the public monopoly might be. Because in most cases the bill is separated from the provision of the service, and because the bills are aggregated so that you pay for hospitals, schools and roads all at the same time, it is difficult for an individual taxpayer to get a handle on how good, bad or awful the value might be for the particular service he is considering at the time. The public tends to underestimate by a big factor just how much it is paying for all these so-called free services. The average tax take in Britain now is over 40 per cent. That means that if someone is earning £20,000 a year, £8,000 of their money is spent on taxes to the government. If a household is on £50,000 a year between the two adults, it is paying the government a whacking £20,000 a year.

So often people only see one visible tax bill, the council tax bill. In my area a typical council tax bill would be £1,500. The local council provides the local roads, pays for the local schools, provides a range of social services, and handles planning and the environment. If it could really do all this for £1,500 per household it would be an extremely good bargain. In practice the council tax only pays for about a quarter of the council services, the rest of the money being supplied from the national taxpayer via the government. Nonetheless, every March, when the council tax bills flood onto the doorsteps, many of my constituents feel they've been ripped off. A retired couple looking at the bill would say, 'Why am I paying this?' They may be too young to need any of the social services on offer but clearly too old to need the educational service for themselves or their children. They acknowledge that they get their dustbins emptied free once a week, and the more discerning know that the roads need mending from time to time. Even so, a pensioner couple looking at their council tax bill might well say, 'It's gone up too much, it is too high and we get very little for it.'

The council tax bill is only the visible part of the large floating iceberg of taxation that regularly bumps into us in our daily lives. Some people have a clearer understanding and memory of how much income tax and national insurance they're paying than others. All who care to bother can see on their weekly or monthly payslips the large deductions the Chancellor takes from them, before they even see the fruits of their labours. The taxes that very few people have any idea about are the cleverer, stealthy ones. Most people do not know that three-quarters of all the money they spend at the petrol pump is taxation by the UK government. Most people forget that they're paying VAT on many of the goods and services they buy, and they overlook all those fees and charges that the monopoly state imposes when you need a planning permission, when the building inspector comes to call for your extension, when you license your car, when you obtain a passport or driving licence, when you register under the data protection legislation, or try to comply with a whole host of other licensing and regulatory requirements. The more laws and quangos there are, the more licences and regulatory fees there are. The more voracious the appetite of the public sector for your money, the more these fees and charges go up well in excess of inflation.

Government regulation can also create the same kinds of problem in parts of the private sector which are not properly competitive. For many years in Britain the water industry was a publicly owned monopoly, organised regionally around particular river basins. When the industry was sold to the private sector two mistakes were made. The first was the refusal of successive governments to introduce full competition into the industry. Instead of letting any potential supplier of water have access to the pipe network to supply water to those who wished to buy, governments enshrined in statute the longstanding monopoly of the individual river basin companies to supply water as the sole supplier to all but the largest of users. The second mistake was to put in heavy regulation, largely influenced by European legislation, which concentrated on the quality of water to the exclusion of the quantity. The industry was told that the only thing it had to do in order to gain the price increases it was seeking from the regulator was to improve the quality of all the water in its network so that any water returned to the river system was of a very high standard.

The results of this policy approach are now becoming clear. A country which has all too much rainfall, especially in the west, and which has been experiencing rising aquifers beneath many of its major cities for many years, is now apparently short of water and had to impose hosepipe bans in February, and threaten consumers with cutting off their supplies in their homes altogether if they don't stop washing their cars. The Environment Agency recommends that we abandon the bath and take a short shower instead. It is an outrage that in the twenty-first century in one of the richest countries in the world people are told that it is wicked to keep themselves and their vehicles clean, and are instructed to kill off their bedding plants should there be insufficient rainfall to keep them alive naturally for a couple of months. Only a regulated monopoly or a state-run organisation could get us into such a state. Indeed, the regulator has got the privatised industry back to the position the nationalised industry usually found itself in summer after summer. When we had nationalised water, far from being better than privatised water, hose-pipe bans were a regular feature and occasionally the water literally ran out altogether. One of the first constituency issues I had to take up prior to the privatisation of water came from the complaints of a number of my constituents living in a prosperous suburban estate, five miles from the centre of Reading, that on Sundays when they turned their cold tap on to have water at their sinks after their Sunday lunch, all they got out was sand. This had come about because the government planning system had forced more and more houses onto the local area, without a thought for the impact this would have on the water supply and water pressure from the nationalised concern, which was busily looking the other way and not putting in any additional capacity.

It is frustration with the poor standards of service in public monopolies and in regulated private monopolies that occupies so much political time. I see my job as MP as having three main elements. The first is that I am a legislator. My primary duty is to attend Parliament regularly and make my contribution to debates on what new laws the country might need. To do this I need to keep in daily contact with my electors, so that I understand their concerns and preoccupations about the laws that the government is wishing to pass and the laws they would like to see passed. My second task is to explain to the government of the day how my constituents would like to see their tax money spent and their public service provision organised. My third task is to explain to my constituents how the government is doing this and how I, as an opposition MP for the time being, would like to see this changed or improved.

Although an MP's role as a legislator is the primary task, the public is increasingly defining the job in other ways. The extent of this came across to me in one of those illuminating doorstep exchanges recently. When the lady saw who was calling she decided to explain to her young children who I was and what I did. She mentioned I was a member of Parliament and realised that was a long phrase for little children, so she summarised it as 'he's the man who does schools and hospitals'. Labour propaganda telling the public over the years that schools and hospitals are the only things that public money is spent on and the only things that matter in political debate has clearly had its impact. It has worked with a surprising number of my constituents who now make the association between an MP and whether they can get their child into the school of their choice, and whether the hospital has enough beds or not. The sad truth is that, whilst I and my constituents would agree about many of the things that need doing to sort the schools and hospitals out, successful election to Parliament does not give the individual concerned any of the powers needed to deal with those problems. School choice is handled by the elected local authority. The government of the school is under the immediate guidance of its board of governors, chosen from amongst the local parents, councillors and other well-wishers. The local hospital is under the control of a quango with boards recruited from local people paid salaries to supervise the work of the chief executive, who in practice has the power to decide how many beds are going to be provided. I can rail all I like in the House of Commons, and often do, about the need for more beds in the Royal Berkshire Hospital but nothing ever happens. Even if the minister agrees, he may discover that nothing happens for him either. The system is unresponsive to the political will, even though in theory it is under direct political control through ministerial accountability.

This association of MPs with schools and hospitals, and the growing frustration of some of the schools and all of the hospitals, is a further reason why people are increasingly dissatisfied with the political process. 'Why can't you get my son or daughter into school X?' they ask me. 'We are paying a lot in tax, school X is within a reasonable travelling distance of our home, so why can't our child have the advantage of going to it? Why does my son have to go to school Y, which we do not like for all sorts of reasons?' One of the saddest things about these debates is the dishonesty they encourage. Constituents coming to see me to request my assistance to get their son into school X and to avoid school Y will give me all sorts of reasons why they want their son to go to school X. They will talk about transport, extra-curricular activities offered, single-sex education and sibling attendances. They do not normally say they want their son to go to school X because it has much better academic results. It is nearly always the case that parents do want their child to go to the school with the best academic results in the local area, or failing that, one of the other schools with pretty good academic results. I see nothing wrong with that – indeed, as a parent myself, that was exactly the view I took. You can never be sure why any individual school does better than another individual school, short of a detailed study. To the average parent what matters is that the school does do better. It may be that your child could rub shoulders with brighter and more motivated children. It might be that he or she would encounter more persuasive and better teachers. It may be some combination of the two. Why, people ask themselves, should they put up with second best when their tax money is as good as the next man or woman's? Why can't the LEA take into account people's understandable wish to send their child to a well-performing school?

As a strong believer in school choice I do what I can. Sometimes my voice, added to that of the parents, does succeed and a place becomes available through the waiting list so their wishes are met. On other occasions our joint efforts are defeated and the parent has to accept a place at a school not of their choosing. I have campaigned locally for more places to be supplied at schools that are successful and popular. In some cases I've been successful with this but the supply of places at good schools never overtakes the demand. Some people still remain unhappy because they are allocated places at schools they do not like.

Labour really did believe their own rhetoric when they came to power. Labour's story of the 1980s and early 1990s was a simple one. They said that a Conservative government had been elected which disliked public services. As a result, according to Labour, the government starved these public services of money in a desperate attempt to drive people into the private sector, and bribed many voters with lower taxes than the public services could withstand. The answer was simple. Labour would collect a lot more money in tax to spend on the public services and all the imperfections would go away. There would be no further privatisation by the front door or back door. The money would not be spent but would be 'invested', public service morale would rise, and everyone would live happily ever after with their local neighbourhood comprehensive school or their local district general hospital.

There was one carefully contrived part to the New Labour case. Whilst New Labour were as desperate as old Labour to spend a lot more money on the public services, they were very aware that offering to increase income tax rates on people would prevent them from winning the general election. They therefore said that Labour would gain all the extra money to spend on the public services by presiding over a much more successful economy, which would mean many more people in work, paying income tax, and many fewer people out of work and on benefit. By this very sensible transformation of the British economy, from high unemployment to low unemployment and from high benefit to low benefit, Labour would generate a lot more cash to spend on the public services without the pain of higher income tax rates.

So what has happened in practice? In office Labour found getting rid of the so-called costs of economic failure was not as easy as they had thought. Indeed under Labour, far from shrinking, the welfare bills have gone up. It is true that unemployment, as measured by the official figures, continued to fall under Labour, as it was falling under John Major in his later years as Prime Minister, until 2004. However, the benefits of reduced unemployment bills have been more than offset by the surge in disability claims and bills, as Labour have presided over an increase in the number of people registered disabled and therefore not working. At the same time, Labour have offered far more generous benefits to a whole variety of different people and families, boosting the cost of welfare benefits still further.

For the first two years in office from 1997, Labour decided to run the public services on the inherited budgets from the Conservative administration. This created an extremely strong economy. Public spending was kept within sensible bounds overall, tax rates were not put up, and the economy continued its strong performance, recording good growth and good productivity growth as it had been doing in the post-Exchange Rate Mechanism phase of the Conservative government. The public spending targets for health and education were tight. Indeed, they were so tight that had the Conservatives been in office, I am sure they would have relaxed them, although I trust they would have relaxed them at the expense of other budgets for other departments. The Chancellor realised that Labour's experiment required huge sums of money to be routed into the public services. His decision to run on Conservative spending targets for two years, and to make the Bank of England independent, was a clearly orchestrated media strategy designed to show that you could trust Labour with the economy after all. He realised that these features would be taken well by the City and would gain him an early reputation for economic prudence which would then enable him later on to launch his major public spending splurge.

To do so the Chancellor recognised that he would need additional tax revenues on top of the extra borrowings that he was prepared to countenance. As a hard-working fiscal anorak, the Chancellor set about researching how he could gain huge sums of money without apparently increasing taxes. He knew that the important pledge was not to increase the standard rate of income tax or the top rate of income tax, a rate being paid by an increasingly large number of people as incomes went up. The Chancellor hit upon two particular measures which made a big difference to his fiscal provisions.

The first was his decision to tax the income from shares collected by pension funds and charities. All previous governments had allowed charitable funds and pension funds to get back the tax paid on company dividends through a tax credit system. The Chancellor decided to abolish the advance corporation tax provisions which could generate the tax credit, claiming this was part of the general corporate tax reform. However, the real import of what he was doing was to remove £5 billion a year from pension and charitable funds that they had previously collected by means of tax relief on their dividend income.

The Chancellor refuses to come clean about how much tax reclaim the pension funds are now losing. At the time of his original decision, he'd put the £5 billion-a-year figure into general circulation but explained that that wasn't just pension funds. All subsequent parliamentary questions to find out how much the tax credit would now be worth if it was still in operation have been blocked. The Treasury's line is that because it has abolished the system it is no longer possible to work out the figures. I can't help but think if the figures were ones the Treasury wanted to be well known, it would find a way of calculating them.

At the time when he made these tax changes I pointed out that they were bound to have an impact upon the value of shares in the stock market. When he announced it the stock market was riding high. In those days people valued company shares at twenty times earnings. If the after-tax profits of a company were running at £10 million, then the stock market would value all the shares of that company at an aggregate £200 million. I pointed out that if you reduce the net profits to shareholders by £5 billion a year over the market as a whole, then you would expect share prices to fall by twenty times £5 billion or £100 billion. That was the clear intention of the Chancellor's move. He had decided that net profits to shareholders in the UK market would be £5 billion a year less because he was intending to pocket the £5 billion. Stock markets have never valued gross profits, as they are interested in the money that is available, either to distribute to shareholders or to reinvest in the shareholders' business, not in the amount of money that the companies collect for the Chancellor. Both Prime Minister and Chancellor pooh-poohed my argument. They pointed out that the stock market was riding high and they assumed it would continue to rise. They thought they had found painless money. They could take £5 billion out of the hands of the pension and charitable funds, only for the pension and charitable funds still to benefit from a rising stock market despite the tax on company income. They were living in cloud cuckoo land.

Subsequently, the UK market fell sharply. The government's defence was that, far from proving that I was right, it just showed that there was a general market sell-off, led by the USA, to which Britain had succumbed. It still saw nothing wrong in its actions here in Britain and started to pity that Britain, with its pre-eminently successful economy, had for some mysterious and unknown reason got caught up in a general capitalist sell-off in the markets of the world. This explanation will not do. If you look at the declines in America, Germany, France, Britain, one thing becomes clear. The United Kingdom stock market fell proportionately by more than the stock markets of our leading competitors and allies. The reason is simple. The British market fell more because in the British market company income was subject to a new and much higher tax charge when profits were distributed than had been the case before.

The Chancellor compounded this difficulty for the pension and charitable funds of the country by his second master stroke as he saw it, the creation of the telecoms stealth tax. Under the Conservative government we had allocated more radio spectrum to all those wishing to set up mobile phone services. There does need to be a ringmaster when it comes to allocating radio spectrum, to avoid conflicts and interference. In Britain huge quantities of spectrum had been kept back for the public sector. Britain had a strong military interest in blanking out large amounts of spectrum for defence purposes, and until the privatisation of British Telecom it also needed spectrum to allocate to its own monopoly telephone business. In addition, the BBC had reserved large quantities of spectrum. With the advent of a whole host of new radio-led services, from radio pagers through security to mobile phones and data transmission, the private sector needed access to some of the unused spectrum controlled by the public sector. The Conservatives offered spectrum to all those coming forward with sensible plans for using it without charging them. The Labour government decided to hold a spectrum auction when a number of existing and potential mobile phone service providers wanted access to much more spectrum, to provide the so-called 3G services. The advent of mobile phones that could receive pictures and data in large quantities required more spectrum to transmit the material rapidly.

The Chancellor took extremely good mathematical and game theory advice on how to maximise the take from the mobile phone industry. By strictly limiting the number of licences on offer and concentrating all the licences in one spectrum auction, he maximised the chances for Treasury gain. By doing it before other countries got in on the act, he also greatly improved his chances of a windfall. Early estimates suggested that the Chancellor would raise between £1.5 billion and £4 billion from the auction of spectrum he had in mind. When the final bids were in he had netted a massive £22 billion from a single auction. It was a spectacular coup, milking one sector of the economy for so much money in one single move. As far as the Chancellor was concerned, they were volunteers. As far as the boards of directors of the companies were concerned, they were being mugged by a monopolist. They argued to themselves that they had to bid for the spectrum to stay in business. They could not, they thought, be serious mobile phone service providers without the extra spectrum it would take to deliver the full range of services under 3G. It was compete or die.

Of course, it turned out that they had overbid. It caused considerable pain and difficulty in the industry for a number of years as they fought to pay the tax bills, repay the borrowings they had to take out, and write off some of the costs because they could never recoup them in full.

The misery of the pension funds was multiplied greatly. Vodafone had been the great success story of the 1990s. The company had powered itself to the position of being the largest in Britain. Pension and charitable funds typically had one-fifth of all of their UK equity money invested in telephone stocks, with the largest portion usually in Vodafone. In the falling market which global events and the Chancellor had helped trigger, telephone stocks were going to be pummelled more than most because of this extra massive tax raid upon them. So it proved. Vodafone fell by more than two-thirds, wiping out huge sums of money in the pension and charitable funds. The Chancellor's defence was that the phone companies had volunteered, that it was sensible to auction a scarce resource like spectrum, and that no damage had been done. It looked very different from the point of view of the businesses concerned. Britain's lead sector with some of its most dynamic companies had suffered a particularly strong tax attack. It set them back several years as they struggled to sort out their balance sheets and pay the bills.

The result of the Chancellor's handiwork is at last becoming clear for all to see. Far from being a victimless tax, the removal of the dividend tax credit for pension funds has proved to be all too expensive. Most pension funds in Britain fell into heavy deficit. Trustees of pension funds found themselves with difficult choices to make. Could they get the employer company to make good all of the shortfall by extra contributions? Did they have to accept their share of the pain for the members of the scheme and accept some change in the pensions promised? Did they have to accept that the employer could no longer afford to carry on with the pension scheme and that the scheme would have to be closed to new members? Did the scheme also have to be closed for future contributions and extra pension entitlements from existing members as they tried to balance the books?

The net result of Gordon Brown's twin tax raids has been to close more than half the pension funds in Britain. We have moved in less than a decade from being a country which could proudly boast of having the best private sector provision of any country in Europe, to being a country struggling to meet the promises it has already made to present and future pensioners, and offering a far worse deal to the new generation than to their parents.

The government again lives in a parallel universe. When asked why it's done so much damage, it usually responds that the fault was with the employer companies who took a 'pension holiday', as it was called, in the 1990s. If only, the trade union and government argument goes, the companies had carried on paying in large sums of money to their pension funds in the late 1990s, there would be no deficit today. Did companies reduce their pension contributions in the late 1990s? Yes, of course they did. Why did they do it? The main reason they did it was that the Treasury insisted they did it because it had no intention of offering further tax relief on more contributions into funds which had quite enough money in them to meet all their pension promises. The Treasury should remember that it was its own rules which required the employing companies and pension trustees to ensure that their fund was not overfunded by more than a 15 per cent margin. Practically all pension funds in the late 1990s were overfunded because the stock markets were rising, because their investments were going well, and because they had the additional money from the tax rebates on the dividend stream they were enjoying. They had no choice but to reduce their contributions in the late 1990s, or alternatively to increase the generosity of the pensions they were offering, to avoid the surplus growing further. It simply was not an option under Labour's own tax rules and regulatory system in the late 1990s to carry on paying money into pension funds to build up a bigger surplus.

Today there are various estimates of the pensions black hole that the government has created. It may be around the £100 billion level, by coincidence exactly the sum of money you would have expected the pension fund assets to fall by, given Labour's dividend tax. Some people put it higher, which would include an allowance for the capital value removed from telecom shareholders by Labour's licence raid. Some put it lower, reflecting the huge extra sums now tipped into the pension funds by employing companies under pressure to reduce the deficits. The uncertainty over the pension deficits is increased by the regulatory system under which pensions now suffer. Under the old system of calculation, producing something called a minimum funding requirement, the deficits of most pension funds are still manageable. This government has decided to beef up the solvency requirements of funds by changing the basis of calculation to a far more cautious one which will increase the size of the deficit. Most funds now have at least three deficits to juggle. They still have the minimum funding requirement deficit, which is the one which still governs their current contribution rate. From 2008 at the latest they will need to make a higher contribution to their pension funds, based upon the new, more pessimistic assumptions in valuing the fund around a scheme-specific actuarial valuation, assuming both the fund and the company can continue in business. There is then the third deficit based upon wind-up, which assumes that the employing company does not survive, and that the pension fund has to be wound up to be replaced by guaranteed annuities or future payments, secured from an insurance company, for everyone in the fund. Deficits on a wind-up basis at current annuity rates are substantially larger than the more pessimistic actuarial valuations the government is insisting on fund by fund.

The government has compounded its errors in overtaxing savings in the hands of pension funds by changing the regulatory system at the worst possible moment for them, in a way which increases the apparent size of the deficits. The truth is that no-one can be sure of how much money you need to place in any given pension fund to meet all the future liabilities. A pension fund with a 25-year-old active member may still be paying out pension to that person in sixty years' time. We cannot know for sure how long the 25-year-old and others like them will live, we do not know what their final salary is going to be, and we do not know what the rate of inflation is going to be when they become a pensioner and expect that inflation increases are made in their pensions year by year. Actuaries are employed to make assumptions about how long people live on average, about how many women are going to be married and will need widow's pensions in the event of their husband's prior death, about what the rate of inflation may be in forty, fifty, sixty years time, and how much the scheme may earn through its investments over the intervening time period. Changing any one of the major assumptions can make a huge difference to the deficit. Assuming an extra 1.5 per cent per annum return on the investments can, for a long-term fund, make many millions of pounds of difference to the apparent deficit.

All these calculations have been made far worse for those providing pension funds by another quirk of the Gordon Brown Chancellorship. Despite needing to borrow substantial sums of money from the marketplace, the Chancellor has presided over a huge surge in the prices of government bonds, meaning that the amount of interest he has to pay on any given amount of money borrowed has reduced sharply during his period in office. This matters a great deal in the pensions argument. When a fund is wound up and an insurance company offers to make given payments to pensioners, it usually at the same time buys government bonds to provide a stream of income to make the payments. Today, because the government interest rate is so low, now around only 4 per cent on long bonds, insurance companies need a great deal more money to buy many more bonds in order to guarantee a given level of income for future pensioners. This has greatly ballooned the wind-up deficits for pension funds.

The Chancellor has created a virtuous circle for himself. Because so many pension funds are now closed for new members, and because so many pension funds are being advised by actuaries and investment advisers who are extremely cautious, these funds are busily switching money out of shares into government bonds. As a result, there is a huge demand for government bonds, in excess of even this Chancellor's appetite to borrow more money from the bond market. It is this merry-go-round which is keeping bond yields so low, paying the Chancellor's bills on the never-never on very easy terms, and greatly increasing the apparent deficits in pension funds as a result. The pension funds are being made to pay twice over for the Chancellor's tax rates. They first of all were hit on the values of their shares and they are now being hit by regulatory action to buy more and more government debt.

What has happened to Britain's private sector pension provision is a tragedy. In the 1980s and 1990s Britain was pioneering a new private welfare system based on generous tax relief. We were spreading the advantages of the few in earlier years to the many. We wanted to live in a world where all who had had employment could look forward to a better old age with a decent pension from their employer, to top up the far from generous pension from the state. Instead, today, we live in a divided world. Those who paid into employer pension schemes and have already retired are going to do much better than the new generation, who in many cases have no access to an employer pension scheme at all, and better than those who are still in work, who may face reductions in their future pension entitlement as pension funds struggle to balance the books.

What could be done to alleviate this problem? The government could offer tax breaks on dividend income back to new funds seeking to provide decent benefits to people currently without employer pension schemes. It could extend these tax breaks to new contributions from people in existing employer schemes, whilst still continuing to collect all the tax on the existing funds. The government could issue a lot more long bonds to meet more of the demand from mature pension funds for these instruments. Above all, the government could issue new instructions to the regulators and the professions that it does not believe that long bonds are a suitable matching asset in growing pension funds on the scale of the present advice. If it does not speak out soon on this issue we could have a second huge pensions crisis when the long bond bubble bursts, and when bond prices go down instead of up. We may discover that this government has come back to have more revenge on the pension funds, by allowing the rapid move of these funds into bonds. If long bonds at some future date do fall substantially in price, pension funds and the members dependent on them are going to be the main losers and the regulators should take their fair share of the blame.

The most common question in British politics today is: where has all the money gone? People can feel the tax take upon them even though they may not be precise in telling you exactly how all the money has been removed from their pockets. They know that on top of the very large increases in the council tax bill there have been big increases in petrol tax, in national insurance, and in various public sector fees and charges. They are told the inflation rate remains very low. It doesn't feel like that when you face the council tax bill, the gas bill, the electricity bill, the water bill, the petrol bill and the mortgage on very inflated house prices. People feel under pressure despite all the government's attempts to prove they've never had it so good because more and more of their income is absorbed in paying for the necessities. The reason so many of the necessities are so high is that they are the result of taxes going to pay the ever-growing public sector bills, or they are regulated monopoly charges reflecting poorly organised and underinvested industries.

We live in a very divided world. If you want to buy a new fridge, a new car, a new television, a new camera or a new mobile phone you're spoilt for choice and can find extremely competitive prices. If it's clothes or food you're buying, you can get some sensational bargains in the main supermarkets and chain stores. Indeed, clothing prices and footwear prices have been falling year after year as a result of a surge in Indian and Chinese competition, and the prices of many so-called white goods, kitchen appliances and the like, have also been going down. The trouble is people don't have enough money left over, after paying all the taxes and necessary charges for the basics, to buy as many of these new and competitively priced products as they would like. Whilst mobile phone service charges are falling, congestion charges and NHS dentistry charges are rising.

Huge sums of money tipped into the public services have mainly gone in increased pay. Any government would make annual pay awards to public service workers and maybe there was a case for giving a rather more generous settlement to the nurses and doctors. What has happened under Labour is not merely a catching up but an overtaking by public service workers compared with private sector workers. The old theory was that people do not earn such high wages in the public sector because they had greater job stability and better pension benefits. You worked in the private sector if you wanted to earn more week by week, with greater risk of losing your job and insecure provision for your old age. You worked in the public sector if you wanted the opposite. Today it seems from many private sector workers' viewpoint that public service workers have everything. A typical public sector worker now gets paid more than the private sector worker, has a final salary pension scheme which also takes care of inflation, and is still very unlikely to lose his or her job. In contrast, private sector workers now may have no employer final salary-based pension scheme at all, may well have lower wages, and be at much greater risk of losing their jobs if the Indian and Chinese competition catches up with their firm.

Recent revelations have shown how the new GP contracts introduced by this government allow some GPs now to earn £250,000 a year working for the NHS, whilst the average has increased by more than 50 per cent from £62,000 a year to nearer £100,000.

The second heavy call on public funds has been the cost and prices of endless reorganisations and managerial advice offered by consultants. There's not a corner of the public sector that hasn't been subject to a very expensive reorganisation. Each reorganisation brings its need to headhunt new expensive people to senior positions, new PR advisers and spin doctors, new logos, headed notepaper, opinion studies and research. The government is currently trying to amalgamate primary healthcare trusts, allegedly to reduce the overhead but in practice likely to increase it, as yet another layer of management is brought in over the heads of the existing smaller trusts. It wanted to amalgamate various police forces. It is reorganising the Learning and Skills Council. The railway industry has been subject to endless reorganisation and partial renationalisation. The Strategic Rail Authority was both set up and then abolished as the government took the work back in house.

The government is also extremely good at squandering huge sums of money on large computer systems that often make the problem worse rather than better. The Child Support Agency computer system has been spectacularly expensive and difficult to operate. The government now wishes to spend a fortune on a national register of everybody in the country as the back-up to its identity card scheme. This could well prove to be another hugely expensive and difficult essay in computerisation. The NHS computer scheme is proving to be both expensive and long winded, with plenty of scope for cost overruns despite the huge budgets already allocated.

The modernisation of services was meant to make them better and more responsive. Instead Labour's modernisations so often mean the creation of more remote, regional managerial units getting in the way of good communication between local management and central government decision takers. This so often means expensive computerisation, which in the early days can disrupt rather than help, and it always means a huge expenditure of moneys on studies, surveys and managerial reports. Hundreds of millions of pounds have been spent on various consultancies casting their eye over both the national railway network and the London Underground. Even more has been spent on endless study of the health service.

It is for these reasons that people are increasingly disenchanted with what their politicians are offering and doing. If Labour had spent more of the extra money on providing extra beds in district general hospitals people would be more sympathetic. If they had spent some of the extra money on getting rid of the worst bottlenecks on the nationalised road network and started to reduce congestion, they would have both made a blow for a better environment and solved some people's daily problems in getting their children to school and themselves to work. If they had not tampered with the NHS dentists' contract, they might have more NHS dentists still practising today than they now have. Instead the adverse reaction to the contract the NHS decided to impose on them drove some dentists into the private sector. The irony of Labour showering the public services with so much extra taxpayers' money is that, as a result, they have succeeded in privatising rather more of it than the Conservatives ever intended.

The direct result of the bungled new NHS dentistry contract is more and more people joining private dentistry patient plans. A result of the continuing delays in getting non-essential treatment in district general hospitals is for more and more people to pay for their own operations in the private sector. The Labour government's own frustration with the lack of progress from the money it's spending has led it to buy in extra capacity for the health service from private sector providers, much to the chagrin of some of the NHS unions. The government has concluded that it can get more cataract operations and knee joint operations done to a higher quality by farming the work out to private sector providers than by constantly shovelling money into the top of the creaking NHS machinery.

The government continues to protest too much. The Chancellor recites barrage after barrage of statistics, reminding people that the standard rate of income tax is still at 22 per cent and the top rate of income tax at 40 per cent but omitting to mention the increase in national insurance at all levels of income. He continues to tell us that he is committed to a free enterprise and flexible economy, whilst doing everything in his power to tie us up in ever more regulatory knots. The one good thing this government has done is to test to destruction the proposition that taxing people and companies more, and spending far larger sums on the crucial public services of health and education, will solve the problem. It has demonstrated beyond any possible doubt that spending all the extra money does not solve the problem. It has not mysteriously banished educational inequalities. However much you spend, it does not suddenly transform bad schools into good schools, and it does not suddenly remove the very long waiting lists for NHS treatment.

Instead of the usual yah-boo of political life over who spent more, we need to have a serious debate in this country about how money could be better spent, and what is the right balance between the money we spend as taxpayers and the money we spend on our own account. The old pension system of allowing people generous tax breaks if they would save for retirement worked extremely well and gave us the best provision of anywhere in Europe. The Chancellor's demolition of that settlement has placed a huge future burden on British taxpayers, as it means many more people will now depend upon the state for pensions and top-up benefits in retirement. Some people are themselves trying to opt out of state education and state healthcare wherever possible. It is the huge expense of paying twice for schooling that means it is not possible for most families on average budgets. More are realising they can opt out of NHS healthcare. Indeed, most people do so week by week when they go to the local chemist and buy over-the-counter medicines to treat themselves, rather than committing themselves to waiting for the NHS.

I would like to live in a world where more people were empowered and encouraged to make provision for their own services, by giving them a reduction in their tax bill if they do so. Of course, none of us begrudge paying taxes to make sure that the old, the sick, the disabled are taken care of and can enjoy some of the prosperity that the rest of us enjoy through our daily working lives. That does not mean, however, that the rest of us have to rely on state provision in all the areas we currently do. I'm quite sure that private sector roads would operate better with far less congestion than the present nationalised ones. The Dartford Crossing showed how the private sector could supply and build a crucial link in our transport infrastructure. The project was so successful that the bridge was given back free to the taxpayer in a far shorter time than originally planned. The government continued charging the toll even though the private sector had long since repaid the debt and taken its profits! The M6 Birmingham Relief Road is a toll highway which provides an excellent fast route around the Birmingham traffic jams at no cost to the taxpayer. If you don't want to use it there is still the free road to the south. We need many more private sector roads to tackle the capacity problems and to offer people choice. They would be built more quickly and to budget, and would make money for those who operate them.

I would like to see everyone attend an independent school. We should ask all state schools to set themselves up as charitable trusts, not-for-profit companies, teacher co-operatives or whatever they choose. All those wanting free places for their children should have money paid by the state to the school of their choice, up to a specified limit, so that there would still be a free place for all those who needed it. People should also be free to send their children to more expensive schools and to top the money up which is theirs by right because they are the taxpayers contributing it in the first place. In this way we could start to bridge the divide between the rich and the rest, for at the moment only the rich have real school choice.

The tragedy of this government is that Tony Blair would agree with some of the things I have written and has been trying to nudge policy in the right direction, only to be thwarted at every turn by the Chancellor of the Exchequer, the true roadblock to reform. It is the Chancellor who's worked out the ways of raiding people without putting income tax up. It is the Chancellor who expects adulation for hurling unheard-of sums of money at the core public services. It is the Chancellor who's taken charge of most of the domestic departments and, with the respective secretaries of state, has made such a hash of spending the large sums of money.

It is this above all which has led to so much disillusion with British politics. The public have been told that the public services were not working properly because the Tories were too mean with other people's money. Now we've had in office for nine years a government which is too profligate with other people's money, only to establish that that does not solve the original problem. We are still short of hospital beds but not of hotel beds. We are still short of NHS doctors but not of solicitors. We are still short of road space but not of cars. The reason is simple. These are monopoly services run by people who are monopolists at heart. Monopolists do not care about providing extra capacity and do not care about the convenience of their customers and clients. Monopolists do believe in overcharging and do believe in spending much of the money on their own comforts. Until we break the monopoly stranglehold of the existing public services we will not get value for our money. Until we offer people real choice there will be a growing gap between the excellence of the best services supplied by the competitive marketplace and the defects of the services provided by the poorer public sector monopolist.

9

Sleazy come, sleazy go

> **I WANT TO MAKE A DIFFERENCE**
>
> *I want politicians to understand how the rest of us feel*
> Write to your local councillor
> Write to your MP
> Write to the newspaper
> Ring up the phone-in radio show
> Join the political party that is nearest to your view
> Go along to their meetings and talk to the volunteers and elected representatives
> Discover that they too want to make a difference – they too believe in public service
> Offer your services as
> - a school governor
> - a health board director
> - a council candidate
> - a committee member on a local body
>
> Discover that you can change things and get things done if you take some time and some responsibility
> Discover that it can be more rewarding to try and do it yourself than sitting at home watching others trying to do it on TV
> Remember you will have plenty of time to watch TV when you retire – so why not be more active when you can?

The decline of interest in politics began with Labour's extremely successful sleaze campaign against the Conservatives in the period

1993 to 1997. Desperate about being out of power for so long, the Labour opposition in the fourth Conservative majority parliament since 1979 stepped up a gear. They decided upon a vicious campaign highlighting every peccadillo, mistake or false allegation aimed against Conservative members of Parliament or, even better, Conservative ministers. They watched to see who was cheating his wife, who did not know the dividing line between a legitimate business interest and an illegitimate one. They kept their eyes open in case there was real corruption. Labour made no distinction between sexual scandals and financial ones. They blurred the line between an MP doing something wrong in his professional life and an MP misbehaving in his private life. They operated carefully, mainly through backbench MPs, levelling the charges and pursuing the quarry. They built up a good network of contacts with journalists desperate for such stories to titillate their readers.

The irony of Labour's sleaze campaign is that it was as unnecessary as it was over the top. Labour were likely to win the next general election anyway. The Conservative decision to impose the Exchange Rate Mechanism policy, backed by Labour, did so much damage to the economy. It meant the Conservatives were going to lose. As the 1990s advanced, people counted the cost in terms of lost jobs, slashed house prices, bankrupt businesses and broken dreams. Although Labour had strongly recommended this policy along with the Liberal Democrats, they made sure they were well away from the scene of the crime by the time its true cost came home to the British public. It was a great example of how consensus policies in Britain can be ruinous, and how the blame will fall almost entirely on the government of the day.

Labour were not going to take any chances. They thought if they could portray the Conservative government as a group of unpleasant people swimming in their own sleaze, they were guaranteed victory at the polls. When they began the campaign I felt it would be extremely bad news for politics. Anything Conservative MPs were up to was likely to be true of Labour and Liberal Democrat MPs as well. There was going to be no monopoly of wife swapping, love cheating or sailing close to the wind on business interests on one side of the House. Labour were digging a sleaze pool that they were going to swim in themselves.

It was clear from the early skirmishes that if you threw enough allegations against individuals or a political party some of the dirt would stick, even when there was no proof to decisively resolve the claims. Whilst newspapers acted as something of a filter because there was always the fear of a successful libel action if they went too far, journalists were also aware that many MPs were reluctant to go to libel lawyers for fear of rough justice in the courts, or for fear of other things coming out during the process of disclosure that could portray them in an unfavourable light, even if they were not illegal or against the rules. The newspapers became emboldened when two of the richer Conservatives, Jonathan Aitken and Jeffrey Archer, both got into more trouble by pursuing libel actions than if they'd not bothered, when they failed to stick to the truth in trying to defend and prosecute their claims in court.

I can remember just how successful Labour were in changing the atmosphere with their sleaze campaign, when, in the 1995 Conservative leadership election between myself and John Major, it became one of the crucial issues which Labour and the press set down for our campaigns. It was not an issue which I wished to comment on at all. I was well aware that half of it was a put-up job by Labour and half of it was establishing new, high standards of conduct by which to judge Conservative MPs, standards against which MPs of previous generations and many Labour MPs would be found wanting. To mention it at all in the leadership campaign was like volunteering the other cheek for a free punch.

Under the pressure of the campaign, I felt I needed something to say to deflect and divert. I came up with the mild and sensible proposal that if I became Prime Minister the one thing I would do is have a private conversation with anyone on the verge of being invited into a government role, to ask them if there was anything in their past that might come out that could embarrass them and the government. This seemed to me to be common sense. In some cases people would have been able to answer, 'No, there was nothing.' In some cases people may have mentioned the odd guilty secret or two, and we might have agreed that a combination of disclosure and confident presentation would cause no problem. In other cases I might have said to the person concerned that the risk was considerable and they might be better off forgoing the pleasure of office, if all it was going to do was to expose a weakness and lead to their destruction following a miserable few weeks being hounded by the press.

This mild proposal was blown up out of all proportion as some kind of new Puritanism which would descend on the Tory Party. As it entirely rested upon self-disclosure and was based on conversations in the interests of the individual as well as the country and the party, it was a sign of just how intoxicated the air was on this subject that it could become so significant and so misconstrued.

The Labour campaign, the press and the natural drift of events exposed several cases of MPs two-timing their wives. David Mellor got into trouble with his private life. Endless efforts to accuse the Prime Minister were blocked, largely because those who wanted to tell the story couldn't find out who the woman was. It was only a long time later that it emerged that the Prime Minister himself had been involved with Edwina Currie. Lesser figures in the party were also dragged through the popular press, whilst Paddy Ashdown showed that the Conservatives had no monopoly over amorous dalliances. Labour managed to keep out of it, partly because the Conservatives were too gentlemanly to return the compliment of the sleaze campaign, and partly because the press sensed that it would be much more fun to go after the Labour figures once they were in government, following the election.

What Labour were really after was some good old-fashioned corruption or graft. Hard as they looked, it was extremely difficult to find any clear-cut cases where individuals or companies had bought changes of policy or favourable government decisions. The nearest Labour got to establishing any financial sleaze was their attempt with the press to sting little-known Conservative backbenchers into asking questions for cash. A couple got into difficulties through this technique but it was a long way from establishing that big money was changing hands to buy government favours.

Labour and the press had their greatest success in the unfortunate cases of Jonathan Aitken and Jeffrey Archer. Both men lived exciting and exotic lives, both had substantial wealth and income, both went to court and both ended up in prison for perjury. The fact that one former Cabinet minister and one former senior official of the Conservative Party had ended up in prison was the icing on the cake of Labour's campaign. To them it proved beyond doubt that the Conservatives were unsuited for government.

When Labour swept to power in May 1997 they realised there were two imperatives to secure their future. Tony Blair as their leader was well aware of how long they had toiled and suffered in opposition. He knew how unforgiving the public had been for the Winter of Discontent and the economic disaster of the middle 1970s that his party had presided over. That had not been based upon consensus policies but had been the free choice of the Labour Prime Minister and Chancellor of the Exchequer. It had gone miserably wrong. He knew in May 1997 that Labour had to prove the economy was safe in its hands. He knew they had to demonstrate that the mistakes of the ERM were well behind the country and were the fault of the Conservatives not Labour. He and Gordon Brown cleverly avoided all mention or reference of their support for the ERM, and instead christened the policy Conservatives' 'boom and bust', a phrase that they endlessly repeated during the first two parliaments to remind people of the mistakes of the early 1990s.

Blair knew he had raised the hurdle of politics with his anti-sleaze campaign. In his first days at Downing Street he stressed that New Labour, with the emphasis on new, would govern differently. They would bring a new whiteness to the political laundromat. They would govern in the best interests of all the people, they would be clean, open and sleaze-free. He must have had a hint, even in those early, euphoric days, that this was going to be a very tall order. I'm sure he had no inkling that within nine years his own government would be scrambling around in a very muddy pool, based on the decisions it had taken and the private and public actions of many of its leading personalities.

To make his task a little easier Blair and his spin doctors immediately redefined sleaze when the baton passed from the Conservatives to the new government. They announced through private briefings that sleaze no longer included people's private lives. In New Labour's world it was fine for a minister or an MP to cheat his wife or her husband as that was a private matter. As long as the MP had not cheated the taxpayer or the constituency all was well. This at a stroke got rid of a large amount of the so-called sleaze that had afflicted the Conservatives, and started to create some kind of barrier against too many allegations of sleaze against Labour. Despite this rule, Ron Davies's wanderings on Clapham Common at night became too notorious and difficult, losing Blair his Secretary of State for Wales. David Blunkett's amorous encounters as Home Secretary and Work & Pensions Secretary led him into other difficulties, leading him to resign twice against his and the Prime Minster's original wishes. Robin Cook, the Foreign Secretary, lecturing the rest of the world on a moral foreign policy, got away with swapping wives at Heathrow Airport under the cosh of the press exposé of his love affair with another woman, and perhaps with the assistance of the Prime Minister's spin doctor trying to manage the story. More recently, the Deputy Prime Minister, John Prescott, remained in post after revelations about his private life. Where the Conservatives had had colourful culture secretaries and chief secretaries of the Treasury, rather junior jobs in Cabinet, Labour was providing press interest at the most senior levels.

Labour got into far worse difficulties when it came to the separation of business interests from ministerial life and the handling of money generally. At the opening of the government in 1997, Blair wanted to appoint Lord Simon, the chairman of British Petroleum, to a position in the Treasury. It is rumoured that Gordon Brown would not have him, so Blair made a job available for Simon in the Department of Trade and Industry. The job was described as being a liaison job between the DTI and the Treasury over such matters as the campaign to introduce the euro in Britain, as well as giving Simon a conventional DTI brief, which included energy. Of course, Simon had resigned as chairman of BP. However, it emerged that he had a substantial interest in BP shares which he had not sold when taking up the ministerial job. Ministerial rules were quite clear. Ministers making decisions on such issues as the allocation of oil licences to leading oil companies and influencing decisions over oil taxation, through the dialogue between the DTI and the Treasury, should not hold significant shareholdings in the oil companies they were regulating and taxing. After a long defence based on the use of a trust, Simon himself admitted that his share ownership was not a good idea and in due course he left the government.

The Bernie Ecclestone row shook the Labour establishment to the core. Ecclestone, the very successful entrepreneurial owner of Formula 1 motor racing, gave £1 million to the Labour Party. Subsequently, Labour ministers decided to exempt Formula 1 grands prix from the ban on display advertising for tobacco companies. When this unhappy conjunction of events got out, the Prime Minister went on television to explain that no policy change had been bought with the money. Ecclestone was repaid his £1 million.

On two separate occasions Peter Mandelson was forced to resign. On one occasion the issue was his mortgage application on his smart London property. It turned out that Geoffrey Robinson MP, himself a Treasury minister, had lent Mandelson an additional mortgage on top of the commercial mortgage. A number of issues were raised about how the mortgage application form had been filled in and the circumstances surrounding the loan of money by one senior Labour figure to another who were both now ministers. An additional complication was that Robinson's former business activities were the subject of an investigation by the DTI. In the end both Mandelson and Robinson left the government. No offence was conceded or proved. Mandelson also had to leave the government following allegations about the circumstances in which the Hinduja brothers had gained access to passports in the United Kingdom. Again, nothing was proven.

There have been numerous cases of ministers claiming House of Commons expenses in a way which has attracted the ire of the press. Some Labour ministers in receipt of grace-and-favour residences have nonetheless kept on two or more residences of their own at the same time, and claimed for one of them on the House of Commons system. Whilst there is nothing illegal or even against the rules in this, some have questioned whether a minister on a high salary should enjoy an additional expense account on a third property, when their immediate requirements in London are taken care of through the grace-and-favour residence.

Tessa Jowell, the culture secretary, has been put through the tabloid mill over allegations surrounding her husband, David Mills, and the receipt of moneys from Italy. Jowell claimed to know nothing about the reasons for her husband taking out a very large mortgage on their joint home, and the subsequent early repayment of the mortgage on receipt of a substantial sum of money from overseas. Various problems in their different accounts emerged. Mills separated from his wife and is determined to fight to clear his name in the Italian courts from allegations surrounding his links with the former Italian Prime Minister Silvio Berlusconi.

Several senior Labour figures made use of offshore trusts and blind trusts, a practice they condemned in others when they were in opposition. Lord Sainsbury has been subject to scrutiny. He has been a substantial donor to the Labour Party throughout his period as a minister. A well-known enthusiast for biotechnology, he put his investments into a trust according to the Ministerial Code, which, under Labour's rules, enabled him to carry on as minister responsible for that area of interest in government. It is only recently that some Labour figures themselves have raised the question of how wise it is to allow a minister serving in a government to lend money to the sponsoring party. Labour figures have asked if this makes it difficult for the Prime Minister to form an objective view of the minister's worth. The official answer is that the Prime Minister is quite happy about his minister anyway so no conflict arises.

Early in 2006 a new and spectacular row erupted. It emerged that prior to the general election in 2005 the Labour Party, desperate for money to fight the campaign, had accepted a series of loans from rich individuals. These loans under the then rules did not need to be declared to the Electoral Commission or as part of the general election returns. No-one disputes that the loans, if commercial, were perfectly legal under the law of the day. Both major parties used them. Both major parties subsequently had to prove that the loans were on commercial terms.

The law was very clear. If a party or candidate was given a grant or gift, it had to be declared as part of the general declaration of sources of money for the general election. It had to be declared to the Electoral Commission, and if it went to support individual candidates, it also in turn had to be put into their statement of election expenses. If, on the contrary, the party borrowed money on commercial terms and commercial rates, that was all in the normal course of business and did not have to be notified.

People became alarmed at so much money being borrowed in such a short space of time. They were concerned lest there were a hidden agreement in any of these loans that the money did not have to be repaid, or the repayment could be so delayed as to be similar to a gift. There was a worry that the interest payments had been waived or were not at commercial rates.

Worse still, some in the press and elsewhere raised the question of whether the people who had lent substantial sums of money to the ruling party before the election were going to be in receipt of peerages. It emerged that lending money to a major party did not debar people from gaining a peerage, and that there were examples in the past of people who had made substantial gifts or loans to the Labour Party receiving peerages in subsequent honours lists. This again is not against the rules, as long as the Prime Minister and his advisers can demonstrate that there were a series of very good reasons why that person was elevated to a peerage, other than the grant or lending of money to the ruling party.

Some tried to conjure up images of peerages for sale, reminding the public of David Lloyd George and his scandalous case of selling the peerages to keep his Liberal Party going at the beginning of the twentieth century. Others were quick to deny that anything improper had incurred, and one or two people let it be known that they weren't seeking peerages anyway. The Prime Minister and the leader of the opposition met to discuss how future party funding could be organised better, with the mutual understanding that leaving open the possibility of people claiming that honours or peerages had been sold was corrosive to the whole body politic and damaging to all political parties. When Lord Levy, Tony Blair's leading fund raiser, was arrested in order to help the police with their enquiries, there was another round of unfortunate publicity about these allegations.

It is almost extraordinary that New Labour, elected on their white chargers just nine years earlier, could by 2006 have been brought low by so many different stories alleging improper conduct, poor judgement or worse. The Prime Minister showed all his usual skills in moving to head off the damage of the peerage row, setting in train work to produce new and tighter rules which would spare the political classes so much embarrassment in the future.

After these brief histories, we must ask ourselves: how corrupt is British politics today and what would we expect from a clean, straightforward and well-organised political system?

All my adult life I've been brought up to believe that Britain has uniquely clean, open and well-behaved government, unlike many countries abroad. People of my generation were taught at school how honest and straightforward our civil service and administration was, how we gave to the Empire, subsequently the Commonwealth, a tradition of honest and fair-minded justice and administration, and how we have continued this tradition in our more straitened circumstances after the loss of Empire. I am pleased to say I have never been approached by anyone who wanted to bribe me with cash payment and I have never witnessed the taking of money for contracts or favours within British government. However, I think we also need to recognise that modern governments handle huge sums of money, make extremely important decisions which have a big bearing on other people's businesses and lives, and build up a very subtle network of friends, well-wishers and partners. These start to blur the clear edges between an independent government coming to an independent judgement and a government acting heavily under the influence of those to whom it owes favours. Whilst there are mercifully very few cases of officials in Britain taking money for themselves in return for favours, there are a whole series of other practices in the grey area which need careful examination. The public has been shocked to learn that thirty-one employees of the Immigration and Nationality Directorate have been referred for prosecution and seventy-nine for disciplinary action following more than 700 complaints about conduct. Allegations include demanding sexual favours in return for entry permits.

Let us look first at how the rules work for a backbench member of Parliament, whether of the governing party or of the opposition. A backbench MP makes no administrative decisions and has no control over any administrative budget of government, other than the decisions relating to the small public budget he administers to run his own office and to provide a service to his constituents. An MP cannot grant an income support claim, cannot change the welfare budget, cannot grant planning permission, cannot decide whether to prosecute an alleged criminal, and cannot award a government contract to a third party. For this reason, Parliament allows back-bench MPs to have interests outside the House of Commons.

There is nothing wrong with an MP being a non-executive director of a company, sitting on a charity board, sitting on the board of his local football club, continuing to practise as a barrister or as a dentist or as an accountant. However, an MP is barred from holding any office of profit under the Crown. He cannot become a paid chairman of his local health trust or the head of a government quango.

An MP has three primary roles. The first is to be one of 646 legislators. If the law needs changing, or if others think the law needs changing in Parliament, the MP is there to exercise his judgement. He can criticise, move amendments, make different recommendations, and ultimately decide whether to vote for or against any part of the proposition, or for or against the Bill as a whole. In practice, if the MP is in disagreement with the government, he is unlikely to change the law in the direction he prefers, as the government usually has an inbuilt majority to do anything it wishes. The MP may have at the margin some ability to influence the government, especially if the view he is putting forward carries favour with sufficient government backbench MPs to warn the government off, testing its majority on that particular proposition.

The second function an MP has is to hold the executive to account. The MP is there, whether of a governing party or on the opposition benches, to ask difficult questions, to expose problems and mistakes, and to find out how the executive is making decisions and spending money.

The third task of the MP is to represent the constituency view and the views of individual constituents to the government, and to get them redressed when need arises.

The constituency MP is regularly being lobbied. Most people recognise that they can best lobby their MP by sending him an e-mail or a letter, or by arranging to see him at his surgery. Very few constituents think lobbying an MP means taking him out to lunch or inviting him to the local theatre. It is clearly acceptable practice for constituents to lobby an MP to get the government to change its view in a direction that favours them, and perfectly reasonable for the MP to decide that he agrees with them and to take up their case. If the MP also has an interest in the matter then he has to be more careful. Under parliamentary convention specialist interests are difficult whereas general interests don't count.

If, for example, a group of constituents argued persuasively to their MP that income tax should be reduced because they were finding it so burdensome, there would be nothing to stop the MP taking their cause up and arguing it passionately, including his own view with theirs, even though he too pays income tax and would benefit from a reduction. Nor would there be anything wrong with an MP taking up the cause of local businesses who wanted a specific change to the tax laws affecting their type of business, if he agreed with them and if he thought it a good idea. If, however, he happened to run or partly own or be involved with a business that would benefit from a specialist change to the tax system, he should not pursue it. He cannot act as a paid lobbyist for a business group wishing to pursue, for example, a specialist tax change that would favour it. In this case he would be nothing more than a hired hand for the lobby group and that has been correctly banned by Parliament.

There are strict limits placed upon hospitality for obvious reasons. If a business in a constituency has not succeeded in its earlier attempts by letters, e-mails and meetings to persuade the MP to take up the issue that most concerned them, it might resort to other means. No-one believes an MP could be bought for the price of a good lunch in a local restaurant. The MP would be quite within his rights to accept a lunch from the company in question and then to come to the conclusion, based on the merits of the case, that it did after all have a good point. The MP, however, would not be wise to accept an overseas trip from the company to see the overseas implications of what it was worried about prior to changing his mind on the issue, especially if the trip involved a long-haul flight in expensive seats in the aircraft and allowed him free time in addition to the getting-to-know-you sessions when he arrived at the company's overseas operations. If the company offered him money in lieu of the overseas trip that would be a bribe. If the company offered an overelaborate overseas trip that too could be easily misconstrued and would not look good on the front page of a tabloid newspaper.

Things get more complicated in the British system when it comes to party funding. Prior to the changes of the last decade, little was known about how local political parties were funded and few questions were asked. It was theoretically possible for an MP to develop a very close relationship with rich individuals or companies in the constituency, who would then pay many of the bills both for elections and out of election time. Honest MPs would not have taken up the issues that mattered most to those companies, using the privilege of their position and the headed notepaper of the House of Commons, but the system was open to abuse. More recently transparency has required the registration of many large donations from rich individuals and companies, which should encourage all MPs either not to lobby on behalf of those people or to make a very clear declaration of interest when so doing if it is within the rules to make the point.

The position of government ministers is much more exposed and has always been, correctly, more strongly policed. On taking office, however junior, in the government, an MP moves into a different world. Now he or she is a member of the machine that decides what legislation will go through the House and what legislation won't. In most cases it is in effect the government which decides what Parliament will legislate rather than Parliament itself. If an individual from within the government can persuade the government to take a particular line then the full weight of the government's majority will be behind it, and barring any accident in the House it will carry. More importantly, even in junior jobs ministers have direct power to make decisions. They have large budgets of public money, where they have discretion in many cases over how it can be spent. They are involved with civil servants in the organisation of tenders and the award of contracts. They make appointments to public bodies, they can review the corporate plans of the quangos within their remit. They can issue private or public directions and instructions to staff in the public sector within their departmental field, and they often have to adjudicate in individual cases where they are tricky and are escalated to ministerial level. A good minister spends quite a lot of his or her time judging difficult disputes, deciding on the course of action when official advice is split, and deciding on people and policies for the future of his or her part of the public sector. It would not be possible to do this and at the same time remain as the director of a company, sit on the board of a charitable trust, or even be on the board of the local football team.

As a result, all incoming ministers are given copious advice on avoiding conflicts of interest and embarrassment. They are told that they should resign from every paid post they hold in the private sector as well as continuing with the bar on any other office of profit under the Crown save, of course, the ministerial appointment. When I became a junior minister at the DTI, I was at the time the chairman of a large quoted industrial conglomerate. On being told the news that I had become a minister I rang my company's office, explained to them that I was resigning instantaneously and told them that to avoid embarrassment both to them and to me I would not be visiting them again. I asked them to send my belongings round from my office and then to take the car back to the company because I could no longer use it. I swapped my company Daimler for the government's rather more modest Montego as I set about complying with all the rules that rightly bore down upon me. I still asked my officials never to refer papers to me that involved that group of companies.

There are some strange quirks in the government's approach to avoiding ministerial conflicts of interest. Whilst the government is rightly firm on saying that you cannot maintain any directorship or active interest in a company, they do not make ministers sell all their shares. Ministers are allowed to continue holding shares but they are advised to place them all in a blind trust, run by an independent third party who does not communicate with the minister about the details of the sales and purchases. In most cases this is a satisfactory precaution. If a minister has a mixed portfolio of shares whose composition he knows on the day he's appointed and he gives this over to genuinely independent management, leaving them free to buy and sell as they see fit, he will after a few weeks no longer be sure what he owns. It is unlikely to influence his decisions. It is more difficult where a minister comes to office owning a very large shareholding in a given company. It is especially difficult if the shareholding or shareholdings are in companies that are not quoted on the Stock Exchange, making it unlikely that even an independent investment manager will be able to sell the shares and put the money into something else. This means that the trust the minister has for his shareholdings is not blind, and he therefore has to be extremely careful never to take decisions which could in some way bear upon those particular companies or interests.

Stranger still is the ruling that ministers can continue to own their own farms. Whilst it would be clearly impractical to make ministers sell their farms as soon as they came into office, there is an obvious conflict if a minister owns a farm and is given a job in agriculture or the environment, making decisions on agricultural matters. When I first went into government officials were only just becoming aware of the dangers of allowing someone who was a member of Lloyd's to be a DTI minister. I was asked when I turned up to be the insurance regulator in the DTI, amongst other duties, whether I was a member of Lloyd's. No-one seemed to think it would necessarily bar me from undertaking the general duties of insurance regulator. I was quite sure it would have prevented me and was delighted to tell them that I had never been a member of Lloyd's.

When I first went into Downing Street as an adviser in 1983, I set up a system for myself and the other senior officials in the Prime Minister's Policy Unit, which I led, to avoid conflicts of interest between the advice we were proffering and any private interests we might hold. I was surprised to discover there was no system in place when I arrived. I told all my policy advisers it was better if they did not buy shares. If they did wish to buy shares or government bonds, I wanted them to report the transaction to myself or to the Prime Minister's principal private secretary, so that we could keep an eye on what was happening and so that they could show they had not behaved unreasonably with any subsequent advice they might give. I was even more surprised to discover that some officials in the Treasury, who were well aware of the policy on interest rates and government funding, talked about buying and owning government bonds. There was in those days no absolute ban on senior officials owning government debt. Whilst I have no evidence that anything wrong took place, it did seem to me strange that people who were privy to decisions in the Treasury over what interest rates should be and how much money the government should borrow were technically free to purchase government bonds themselves.

We have to ask ourselves: what influences is it reasonable for ministers to accept or to take seriously, and which influences must they exclude from their decision taking? At the extremes it is an easy question to answer. No minister should accept a large sum of money into his personal bank account from someone seeking a policy change from his department, or a planning permission which is under his influence. At the other extreme, it is perfectly reasonable for a minister to hold a meeting with businesses or individuals interested in the law or decision he's going to take, to hear their case before deciding. It would be perfectly reasonable for him to be swayed by the case if there are no other behind-the-scenes considerations. He should offer all the relevant interests the opportunity to put their case before deciding. The issue gets more difficult with all those grey areas in between. How can a minister be sure that his motives are right in changing a given policy if the leading proponents of the policy change happen to have given large sums of money to his political party to help him win the general election? Can the minister be sure he's making the right decision in favour of a particular industry and against another industry, if the industry he favours by his decision happens to be the one that is more important to his own constituency? If a minister borrows substantial sums of money that he could not get on commercial terms from a bank or building society to sustain his own lifestyle, he should expect close examination of any decisions he subsequently makes to see if there was any favouritism towards the people or interests who had come to his aid financially. If a minister has a significant shareholding in a trust which is likely to still be in that trust, he would be unwise to make decisions which favoured that company or sector.

Throughout the civil service there is the thirst for knowledge or rather a rush to protect positions against the charge of ignorance. The British system has traditionally rested on the idea that any MP can ask the government anything he likes about how it operates, or about the impact its policies and programmes have upon the wider community, and expect an answer. The civil service has also thrived on appointing generalists to its ranks and then moving them onwards and upwards, regularly changing their jobs at two- or three-yearly intervals. As a result, many people in the civil service often feel they do not have enough knowledge or information to carry out the particular task they are doing, and are worried in case an incoming question reveals too much ignorance. The civil service builds up a network of contacts amongst the businesses and people, the lobby groups and interests which it is regulating, presiding over or awarding money to. This is the civil servant's way of keeping in touch and of having sources to go to should a difficult question come in or should a tricky policy paper need writing.

Properly handled this just makes better-informed government. Improperly handled it can lead to undue influence. Whilst the civil servant coming into a new job inherits a lot of the contacts from his predecessor, for they are contacts with the civil service as a whole and not specific to one individual, quite a lot rests on the senior civil servant and how he maintains, develops and grows that contact list. If the contact list is skewed, partial or inadequate it can mean that that branch of the civil service is badly informed. If there are insufficient contacts it can also mean that the civil service may feel it needs to genuflect in the direction of those contacts rather more, fearing that it might get cut off from its source of information if it made life too difficult for the contacts and their businesses, or if it did not accept enough of the incoming advice.

The civil service also has considerable power over the award of contracts. If you are buying paper clips or computer consumables it is a relatively straightforward task to organise a competition, ask for quotes, and to award the contract to the least-cost bidder. The product is relatively homogenous and the specification common. But so much of civil service procurement now is more complicated than that. At the other end of the spectrum, when the civil service is buying in management expertise and professional advice, it is very difficult to pin down who will be the least-cost supplier. You can organise a competition, setting standards for basic knowledge and expertise, and asking for tenders based on hourly rates. You may even be able to include in the tender the total number of hours that you will be awarding. What you cannot do to justify the price is specify exactly how much work is going to be done and guarantee that the work will be done to a sufficiently high standard in the way that you would like. A great deal of judgement comes into complex tenders and procurement which can give rise to more subtle influences over officials making the awards. Ministers are well advised to keep out of these decisions but on occasion they too may get involved and will need to make sure that they themselves are judging things objectively and protecting themselves from any allegation of favouritism.

My close observation of governments over the last thirty years tells me that incompetence is much more likely than soft corruption or undue influence, which in turn is much more likely than direct corruption. Politicians are more open to suspicion that they have cut corners or turned a favourable eye or ear to those who look kindly on their party and offer it money and other support, than to those who have favoured them personally. All but the crassest of ministers understands it's not a good idea to accept lavish holidays, mortgages or other favours from commercial interests who may be seeking a decision from them about something that matters to them. On the other hand, many ministers are probably tempted to favour interest groups that their party likes, constituency interests and others who might not win the argument on its merits.

All of this has been called into question much more by Labour's campaign against sleaze. Prior to the 1990s people accepted the weft and warp of political relationships and influence. They accepted that if people were in the know, had good contacts, had successful networks, they were more likely to do well. People openly spoke about the so-called 'old school tie network' which they thought operated at the top levels of commerce, government and the professions. People knew that in a society things rubbed along by one person scratching another person's back in return for a favour. This was not sleaze, this was just good neighbourliness, partnership, reciprocal conduct. Labour's sleaze campaign has shone a lot of light onto these issues and asked people to make hard and fast decisions where often the issue is grey or difficult to define. Prior to the sleaze campaign all MPs were honourable. If the occasional rogue turned up the club soon found him out and usually took action to expose him or expel him. For the rest, people accepted different MPs, and made different judgements about how far they could go and how they balanced their public and private interests. People accepted that ministers were likely to be sympathetic to their own constituencies and people in their own parties as long as it didn't become a scandal.

In the post-sleaze-campaign world everything has to be quantified, defined, put under rules, and judged by so-called independent figures. Parliamentarians' conduct is now subject to potential investigation by the Commissioner for Parliamentary Standards. Councillors' behaviour is similarly subject to complaint and scrutiny by an independent body. We are now discovering that some in the political game think they should hurl serious allegations around about members of other parties in the hope that some of the mud will stick, constantly appealing to the regulator or referee to find against the other side. This in turn builds stronger and stronger demands for ever more specific and clearer rules. Instead of living in a world where we trust people to make moral judgements based on their own under-standing of what they and their constituents regard as reasonable, we now have more and more things defined in the rules and subject only to the test 'were the rules broken?'. People who give large sums of money to a political party can qualify for peerages with no rule broken. Ministers can make decisions in favour of people who have given large sums of money to their party with no rules broken. Ministers can claim substantial expenses from their parliamentary allowances whilst also having grace-and-favour residences with no rules broken. This just encourages the press and some of the political campaigners to make a bigger fuss and throw more allegations. It is dragging politics down further.

So where should it all stop? It is quite difficult to see where the new lines should be drawn, given the growing prurience of the system and the way in which more and more people are using the rules, both to protect themselves from charge and to hurl charges at others. Let us take the case of party political funding. If people think it unseemly for someone to give £1 million and then coincidentally for that person to be granted a peerage or his or her company to be granted a planning permission, at what level does it become acceptable? David Cameron, the leader of the opposition, has suggested that a new, absolute limit be placed on any given donation or grant of only £50,000. I'm sure most people would agree that it would be difficult to believe that any minister of the Crown could be bought for only £50,000 given to his or her political party, and difficult to believe that the market value of peerages, should they be for sale, would be as low as £50,000. A party would need a lot of £50,000s in order to maintain anything like current levels of spending, which would reduce the significance of any donor very considerably.

However, in the context of an individual constituency the limit might need to be rather different. In a world where an MP can only spend around £12,000 to get re-elected, maybe the limit for any individual subscriber has to be placed much lower. Under the current rules an MP is not allowed to accept a gift in cash or kind in excess of £250. This may be unduly low. I know very few MPs so hard up that £250 would buy them. It means that an MP can accept lunch in a reasonable restaurant without having to register the interest but may well have to register a day at a prestige sporting event, as these days you wouldn't get any change out of £250 for good seats, high quality entertainment and food.

There are some who think that MPs should not have any outside job. Banning all outside interests would certainly ban any possibility of conflict between how an MP earned his or her top-up money and his or her prime job. However, it is likely to produce a worse type of influence or possible corruption than it is designed to prevent. If MPs have no outside interests they are completely dependent upon their income from the House of Commons. Winning the seat again becomes ever more important. Not falling out with the political party that endorses the MP as candidate and makes that MP's victory possible becomes crucial. Creating a career out of Parliament for political professionals guarantees that they will have to stay true to their party whip, obedient to their party's changing views, and keen to raise as much money as possible for their party to perpetuate its success. It is those who know least about the outside world in politics who are keenest on the biggest budgets, the most lavish advertising campaigns, and the most ample staff numbers at party headquarters and on their own staffs.

In order to guarantee their purity from business lobbyists, MPs who are full-time professional politicians will know nothing about the rest of the world. They will be cut off from that experience and wider view which MPs enjoy who have done other serious jobs in their time, and who keep their hand in in certain specified fields. The House of Commons is a richer place for having people in it with recent or active experience of business, social work, accountancy, the law, teaching and the university world. If we ban all those links there will be a new generation of MPs who are entirely dependent upon the lobbyist, the PR professional and the working lunch to learn what little they know about the other worlds that they seek to regulate and control.

The House of Lords in recent years has gained greater glory from two things. The first is that it has had the power to vote down the government of the day at a time when the Commons with such large Labour majorities has very rarely been able to. The second is that because the Lords has so many people in it who have other jobs and real expertise, their debates have been broader and deeper. They have been assisted in this by the absence of very tight guillotines used in the Commons. The Lords has shown that people who know things about areas of life outside Parliament can make a more valuable contribution to analysing problems, scrutinising government policy and formulating new laws. The presence in the Lords of the very powerful Law Lords sharpens minds when it comes to discussing formulations of new law codes. The presence of many senior generals, admirals and Air Force officers of recent prominence provides depth to the defence debates, whilst the presence of serving senior clergy provides interesting insights into moral and life issues such as abortion, single-parent families and the relief of poverty.

It would be even more difficult for the Commons to match or balance the depth of the Lords debates if anyone were excluded from the Commons who wished to carry on in one capacity or another as a barrister, as a director, as a professor or in some other professional capacity. It would mean that all MPs were very vulnerable to political lobbying, to the party political dogfight, and to the relentless need to raise more money to fight better elections to keep their seats. It is quite easy portraying things as sleazy. It is much more difficult finding ways of banishing sleaze altogether.

So how then are we to clean up British politics? The public are sore about the poor performance in power of the two main parties between 1992 and today. Just to show the Liberal Democrats would be no different, their recent leadership campaign saw one candidate forced out of the race because of the extraordinary double life he was leading with a rent boy as well as his wife. Another senior contender was damaged by denying that he was homosexual, only to confirm at a later stage that he had enjoyed homosexual experiences in his time. The Liberal Democrats found a question mark hanging over one of the largest contributions to their campaign funds as to whether it met the rule of payment from a British source or not. They are adamant that it was an entirely legal payment but a lot of press ink was spilt examining it. The Liberal Democrats showed that even spending far less than the other major parties raising the sums they need is still a struggle, requiring dependence on a few large donors in exactly the same way as the major parties.

There are three possible solutions to the difficulty of party funding. The first and best answer is the one that will not be tried and is unlikely to succeed. The best answer is we should return to the age of mass democratic parties, where a large number of people each give a small amount to belong to the party, providing the wherewithal for that party to campaign strenuously and employ good-quality people. If we assume that in a normal election Labour and Conservative parties should each get around ten million votes, and if one in ten of all the people voting for those parties could be persuaded to join through a subscription of only £10 a year, it would give each of those major parties £10 million a year to spend. You could run a very successful major political party on £10 million a year. In the non-general election years you could put a little by so that in a general election year you had a bit more to spend on the campaign. You could also once every four or five years have a general election campaign fund appeal, which would easily bring in another £10 a head on average from your million members, giving you ample funds.

The aim of enrolling at least one in ten of a party's voters used to be the stated aim of the Conservative Party and it was an achievable aim in many parts of the country. Today the parties are hard pushed to enrol as many as one in twenty of their voters because people are not attracted to what a general party has on offer. We shall in the next chapter look at ways in which a party could try and revive its fortunes, relate more directly to the way people currently wish to do their politics, and engage with those who do wish still to make a difference.

The second proposal on the table which is attracting many professional politicians is the idea that the public should pay for their political parties through taxation. The argument runs that the bill on the taxpayer would be quite small. In a world where the government spends £550 billion a year the odd £10 or £20 million to pay for the political parties would be a drop in the ocean. To those who say they have no wish to make a compulsory contribution to a party not of their choosing through the tax system, the answer goes that they could if they like assume that all of their tax contribution is going to the party nearest to their preferences. To those who say they don't vote and don't like any of the parties, the political parties may well be arrogant enough to say, 'Well, that's your fault and we want you to participate.'

It is exactly that spirit that I do not like about the proposal of compulsory state funding of political parties. I think parties should have to work hard to raise their money from as many people as possible. If parties are not able to raise enough money by voluntary donation, they should think very carefully about what they are doing wrong and why they are not engaging with sufficient people in the right way. As a taxpayer myself I have absolutely no wish to help fund the Labour or Liberal Democrat parties. I even have a reluctance to have to pay my money to the Conservative Party through taxation. I willingly give some money to the Conservative Party at the moment but that is my choice. I do not think it is right that I should have to pay it on threat of imprisonment as part of the tax deal. I respect all those who do not like the current party political offering and even those who do not vote. I believe it is the job of candidates and political parties to engage enough interest. I do not favour mandatory voting by Act of Parliament and I certainly do not favour the mandatory support of political parties by individuals who dislike them.

We already have quite a lot of back door state funding, taxpayer funding, of politics in Britain today. It is dressed up as not being party political funding. Substantial sums of money are paid to the opposition parties based on the votes they received in previous general elections through the so-called 'Short money'. This money, granted to the Conservatives and the Liberal Democrats, enables them to hire researchers and other support staff to conduct opposition to a higher standard. Whilst it is not meant to be spent on party political campaigning, it does enable shadow spokesmen and women to have at their beck and call talented people paid for by the taxpayer to help in at least part of their role. Similarly, expense allowances have been generously increased to MPs to carry out their constituency and parliamentary duties. It is now quite possible on the staff allowance to engage a constituency case worker and a researcher, as well as a secretary to type the letters and handle the e-mails. Whilst again these staff are not meant to be engaged in any party political activities, it greatly eases the life of the MP, who is freer to undertake party politics himself or herself, in the knowledge that the taxpayer-supported individuals are doing large parts of the rest of the job. I would regret any further development in these directions.

One of the problems with taxpayer funding of opposition parties is that it can make professional performances by shadow spokesmen more difficult rather than easier. Prior to all this money coming into the system shadow ministers had to brief themselves, versing themselves in the subject that they were shadowing, meeting the right people, learning from outside interest groups and other knowledgeable people, reading the documents, taking a lively interest in their subject. Now that more shadow spokesmen depend on professional researchers it can mean that in that spontaneous moment, or in that unexpected debate, a shadow spokesperson is at a loss because the researcher is not there to make the relevant point available to him or her. Researchers in their turn, like civil servants, can often be very dependent on too few sources of information in the outside world, which they repeat sometimes without credit so that the shadow spokesperson is voicing the lobby group's interest without always being aware of what he or she is doing.

The third route which has been put forward by the leader of the opposition is tighter controls over what political parties can spend. This is a productive line of enquiry. I'm quite sure that the major political parties spend more in a general election than is sensible or desirable. Spending £20 million each on research, PR, press stunts and advertising does not necessarily improve the product, produce better policies or wow more electors. As we've seen, in 2005 the most expensive election fought so far on British soil produced a great deal of apathy and anger about the quality of the campaign, and failed to find sufficient reason for almost 40 per cent of the electorate to bother to vote at all.

In the United Kingdom, unlike the United States, there is still a national media although, as in the United States, the media is becoming more diverse and the audiences for any particular television programme, radio show or newspaper getting smaller. It is still possible for the main political parties to get over a single message through the main news channels and through the main national newspapers in a single day, with the minimum of effort. One good press conference with the right message would ensure a strong communication through all the main media outlets without needing to spend money on additional PR or supporting advertisements. During a general election campaign the main news outlets are going to produce at least one political story every day, and in that political story they will be required under British electoral laws to say something about each of the major parties, however poor the message may be from that political party on that day.

The main parties have recently developed a habit of making a news story out of establishing a big poster site. This is an expensive way of putting forward a simple proposition. In order to speed it up and reduce the cost a bit, the main parties have sometimes scaled back the run-out of a poster campaign across the country. Nonetheless, they have still had to pay substantial sums for top poster sites in London, where the press stunts are held, and go to the cost of employing the advertising agency, sorting out the copy and producing the mega-poster for unveiling. It would be quite possible to get as good or better coverage out of a well-aimed press conference at party headquarters on the same occasion, if the party has something useful to say and says it well. It would also be a great deal cheaper.

David Cameron suggested cutting the cap on national general election campaign expenditure to £15 million for each main party. I would be happy with that, indeed I'd be happier still if it were cut to £10 million. That would still leave plenty of money to employ decent-quality staff, to supervise the e-mails, the legal checking, the daily press offerings and the literature that make up a modern campaign. It would enable the party to give full support to its leader and other leading figures as they toured the country, and to organise suitable photo opportunities, public meetings and events. It would not leave the parties with a budget to spend on national advertising but that, I think, would be a good thing. The national media outlets are going to have to follow the campaign anyway.

If the main political parties were eased of the burden of raising between £5 and £10 million in general election year, that would in itself limit the number of obligations they could run up to very rich individuals and companies. I suspect, however, it will not solve the whole problem. The leader of the opposition certainly does not think so, which is why he has allied it to the need to impose a £50,000 cap on individual donations. This immediately raises the issue of the trade unions. The trade unions have traditionally been the main source of Labour support just as big business used to be the main source of Conservative support. In recent years the combination of the relative decline of the trade unions with the voracious demand for more money from the Labour Party has meant that Labour have increasingly relied on a narrow range of big business donors, in exactly the same way that the Conservative Party did when in power.

Labour believe that if there is a limit placed on individual donations this should not apply to the trade unions. They argue that in effect a trade union donation of £1 million represents individual donations on behalf of the thousands of members that the union has. I think this is impossible to sustain morally, unless every individual member of the union has been asked and has opted in to paying the sum to the Labour Party. If union members are asked and if they agree that they wish to make an individual contribution of that sum to the Labour Party, then Labour has returned to being a mass membership party, which is the best possible way of financing political activity. Similarly, companies could give more if they asked all their shareholders and the shareholders individually opted to give more. Alternatively, in both cases the rules should ban companies and trade unions giving more than £50,000, on the grounds that the individual members of the unions and shareholders of the companies could give their own money direct if they wished.

Do we need to take any further action to clean up the pursuit of personal gain when holding public office? One thing which would remove quite a lot of the allegations would be to subsume within parliamentary pay the living-away-from-home allowance, paid to all MPs who need to keep more than one home because of their jobs, working in two different places. If MPs' salaries were increased by the average allowance paid for second homes or even by the maximum allowance paid for second homes and the allowance abolished, all scope for marginal calls and difficult decisions over what was a reasonable expense for a second home would at once be removed. There would doubtless also be a huge row about it in the short term as the public never likes to see their MPs getting large pay rises. No doubt any consolidation of the allowance would be presented as a pay rise, even though if the average amount were taken the total cost of MPs to the public would not change.

I would be prepared to back such a scheme but only if the number of MPs were reduced substantially. I do not think a medium-sized country with sixty million people and devolved Parliaments in Scotland and Wales needs 646 members of Parliament. The United States, with four times as many people and far more power and wealth, gets by with 100 senators compared with our 740 peers in the upper House, and 420 congressmen compared with our 646 MPs in the lower House. No-one suggests that America is short of politicians.

Until the boundary changes in 1997 I looked after almost 100,000 electors in my Wokingham constituency. The boundary changes took me down to just a little below the average of 67,000 voters, a cut of almost one-third. I know from experience it is quite possible to look after 100,000 people to a standard that they find acceptable. If we went over to such a scheme we could remove some 200 members of Parliament from the current tally. As many would think this was too extreme a move, the Conservative Party has proposed the middle course of removing about 100 at the next boundary review. This would give the taxpayer considerably better value for money and would be a suitable offset for any consolidation of the living-away-from-home allowance into the pay. The taxpayer would save about £250,000 a year on every MP who was removed, producing a total saving of £25 million a year. Most of the £250,000 is spent on back-up staff and support services in addition to the £58,000 annual salary. The stated cost of an MP is higher than £250,000, but these figures include each MP's share of the cost of the support services at Westminster, which would remain for a smaller number of MPs. At the same time we should introduce English votes for English issues so that MPs from Scotland do not help to decide laws for England in areas that have been devolved to the Scottish Parliament. This should also lead some reappraisal of the level of salary and expense allowance that Scottish members of the Westminster Parliament need, given their much-reduced duties compared with an English member.

I would also wish to see the abolition of all regional government in England, removing the quango state which has sprung up. We do not need the unelected assemblies throughout the so-called English regions. We do not need the regional development agencies, the regional strategic health authorities, and the regional housing and planning bodies. This too would represent a substantial saving whilst improving the honesty and integrity of the political system. It would mean that local elected councillors were answerable locally for decisions made in the county hall or town hall, whilst national politicians were answerable for national decisions made by the UK government and by Parliament as the legislature.

We have a similar problem of sleaze rows at local government level in modern Britain as well. The advent of the independent regulator of councillors and the more prescriptive regime over councillor declarations of interest has given the impression that local government has suddenly become much sleazier. The tradition in British local government is to employ amateur part-time councillors who earn their living by some other job. Britain over many years has been well served by business people, trade union officials, housewives, college lecturers, and retired military and civil service personnel coming together to meet as a council in each local area. For many years they did so for very modest expenses. More recently they have also received more adequate attendance allowances but these allowances still fall well short of a professional salary for a full-time or serious part-time job. It means that most councillors have some other way of earning their living. It means that they have savings and investments or pension entitlements if they are not still employed. All these things now have to be declared and on many occasions when a debate gets interesting a councillor has to declare an interest and exempt himself from either the debate, or the vote, or both. Indeed, the interest rules are so narrow that you can get to the point where a councillor cannot take an interest in and vote on a planning application in his own ward because he happens to live in the ward as well. This can be very frustrating to the people he represents as well as to the councillor himself.

At the same time that the interest rules have become tighter the demands on councillors have become greater. We have created a very technical and risk-adverse world. There is now a serious possibility that the council will be sued if there are too many road accidents on a stretch of highway that the council is responsible for designing and maintaining. If a local building is improperly constructed, the council may be liable through its building inspectorate and planning services. If local waste is handled badly it could lead to a substantial environmental claim, whilst if parents are unhappy about the way their child is being treated at school that too could lead to lawyers at dawn. Councillors are under more and more pressure from professional advisers, officers and the many private-sector consultants they employ to protect themselves over the direction in which they must lead the council.

So what then is the answer? I do think we need to reduce the number of councillors, as all the political parties are struggling to find enough suitable people to fight all the different seats on offer, at all the different levels. We should then consider paying better salaries to the councillors that remain so that they can treat it as a serious part-time job, and be paid according to the professional responsibilities they are now carrying. We should also consider buying them professional indemnity insurance in the same way that directors of companies now expect such insurance to be in place when they carry out their onerous duties. Reducing the number of councillors and layers of government would also help in areas of the country where there are not unitary councils. This should be done on a voluntary basis but I'm sure there are other parts of the country which could reach agreement on reducing the too many layers of government they currently suffer from.

Simplification, clarification, making responsibilities clearer and rewarding people sensibly for what they do are crucial to getting rid of the image of sleaze that has now surrounded local as well as national government in some cases. Some of the sleaze is self-generated by political parties, now regarding it as part of the hurly-burly of the modern political fight. However, some of it is people getting more worried about the grey areas of life that used to represent accepted influence and now represent unreasonable influence to the public. In such a world there does need to be greater transparency and some rules. Above all, there needs to be a reduction in the amount of money that needs to pass from large companies, unions and institutions to political parties, to get people away from the idea that it is sleazy come, sleazy go.

10

Conclusions

The voters are frustrated with party politics in Britain. We have charted the depths of their ennui, showing how turnout in the last two general elections has been poor and how turnout in local elections over the last twenty years has declined to derisory levels. Whilst polls tell us that people remain very concerned about issues where government impinges on their daily life, they do not feel that exercising their vote for a councillor or a member of Parliament will achieve anything.

British voters are concerned that the National Health Service is not well run and is not delivering all of the treatment free at the point of use in the timely way they would like. They are concerned that there is still too much lawlessness and disorder on our streets, and that they might themselves be in danger of suffering from burglary or a crime against their motor vehicle. People are concerned that their local environment will be damaged by too much building or by bad neighbours being moved in. People are worried that their local school may not offer the excellent education they expect for their children.

These issues are nearly always in the top half-dozen in all the polling that is undertaken. People do understand in Britain that they need to look to the state for an answer to the problems of law and order, education, health and the local environment because they realise that some combination of decisions by the European government, the British national government and the local council will determine how good the local hospital is, how much money the comprehensive school spends, who can go to the local school, how many police will be on the streets, and what development can take place in the locality.

So why do most spurn voting in a local election to choose a group of councillors who may sort things out? Why do as many people as vote Labour and Conservative in a general election now decide it is better to stay at home? Countless doorstep conversations and correspondence by e-mail and letter with a wide range of my own constituents and others tells me that people are cynical about the claims of political parties, and despair of the political parties ever being able to deliver what they promise.

All three main political parties – Labour, Conservative and Liberal Democrat – now share the same distrust. Two have been tried in government in recent years and found wanting. The Liberal Democrats have been tried in many parts of the country in local government and often found wanting. In an increasingly consumerist world, where people are used to good standards of service, high-quality products and ever better value in the competitive market-place, they despair of getting similar treatment from their public services under whichever party may be in power locally or nationally.

The Conservatives did much damage to their credibility when they accepted Labour and Liberal Democrat advice to enter the Exchange Rate Mechanism in the early 1990s, which reduced house prices, drove people out of work and damaged businesses. Labour undermined their credibility by failing to deliver welfare reform, better schools and a more responsive health system, for all the extra money they channelled in. Both parties in power put taxes up, Labour by rather more than the Conservatives, when they had both promised not to. More and more people in Britain feel they're paying the bills but not getting the results. They say to themselves, 'We tried the Conservatives and in the 1990s they made a mistake. We then tried Labour and they did not live up to their fine words.' In many cases they've tried the Liberal Democrats locally and discovered exactly the same problem – bigger bills but no better public service delivery.

I WANT TO MAKE A DIFFERENCE

I want to sort out the water shortage
Things you can do:
- Don't run the taps unnecessarily
- Turn the tap off when brushing teeth
- Do washing-up in a dishwasher or a bowl
- Keep your rainwater in a water butt for watering the garden
- Reduce the size of large toilet flush systems
- Repair leaking domestic pipes and dripping taps

Things the government should do:
- Introduce competition to the regional monopolies
- Ask the regulator to require more capacity as well as good-quality water
- Grant planning permission for the desalination plant Thames Water wants to build

Things the water companies should do:
- Mend their pipes to cut the present massive leakage
- Seek planning permission for extra reservoir and desalination capacity
- Examine schemes for extra pipeline capacity from the wet parts of the country to the drier parts

The paradox of the position in Britain is that whilst the reason for the frustration is very obvious, there is still no political consensus in favour of the changes it would take in order to tackle the underlying problems. Many of the problems could be dealt with by introducing choice and competition into the delivery of services that remain in the state sector, or still contain large monopoly elements. If only we had a competitive water industry where new water suppliers could use the pipe network of the existing regional monopolists, I doubt we would have a water shortage. New water suppliers would tap into boreholes, construct reservoirs and pipe water from the wet areas to the dry areas in order to supply the market. It is the regulated refusal of the regional water companies to mend their pipes, tap the boreholes and construct the reservoirs needed that means that 21st-century Britain is short of water in its most populated and dynamic part. The problem is egged on by Ofwat and the Environment Agency. They have placed too much emphasis on water quality, sending signals to the regulated monopolies that the quantity of water does not matter. If the regulator had told the water companies that they could not put their prices up unless they sorted out the shortage problem, I am sure it would have been sorted out by now.

The Labour government has looked at competition in water and, like its Conservative predecessor, has edged in favour of more water competition for the larger users. As a result, the companies are providing a better service now to the very big industrial users of water but failing to transfer that into a better service for smaller businesses and residential customers. Competition has produced phones for practically everybody at a price they can afford. Competition could produce water for everybody so that the bedding plants could be tended in the spring and the cars washed in the summer.

Tony Blair's antennae have picked up the public frustration with the lack of responsiveness of the schooling and hospital system to the needs of modern voters. He has been desperately trying to lead his party in the direction of public service reforms, only to discover that the Chancellor of the Exchequer and many others in the government still speak with the voice of the public sector trade unions, doggedly defending every restrictive practice and every monopoly interest. Blair only has himself to blame. It was he and his colleagues who tore up the hesitant but well-intentioned reforms of the outgoing Conservative government in 1997, removing the so-called internal market in the health service, which was designed to give patients more choice, and threatening those schools set up by the Conservatives or continued by the Conservatives which offered a better education and some choice to parents.

Again, the solution to the problem is technically straightforward. If parents were given choice between a wide range of different schools, the power of competition would lift the standards of all. If we continue with the monopoly local comprehensive and insist that pupils go to it, there is no pressure on the incumbent governors and head teacher to lift their game and make their school a place of excellence which people naturally wish to go to. I would like everyone to go to an independent school in Britain. I'm fed up with the apartheid which means that the rich minority have a choice between a number of truly great schools where their children can get an excellent education, whilst the children of the poorest are sent to local comprehensives where standards are poor, ambition is low and the results often depressing. Children of middle-income parents fare better in the state system through house ownership in the more expensive catchment area of the better comprehensive. If everyone could take the amount of money the state can afford to spend on education and spend it on a school of their choice, with or without top-up, whilst guaranteeing that there are enough completely free places for all who needed them, we would find that our educational system was transformed in the direction of much higher achievement and greater quality.

We need to tackle the grave damage done to our democracy by the strengthening of the state, the growth of the quango, the transfer of power to Brussels and the growing feeling of powerlessness on the part of many backbench MPs and most councillors. In recent years the government has persuaded people that if things are going wrong in the public sector the answer is more government not less. Labour's big experiment has been based on the proposition that there was nothing wrong with the British public sector that the expenditure of huge extra sums of money and the recruitment of more people would not put right. For every problem that hit the headlines there has been a new quango, taskforce, tsar or other intervention. For every set of frustrated public service consumers that get into the media there has been more targeted money, new grant programmes and ministerial statements. As a result, we now have a labyrinthine bureaucracy stretching from Brussels at the top through to the local quangos at the bottom and encompassing a whole new army of regulators, grant assessors, case reviewers and private consultants.

We need to restore democratic accountability to the system. Instead of six layers of government, stretching from the European

Union through Whitehall to the region, the county, the district and ultimately the parish, we should aim to get down to four. The regions should be swept away in England as they are not needed. English local government should be invited to consider again the possibility of going to a single unitary council in each area. It should not be forced upon the reluctant but I suspect there are more parts of the country where a consensus could emerge in favour of a single, unitary tier of local government, just as we have in most of the big cities and in the county of Berkshire today.

We then need to change the relationship between central government and local government. If we went over to a national scheme for education we could expect local government to collect most of the money it needed from a combination of the council tax and local business rates, to provide the other local services. Getting away from the dominant dependence upon central government grant would increase the freedom of local councils considerably. We should also move away from a system of targeted specific grants and strong guidance from central government to local government over how the money should be spent, to a system of residual block grants in cases where we need to transfer resources from rich parts of the country to poorer parts of the country, leaving the councils free to make their own decisions on the priorities for spending the money.

We should reduce the number of councillors and raise the status of the job. We have too many councillors and we should move to a system of far fewer. With proper back-up a councillor could easily represent 10,000 people instead of the 5,000 or so of a typical ward today. Single-councillor wards would strengthen accountability compared to multiple-councillor wards. The councillor's job should combine three elements. The first is that collectively the councillors should determine the strategy and priorities of the council. The second is that they should supervise the efficient delivery of the policies and public services through the executives they hire to assist them. The third is that they must deal with the day-to-day issues of their constituents and make sure their ward is properly represented.

This is a demanding and interesting job. It is more demanding than a non-executive directorship. A councillor needs to be as good as a professional, non-executive director at supervising the executive, ensuring regularity and supervising audit. The councillor also has to be a strategist with his or her colleagues and good at individual and public representation. To attract people of sufficient calibre we should now offer a salary and make it clear that we would expect a couple of days a week in return. We should be looking to attract a range of people, perhaps aged in their later forties and fifties, who have experience of the business, charitable and public service world but who wish to combine two or three part-time roles and draw on their experience for the benefit of the wider community. A couple of days a week on a principal council spending over £100 million a year should command a salary of, say £25,000 or more. The council as a whole should also be able to draw upon a small number of officers to support it as case workers and secretaries when dealing with constituents' problems.

National parties should do more to support their ruling groups of councillors around the country on strategy and direction. All too often ruling groups of all of the main parties arrive in office ill equipped for the pressures of day-to-day handling of their officials and the constituency issues that arise. All too often councillors, like their senior colleagues in Westminster, define their role in relation to the media rather more than by how they run a large organisation spending big sums of money producing a service that often disappoints those who pay for it.

We will only get interest again in local elections if people feel that the individuals pitching for election are battling for serious jobs that can make a difference. If there are fewer councillors they will each have a higher public profile as a result. If they have more control over the expenditure patterns and the policy direction of their council, they will be taken more seriously by the electors. If electors see they are having to pay salaries above the average of the locality to secure their services, they will be more critical and more interested in seeing what they are getting for their money.

We could go one stage further and elect the chief executive. This is the idea behind the proposal for elected mayors. The elected mayor is meant to bring together the representational side of the council with the power to choose and to make decisions. Whilst the elected mayor in turn may hire a chief executive to implement his policy, the elected mayor is the fount of power and can be his own chief executive, if he wishes to pursue his own strategy and choose his own team of senior officers. An elected mayor can intervene daily in the detail as well as the general thrust of what the council is doing. I would suggest a transitional period during which councils can still opt for the elected councillor model, where the leadership may well become a full-time job and be rewarded accordingly. Local people and their elected representatives would then retain the right to choose. They could either go over to the elected mayor system, or they could continue with the more traditionally elected council but accept that the leader of that council, who would be the leader of the majority group, was effectively an elected chief executive. He or she would be responsible for proposing the strategy, for supervising the executive team and for ensuring delivery of the policy and service offered.

To make this work better central government and local government need to go on a quango cull. Too many decisions that should be taken by local government are either taken by, or heavily influenced by, other quangos. Removing regional government would deal with a lot of this problem. We need to restore to local councils the right in most cases to make their own planning decisions. The abolition of the regional planning bodies would help with this. There are many issues tackled by the Environment Agency that could be given back to local democratic control, so that councillors, who should be more responsive to public opinion, can make the day-to-day decisions affecting the local environment. We should remove a lot of the bureaucratic infrastructure that has grown up on the boundaries between the health service and the local council. Huge amounts of time and money are now wasted in conferences, seminars, joint working groups and meetings. It would be better to establish clear responsibilities and make the people running the respective services accountable for what their service is meant to do. Partnership working is so often a means of blurring responsibility and accountability and driving the service users mad, rather than a way of smoothing the rough edges and getting the services to work together in a seamless way.

How do we similarly revolutionise democracy to make the

backbench MP's job worthwhile, and to make his or her constituents feel it is worthwhile voting for him or her? That too requires a substantial number of detailed changes. If Parliament is to be effective again the forces of opposition, which may include backbenchers on the government's side, MPs need more weapons than they are currently allowed by the present government.

The traditional weapon that Parliament has had to bring a government to account is the weapon of time. The single most undemocratic change this government has made to parliamentary procedure is the automatic timetabling of all Bills in the Commons, greatly truncating the time available for proper consideration of often detailed, prolix and complicated legislative matters. The government should be made to fight to get its Bills through. Legislation is often not the answer to a problem. I dread to think how many law and order Bills I have been asked to vote for by ministers of both parties during my time as an MP. Each one of them is advertised as the means of cracking down on criminals and tackling the same old problem. All my time in the House of Commons it has been against the law to steal somebody else's property or to violently attack another person. Constant redefinition of the offences and shuffling of the legislative furniture does not seem to have come up with better results, when the issues that are going wrong are probably connected rather more with police resources, police priorities and the instructions sent by ministers to police than with the words of the law.

The second big change that could make the job of a backbench MP more worthwhile and more interesting to his or her constituents would be the introduction of more free votes. There is a wide range of issues today which divide the parties themselves rather than creating new faultlines between the parties. It has long been held that capital punishment and abortion are matters which should be left to the individual consciences of MPs. This is a pompous way of saying there are people who believe in making abortion easier and people who believe in making it more difficult within the Labour Party, and similarly there are big camps on both sides within the Conservative Party. The whips accept that they cannot come to a common view and force MPs to vote for it. As soon as we have a free-vote issue democracy takes off. The letters and e-mails flood in. People realise it's worthwhile engaging with their MP. Nobody can be sure what the likely outcome of the vote in the House of Commons is going to be with the whips off, so it is worth the public's while to lobby, push, cajole and encourage any individual MP, as it may be that individual MP who finally swings a decision nationally.

I do believe that parties still have a role to play in a successful democratic system. Well-run parties offer the electorate the vision of a disciplined government following certain principles that the electorate should be able to understand. Well-run parties impose order on what would otherwise be chaos. It would not be easy to pass a Budget based upon a whole series of free votes on what taxes people would like and what taxes they wouldn't like, and what spending they would like and what spending they wouldn't like. There is a lot to be said for there being a Labour Party view of the Budget and a Conservative Party view of the Budget which can inform the public debate, and a great deal of sense at the end in party discipline being applied to the principal votes to ensure a Budget is carried. It also makes sense for there to be party discipline on an issue such as Europe. We now have two pro-federalist parties, Labour and Liberal Democrats, who are usually whipped to vote to pass more power to Brussels, and an anti-federalist party, the Conservatives, who are now successfully whipped to oppose the Amsterdam Treaty, the Nice Treaty, the euro and the European constitution. It is healthier for British democracy if those divisions do cohere within the party framework, so that the public knows that if they want more European government they should vote Liberal Democrat and if they want less European government they should vote Conservative. When all three parties were in favour of more EU power there was a case for free votes.

Outside these large fields there is scope for far more individual differentiation. Issues as wide-ranging as hunting, licensing hours and nuclear power cause divisions that do not run easily along strict party lines. There is something artificial about turning the Labour Party into the party for nuclear power or the Conservative Party into the party against extended pub licensing hours. There will always be a large number of people in Labour who dislike nuclear power and there will always be free traders in the Conservatives who think that, subject to planning and local approval, people should be able to trade the hours they wish. If we can find more of these issues where the major parties agree that it should be left to the individual consciences, prejudices and decisions of MPs, we would rekindle more local interest in the actions of each individual member of Parliament and make debate in Parliament itself more lively and interesting.

There is already a very big contrast between the quality of debates and the interest in them on free-vote issues, and the quality of debates on party-whipped matters. There can be something very tired and repetitious about seeing endless Labour backbenchers standing up in whipped debates, reading out the same old bullet points and banal, well-researched phrases that constitute the government's case. It is altogether more informative as well as entertaining to hear a debate on abortion or fox hunting, where the whips are off and where people come out with some surprising attitudes and views that fascinate the public.

The third thing we need to do to make it more worthwhile to vote in general elections is to put more things under the direct control of Parliament. Far too many issues have now gone to Brussels. All too often today Parliament is legislating because it has to. Bill after Bill, statutory instrument after statutory instrument, is being put through to catch up with the need to implement the directives that ministers have agreed many months earlier. It means our democracy is hollowed out. It makes Parliament a sham, the proceedings meaningless, and increases the disillusion with the whole process. What is the point of lobbying Parliament to change the law if the law can only be changed in Brussels? I favour a substantial transfer of power back to Britain to tackle this democratic deficit.

In the meantime there are things that could be done to make proceedings in Parliament less futile. Instead of concentrating the debate on the statutory instruments or legislation that follow the agreement in Brussels to put through the new law, the government should allocate much more time to a debate about whether we want the proposal in the first place, before it goes off and agrees it in Brussels. At least that would make the debate more worthwhile. If Parliament could have a more direct say in fashioning the UK government's position on a new directive or other EU legislative proposal, MPs and those interested and those lobbying them would at least feel there was some point in the exercise. It could also be of benefit to the negotiating minister. If Parliament is adamant that certain powers cannot be surrendered or certain types of law cannot be enacted, this will strengthen the minister's hand in Brussels negotiations in what is meant to be a union of democratic nation states with ministers answerable to their own Parliaments.

National party democracy at Westminster could learn something from the successful local party democracy operated in some councils. When I was a county councillor my colleagues regarded the Conservative group as sovereign. We had a small majority so we held the crucial chairmanships of the committees which were the then equivalent of today's members of the executive of the principal council. I myself was chairman of a committee so I had authority over the capital budgets of the county council as a whole. Nonetheless, I welcomed the fact that every major move that I and my executive colleagues were going to make was first discussed with the group to make sure that either we reflected the consensus of the group, or we had given our opponents in the group ample opportunity to put their case before settling it on a vote. The system worked very well. Practically every councillor accepted that in return for having their right to put their case against the executive's policy in the group and take it to a vote in the group, they would then vote for the group decision come the full council meeting.

There is no such mechanism in either major party in national government. There are occasions when backbench pressure through the Parliamentary Labour Party or the 1922 Committee can change government policy. If a minister has got very out of touch with the backbenchers, if the policy has got into disrepute with too many constituents and therefore with too many MPs, then it may be possible in the relevant backbench weekly meetings to mount an attack upon the minister and the policy and to force a change. By the time things reach that stage it means the government already has a serious problem on its hands. There will be stories in the press of divisions, the minister's future may be in doubt, and tensions between the backbench members of the party on the one hand and the whips and ministers on the other become large.

Some of this could be avoided or improved if it was accepted more generally in both the PLP and the 1922 Committee that ministers or frontbench spokesmen had a duty to brief their party in advance of a shift of policy or new idea, and to carry them with them. If a minister or a shadow minister is so lacking in political skill that he cannot command a majority within his own party caucus, then you do wonder either why he is doing what he is trying to do or why he is a minister in the first place. In national politics it would not be a foolproof system. There would be still be occasions where a minister or shadow minister had won a vote in the backbench meeting following sharp division of opinion, where nonetheless backbench MPs were still not prepared to toe the party line. One would have to accept that. However, I do believe that there would be fewer serious rebellions and much better working in the interests of constituents if more matters were taken to party caucuses by ministers and shadow ministers at an earlier stage in their development, if more robust exchanges took place within the party caucus meeting, and if occasionally votes were taken to settle the issue.

We expect a lot of ministers. Many MPs are parachuted into ministerial office with no grounding or preparation for what they are about to take on. A member of Parliament may be very good at running his local surgeries, keeping in touch with his local electors, wining his election with a decent majority, being liked by the local community and effective at taking up matters for them. Those skills should be remembered and applied to the nation as a whole when becoming a minister. They are skills not to be sniffed at and they are the skills that are often missing in business people, who are sometimes also parachuted straight into government, often with bad effect. If a backbench MP who is good at all those things takes on a junior ministerial role, he or she could do much worse than apply all those same skills to looking after and representing the interest groups within his or her bailiwick, and ensuring fair decisions and regulation of them.

However, a minister needs many other skills besides those of a good backbench MP. He needs to know how to lead and motivate the civil service team to ensure the smooth delivery of policy and new law, the day-to-day administration of the existing law, and the running of a large budget. He needs to be able to do this without directly hiring and firing most of the individuals involved, and without being able to set their salaries or offer them bonuses. The minister's job in running 'his' staff is far more complicated than the chairman or chief executive's task in a major company. Most of the checks, balances and levers which an executive chairman or chief executive enjoys are missing from the control room in the minister's office. He has to proceed by persuasion, by building a successful relationship with the senior officials in his command, and making sure that they in turn are good line managers with the many officials the minister needs to use, to ensure the smooth delivery of the service he is offering.

The minister needs to know the questions to ask to ensure wise expenditure of money, delivery of the policies he and the government want, and the cancellation of the policies and actions that they have inherited or which they no longer want. The minister has to understand that making the speech, issuing the White Paper, passing the law is only the start of the process. The public will judge ministers more by what they achieve and do on the ground than by what they say. Indeed, one of the main reasons why people are so disillusioned with politics is there is such a huge gap between the fine aspirations that many ministers set out, often quite genuinely, and what is happening on the ground, village by village, suburb by suburb, as a result of the commands issued from on high. Ministers need training in how to balance the demands on their time, how to motivate and encourage the right kind of official machine, how to establish priorities, how to ensure that policies are properly followed up, and how to inspect and supervise sufficiently to guarantee the smooth delivery of public service on the ground.

Ministerial life is often considered in relation to one of the minister's important duties, answering to Parliament. There is a feeling that ministers can go abroad on fact-finding trips or go on holiday when Parliament is not in session. There is a wish to organise ministerial briefs and roles around the adjournment debates, the questions and the legislative debates that form part of the ministerial life. All this encourages a feeling amongst ministers that the rest of the job, what should be the bulk of the job, the supervision of huge budgets and the daily grind of ensuring a quality service under the existing rules, can be downplayed or neglected.

So what should we do? We probably have more ministers than is desirable. Having more than 100 people involved in ministerial and whip roles within the government seems excessive. It means there are quite a number of junior people without real responsibility and challenge. If we wish to carry on with as many ministers for patronage reasons, then a much bigger effort should be made to give those junior ministers proper roles. If we want that many junior ministers some should be expressively given jobs that entail sorting out difficult administrative issues, travelling the country to encourage better service delivery and working closely with senior officials on how the public service generally in their area could be made more responsive. There should be ministerial training for new ministers, drawing on independent sources of advice outside the civil service. Former ministers, former senior officials, senior executives of big businesses that deal daily with government, consultants who come into government would all have interesting perspectives that could be welded into a useful course, to prepare the minister for what comes next and to ensure he gets the most out of each day.

Many ministers lose on day one by failing to gain control of their diaries. If a minister allows the diary to be filled up with a whole series of visits and overseas trips which don't have a clear focus or purpose to them, he or she will find it extremely difficult to do the real job well. If a minister accepts that officials are going to fill the diary with a whole series of internal departmental meetings, rehearsing low-level arguments over things that people don't really disagree about very much, that too will make it difficult for him or her to make progress. If the minister himself defines his role only in terms of a personal career and exposure in the media, and spends a disproportionate amount of time planning the next press release or the next initiative, that too means that he will find it very difficult to get anything done in the department because officials will soon sense the mood and realise that they can get on running the place unencumbered by ministerial questioning and attention.

To make a success of a better ministerial system, there does need to be some greater emphasis on career planning and appraisal. The present system combines gross amateurism with barbarism. Ministers may read in the press of their impending departure from government through well-orchestrated leaks from the centre, when they have never been warned about unsatisfactory performance or given an opportunity to lift their game. Under the Blair–Brown regime the allocation of ministerial jobs looks little better than the allocation of spoils in a gang warfare system, where friends of Tony have to be almost balanced by friends of Gordon, and the definition of their position vis-à-vis the two main forces in the government is the main issue over selecting them. People do not work at their best if they live in fear of the annual reshuffle, are not sure whether they are doing well or badly, and often haven't been told what their bosses expect them to achieve.

A more enlightened approach to ministerial management would give people greater guidance about their career path. As a rule of thumb, one could say to an incoming minister that he or she was likely to spend four or five years as a parliamentary under-secretary of state, maybe in two different departments testing different skills, and another four or five years as a minister of state, again possibly in two different roles, before being promoted to the Cabinet if he or she was thought of sufficient calibre. In a government with a small majority there will be opportunity for most people who want to be ministers to be ministers at some point or other if their party stays in power. Some of the jostling is unnecessary. There will always be some people who don't want to be ministers because they have been ministers before, or because they enjoy the combination of backbench MP and other interests they may be pursuing. There is nothing wrong with that. Some people are more natural at opposition or scrutiny and others better at people management and public service delivery.

Parliamentary under-secretaries of state should learn the difficult craft of being ministers. They should learn how to handle the House of Commons. They should learn how to handle the press and media. Above all, they should learn how to handle a limited number of officials in a specified area, and show that they can make improvements and achieve delivery of what the government is setting out to do under the supervision of their minister of state. They should be given annual reviews, by the minister of state or the secretary of state in the department concerned, to be told how they are getting on, with suggestions for improvement. If there is a danger that the secretary of state and the Prime Minister think they are not delivering nearly enough, they should be given adequate warning. If the yellow card does not work the red card should not then come as a surprise, and there should be an agreed exit from government at a mutually agreed date wherever possible, to minimise the damage both to the government and to the individual themselves. Similarly, junior ministers should be offered seminar and course support, and required to go on one or two of them to open their eyes to the magnitude of the task they are taking on. They should be expected to read the main legislation which their department is enforcing, to read the departmental annual report and accounts, to master the main budgets that they are responsible for, to visit every one of their senior officials and understand who they are and what they are doing for them.

These may seem straightforward and obvious things but practically none of these happen as a matter of routine in modern Whitehall. I found as a minister wishing to meet all my staff it caused enormous consternation, as the official line was, 'Minister, we will come to see you when you need to see us.' I said I wished to see them in their own offices as I wanted to know how many people were there, what they thought they were doing, whether I thought that was a good idea or not, and I wished to show the normal courtesies of a leader by going to visit them. You get so much more understanding of what they are experiencing, whether they have the right building and facilities, and whether their jobs make sense or not, if you go and visit them and talk to them in situ. I also found it was possible to influence how many staff we had and where they were employed, even as a junior minister, but it required careful negotiation with the permanent secretary, who has the named responsibility within the department for pay, rations, hiring and firing.

Improving the performance of ministers is crucial to improving the accountability of government. It is only when you see an experienced, capable, confident minister at work you realise how bad many of the others are. A confident minister is happy to debate how he is running the department, what laws he is proposing, and how he is supervising the existing panoply of powers and controls he enjoys.

A confident minister does carry enough officials with him to ensure good quality work from the many bright people who work within the civil service. The confident minister does not get into trouble with his colleagues and friends in the House of Commons, because he is constantly carrying them with him, especially if there is something difficult or untoward happening. We need to raise the levels of ministerial competence and confidence. We could make a big stride towards that by putting in a rather more sensible career structure, being much clearer about what is expected of ministers, and living with them and their mistakes when they are honestly made and won't recur.

Rebuilding democracy is a huge task. It requires a major renegotiation of the powers between Brussels and Britain. It requires Parliament meeting for longer hours to hold the executive to account, and Parliament having longer hours to debate difficult legislation. It requires more influential and important ministers who have more control over the official machine and as a result are more accountable to Parliament. It requires more influential and powerful backbenchers who can challenge those ministers, who can use the weapon of time in the House of Commons when ministers are not performing well, and who can use free votes to change policy and direction in a number of areas that do not reflect the party political faultlines. All this would make debate more worthwhile and interesting in Parliament more often, more uncertainty over voting would make Parliament more interesting, and ministers would have more worthwhile jobs.

So why would this make it more likely that people would vote in elections and engage with party politics? If people could see the councillors and ministers in charge and making a difference, they would think it more worthwhile participating in elections and engaging in debate with those senior politicians to try and get the changes they want for their local or national community. If they could see their backbench MP having an influence through the party caucus over government or shadow government policy, and if they could see that same MP directly participating in decisions over new laws through more free votes, they too would be more interested in a continuous dialogue and participating in the ensuing election.

Today the escalation of cases from councillor to MP and from MP to minister or Prime Minister has completely undermined the councillor's role and is substantially undermining the MP's role. If we can get back to a position where the buck stops with the councillor on planning matters, on the organisation of local social services, on local highways and traffic, and on local environment issues, the councillor's job will be more worthwhile and the MP's job more feasible. If the buck can stop with the MP on a wider range of issues that are settled by Parliament through free votes, and if the MP is seen more widely as the gatekeeper or principal channel of influence over government and shadow government, that too can buttress the democracy. We need far less unaccountable power resting with consultants, with officials, with Brussels, with quangos, with taskforces and reviews. We need more accountable power resting with ministers, with executive members of councils and with legislators.

The background to this debate in Britain about engagement or disengagement with party politics is the ceaseless drive towards globalisation. The political systems of the main western European countries are finding it difficult to adjust and respond. Proud nations such as Britain, France, Germany, Italy and Spain were used to being important forces in the world and used to making many of their own national decisions in the twentieth century. There is a growing feeling of helplessness amongst some politicians and many electors in these countries that they are no longer in charge or control, that the forces of global capitalism are taking over, and that this makes their endeavours futile or difficult. Some have foolishly thought that the answer to this problem is to club together in a new mezzanine level of government, the European Union. They are doing this at exactly the time when the EU's economic power itself is rapidly waning, meaning that it will be no more likely to be a controlling influence on world developments than the individual countries France, Germany, Spain or Italy are. The problem in countries such as Germany and France has been compounded by the interaction of the electoral system and a divided electorate. In Germany the proportional representation system means that no single party ever has a majority to run the country. In the most recent German election a divided country was unable to decide between the Christian

Democrat-led coalition and the Social Democrat-led coalition, resulting in a grand coalition of all the principal parties. This is a recipe for indecision and lowest-common-denominator politics, unlikely to take the tough decisions needed to allow Germany to compete, to get people back to work, and to prosper in the way that she did in the latter twentieth century.

In France, frustration and anger has boiled over to produce substantial voting for stridently nationalist parties of the right, led by the National Front, and stridently socialist parties of the left, including the Communists. The resulting mayhem through the French electoral system produced the extraordinary sight of a right-of-centre President being elected on left-of-centre votes to keep the National Front out. As a result, the presidency and the government spawned beneath it have lacked intellectual coherence and a vision of how to deal with France's problems of unemployment and social deprivation, and how to respond to the challenge of the global marketplace. Italy, a similarly divided country, found it difficult to decide between Silvio Berlusconi's coalition of right-of-centre populist parties on the one hand, and Romano Prodi's centre-left coalition of more Euro-enthusiastic parties on the other.

Electorates are undecided how to respond to globalisation, partly because they are being given unsure signals by those who pretend to lead them. One of the great weaknesses of the now dominant politics driven by focus groups and opinion polls is that it makes parties less willing or able to tell the truth to the people and to make proposals that are unpopular or poll badly. When Margaret Thatcher set about her task of reforming Britain, she made no secret of the fact in the opposition years that she would need to reduce public spending and she would need to tackle the overmighty power of the trade unions. It is true she did not go into detail of how she would do this, although there were extant a large number of plans that had been worked on in private. It was sufficient to tell the public what was needed. Three election victories in a row demonstrated that it was possible for a democratic politician to do some extremely unpopular things, like cutting public spending and curbing inflation by strong medicine, and still keep enough of the public behind her to keep on winning. Indeed, Thatcher made it more difficult for herself by failing to curb the public sector in her first two years in office, and intensifying the credit squeeze as a result.

Today politicians are extremely nervous about stating the obvious. It is quite clear that the British public sector is living beyond its means and is not nearly productive enough. It is self-evident that if the British public sector got up to anything like the levels of productivity and performance of the best of the private sector, we would have much better public service and at much less cost. Polling tells politicians that people do not believe their claims. They don't believe them because over many years they've watched as politicians have failed to get a grip on the public services and have failed to improve them in the way we would like. Experience currently triumphs over hope. Politicians in their turn become more cautious about trying to persuade the public of something they do not believe and so, as a result, we have a stand-off.

When the Conservatives first introduced the idea of private sector telephone services in Britain the public was very worried. A big majority of the public was against the privatisation of British Telecom. A big majority of the public worried that the service would deteriorate in private hands, that the prices would go up too much, that the poor would not get access to phones, and that their local red telephone box would be cut off. How old fashioned and wrong this all looks twenty years later. People are no longer worrying in the streets at the state of the local red phone box because most people now have phones at home or mobiles in their pocket. Far from the prices going up, since privatisation waved its magic wand the prices of telephony have fallen. Instead of having to wait months for the BT monopolist to install a new phone in your home, today you can go into a shop and buy one that will be working five minutes later. This took a leap of imagination, an act of political will, a little political courage, which are often lacking in today's politicians facing similar poor delivery issues in other public services to those we faced in the 1980s when looking at the incompetent and out-of-date phone system.

The lack of courage and vision throughout the EU is the most worrying feature of the present European political scene. The French government caved in over a very simple idea to encourage youth employment. Why not, it reasoned, let employers take people on for a limited period of time and if it didn't work out get rid of them? You wouldn't have thought anyone sensible could possibly disagree with such a proposal. Without such a change the young people will not have access to jobs. With such a change quite a few young people will be given the chance and many, I am sure, would be able to persuade their employers that they were suitable for long-term employment. The best way to get a job is to have a job. The tragedy for so many of Europe's young today is they don't get on the first rung on the ladder to begin their career climb.

There is still throughout the EU, including many people in Britain, the strange feeling that globalisation is a threat and that the answer to that threat is more protection. We have in charge of many governments in the EU, and in charge of the European Union itself, a group of Canutes who believe that if they stand on the seashore and command the waves to go away the waves will go away.

The irony is lost on so many people. People will stand on doorsteps arguing with me about the threat from China and India and how we ought to be doing something to protect ourselves from it, wearing T-shirts and trainers made in China. Many of their services may now be routed through an Indian call centre. On their driveway may be standing a foreign-made car. They are all enjoying the lifestyle of a globalised world to the full. They expect to go abroad on holiday, to buy good-quality household and personal textiles at world-beating prices, to enjoy global communications from their mobile phone and their landline, to see everything on television that occurs of interest wherever it may be in the world, and to enjoy the cuisines of many different parts of the world routed to them over many thousand miles of ocean by the international trading system. Many simply have no idea of how much poorer they would be if we voted in a Communist government who closed the ports, stopped foreign travel and trade, and said we could only live on what we can produce internally.

One of the most successful lobby organisations of recent years has been the fair trade campaign. This has brought together environ-mentalists, some professional campaign organisations and the churches to lobby for a fairer deal for the world's oppressed and poor.

It has been fascinating to watch this movement. As it has got more involved it has come to see that the EU's Common Agricultural Policy (CAP) is one of the major roadblocks to enfranchising the poor of Africa. It has come to see that restrictions placed by the EU on imports deprive Africans of a potential livelihood. It has come to join us free traders in opposing tariffs from the rich West, subsidies from the rich West, quotas and other restrictions. It sees that blocking imports from poor countries makes it very difficult for those poor countries to develop their economies and create the jobs they so desperately need.

The movement has not been quite so clear sighted when it comes to dealing with restrictions in the developing countries themselves. Some of its leaders argue that we should both remove our barriers to trade whilst encouraging barriers to trade in the poorer countries. This shows a fundamental misunderstanding of how the free trade system works. I don't make Britain poorer by removing the barriers to African trade. Of course I, like them, would like to do it because it is morally right and would be good for all those Africans who could move into gainful employment, supplying us with the things we need, if the CAP barriers were removed. But I also like it because it will mean that people in Britain can buy a better range of food at a quality of their choosing at a lower price. That in turn will leave us more of our incomes to spend on other things, which in turn can generate more jobs in Britain as well as abroad, as the marketplace brings forth the supply to match that new demand. This is the magic of the free enterprise system, Adam Smith's famous invisible hand which lifts many up if you allow the market to function.

The fair trade movement has learnt that it does need to lobby the Labour Party and the Labour government. It has found that lobbying Brussels, the people who really handle our trade policy and trade arrangements, is so much more difficult than lobbying the relatively open, British democratic system. It has also, doubtless, discovered that because we do not elect our commissioners they are not as answerable as our Prime Minister and senior ministers, who do need our favour every four or five years to stay in office. The fair trade movement has shown that there is a role for an intelligently organised pressure group to push all three major parties into a set of policy viewpoints that makes sense for the poor of the world. The campaign group has done a good service in highlighting what is a huge moral and political issue that should worry us all.

The climate change lobbyists have also had a big impact on modern British politics. All three main parties now claim to take climate change extremely seriously. All three have worked up policies to improve our performance in reducing harmful emissions into the atmosphere. All three main parties accept that Britain should be a leader in developing new climate change technology, and in persuading others around the world that they need to take action.

The might of America, coupled with the rising might of China and India, should tell anyone interested in the subject that we are not going to solve this problem without the consent, agreement and positive commitment of those three big economies. At the moment all three of them are outside the Kyoto agreement and see the problem from a rather different perspective. Britain could play a role, as she is trying to do, as an honest broker of a new agreement. The Americans are primarily concerned about energy security. They have been used to producing their own oil and electrical power free of the need to be nice to others who might supply them. America now needs to import substantial quantities of oil from the Middle East and is nervous about its dependence upon a part of the world that looks at political problems so differently from the United States herself. That gives Britain an intelligent entry point into the discussions with the USA. We should couch the argument in America not in terms of the impact on the climate of burning energy, where the American administration is unsure, but on the need for America to curb her appetite for foreign-bought oil and gas, an argument that America will respond to very favourably, to give her greater security of supply.

In China, a country in need of huge quantities of oil and electricity to power her industrial revolution, the appeal has to be to her wish to be at the leading edge of new technology rather than merely catching up with out-of-date technology others have already developed and exploited. China would be a serious candidate for large-scale technology transfer so that she can demonstrate to the rest of the world how clean coal, nuclear and renewable energy technology can be developed on a grand scale to power her industrial revolution.

What can we learn from the success of campaigning organisations in channelling political energies that might previously have been channelled through political parties? We can see that people respond to clarity about a major concern. It shows that many British people are generous and altruistic in their views. They are quite prepared to worry away at a problem which has no direct impact on them. They hate to see the pictures of starvation, civil war and disease in Africa. They are naturally affronted by the contrast between their own lifestyles and those of their fellow human beings. Their generosity and anger combine to make them want to do something. The appeal of the charities and campaign groups is immediate. They share that same sense of anger and moral outrage. They are not constrained in the way that governments are by the need to use diplomatic language when talking about African states, and the need to think about the practical solutions that might make a difference on the ground. Campaigning groups can respond to the feelings of people where the political parties also need a hard-headed realism about what can be achieved. Campaign groups show that there is a role for passion and conviction in politics as well as brokering deals and trying to find solutions.

Campaign groups have made very intelligent use of traditional and modern techniques of political campaigning. They are good at fund raising by appealing to the right instincts of the people who are their natural followers. They use web and e-mail technology very successfully, building up big e-mail address lists to keep in touch with their members and well-wishers, and directing them to the website to give them more information and ammunition. They spread their national campaigns down through each locality via local organisers and local newsletters. They are very active in traditional ways with public meetings, stalls, leaflet drops and photo opportunities for local and national media. They have a good news sense and use public relations to good effect.

None of these things are foreign to the party system in Britain either. Party politicians have to get better at using these self-same techniques to channel those same emotions and wishes into party political channels. The party political offering should be better than the campaigning group. The political party should be able to communicate the same sense of outrage and moral indignation about the poverty in Africa. It should be able to use the same techniques to highlight the problems or to channel support. In addition, it should be able to offer part of the solution. The political party can say, 'We can do all that the campaigning groups can do and we can give you direct access to those in Britain who make the decisions, who form our diplomatic policy, who develop our trade policy with the EU, and who go to the international forum to seek international progress and agreement.' It is the failure of the political parties to do this which is so disappointing for party politics-based democracy in Britain. It is a failure based on disappointment and disillusion with the political parties in the way this book has described.

It is a big task to restore democracy to Britain. We have too long taken for granted that we are an active and flourishing democracy. We have been complacent, having come to democracy early. We have lived on the past glories of votes for every man in the nineteenth century and votes for every woman in the twentieth. We have rejoiced in having the mother of Parliaments, we just assume that the rule of law is always there and is free of corruption or unreasonable influence, and we have dined out on our electoral system.

It is healthy in a democracy that people are critical of their politicians and think their political parties could improve. It is unhealthy if the breakdown in relations reaches the point where many millions are simply disengaged and millions more are desperate for something better but do not know how to bring it about. The political classes themselves should look in the mirror and realise that they are part of the problem. There are too many politicians, senior officials, consultants and advisers. There are too many layers of government. There are too many people sending out press releases and too few getting on with the job of improving public services. There is a huge, unreformed monopoly public sector which is failing to deliver what people want at a sensible price. There are too many rule makers and regulators getting in the way of those who would like to lead decent lives and make their contribution to the enterprise economy. There is too little accountable power.

In this book I have sought to describe the problem and to set out some of the ways it could be put right. Parliament itself needs reform. More time for debate, an end to the automatic guillotine, more free votes, more involvement of backbench MPs in government policy formation, and more confident, well-briefed and competent ministers to keep us informed. Local government needs reform, making sure that it has to raise more of the money it spends, and granting to a more limited number of councillors more serious power to supervise and run the council and to answer for what they've done. We need a new settlement with Brussels so that the important matters that people expect to be decided democratically in Britain are so decided. We need a new honesty in the debate about Brussels so that people are aware where Brussels has acted and where Britain can act alone.

There is at heart a strong wish for fairness and democratic answers in Britain. I detect that people would like stronger leadership and more honesty and directness from their politicians. The political classes should spend less on themselves, less on focus groups and less on opinion polling. They should be less interested in studying what the public think about solving the problems and more interested in grappling with real solutions that would cheer the public up. If you want to win a general knowledge contest it is best to know the answers yourself. You cannot normally ask the audience and expect the right answer every time.

I hope democracy is merely taking a nap in Britain. It is desperately important that it should not be dead. It is there somewhere in the hearts of many of the voters, which is what matters most. It is now up to the political parties to rise to the challenge, reform the institutions and show they've got the message. If we cannot rekindle active political interest in political parties, then the party system itself becomes the problem rather than the solution.

Index